Australia's Liquid Gold

Australia's Liquid Gold

Nicholas Faith

MITCHELL BEAZLEY

Australia's Liquid Gold
by Nicholas Faith

First published in Great Britain in 2002 by Mitchell Beazley, an
imprint of Octopus Publishing Group Limited, 2–4 Heron Quays, London E14 4JP

Originally published as *Liquid Gold* in 2001 by Pan Macmillan Australia

A CIP catalogue record for this book is available from the British Library.

ISBN: 1 84000 794 X

Phototypeset in Berkeley Book by Intype London Ltd

Printed and bound in Great Britain by Mackays, Chatham

To Hazel Murphy,
who sent me to Australia in the first place

Contents

Acknowledgments

This book was sparked off by Hazel Murphy, who introduced me to the story. But it only became a reality through a combined brother-and-sister effort, when Sophia Gilliatt introduced me to her brother, Tom Gilliatt, non-fiction publisher at Pan Macmillan. He and his team – above all, the editors, Rowena Lennox and Simone Ford – proved themselves true professionals. Without blinking they managed to cope with the numerous complications involved in publishing a book where the author is 15,000 kilometres away, as well as dealing with my worries – sometimes expressed in a rather intemperate fashion, it has to be said.

An enjoyable aspect of researching the book was the enthusiastic collaboration of the many people I interviewed, who are quoted in the following pages and whom I want to thank collectively for their patience in dealing with an interviewer who sometimes crossed the line from persistence to intrusion. Researching the written sources was made a pleasant task thanks to Valmai Hankel, former specialist librarian at the State Library of South Australia in Adelaide and the best authority on Australian wine literature. Thanks also to Valmai for reading the text and correcting so many slip-ups.

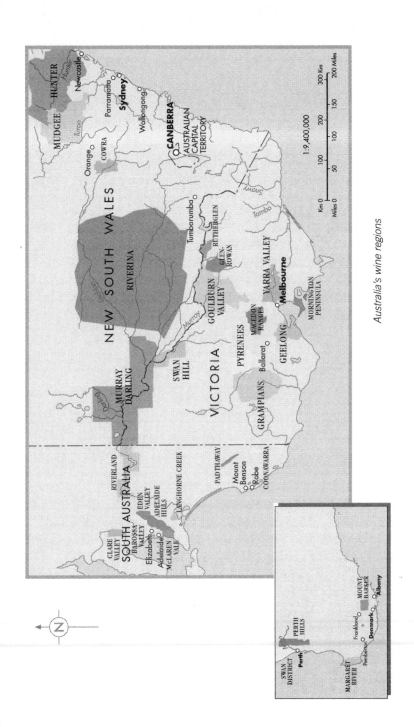

Australia's wine regions

1

Why Australia?

*The Australian wine industry has virtually reinvented itself. . . it has
proved a great ambassador for Australia.*

BRIAN CROSER

This book is an attempt to explain the success of Australians in the international wine market since the early 1990s, and to explore the historical
underpinnings of a phenomenon almost without precedent in the long
history of wine.

The story of wine in Australia is largely unknown, yet it is of increasing interest as the fame of Australian wine spreads throughout the world.
Indeed, wine is one of the few consumer products in which Australians
are setting the pace worldwide. Not surprisingly, the story combines
many of the most typical elements in the Australian character, from a
willingness to innovate and "have a go," to a total disregard for tradition
and the opinions of well-established experts in other countries. It is the
story of the increasing sophistication of wine-lovers the world over,
including Australia, and their growing thirst for ever-improving wines,
together with the winemakers' increasing ability to impose their own
ideas, their own styles, on the generally conservative world of wine.

The rise of Australian wine is astonishingly recent. Since the mid-
1980s, wine exports have increased from little over a million cases to six
million by 1990 and an astonishing thirty-five million by 2001, a rate of
growth unprecedented in the history of wine. As recently as the late
1980s, Australia imported more wine than it sold abroad. Part of the
dramatic surge in exports is undoubtedly due to the continuing weakness
of the Australian dollar since it was floated in 1985, but this does not
provide more than a very partial explanation of the phenomenon.

The most obvious effect is economic. By 2001, wine had emerged as the only one of Australia's seventeen top export industries that is a finished, manufactured product. Wine is sold on average at six times the value of the raw material, the grapes, from which it is made. As Jeremy Oliver pointed out, this makes it "the most successful manifestation of the 'Clever Country' syndrome" – lucky and clever with it, you might say. The transformation process is important not only economically but culturally as well, for it demonstrates, as does no other Australian product, Australia's capacity to satisfy increasingly sophisticated customers the world over.

The "Australian revolution" has made the country the leader in the (sometimes rather artificial) battle between wines made in the New and Old Worlds. Australian winemakers simply don't realize the fear they inspire in the Europeans, fear conveyed in the phrase used by Jacques Berthomeau, a senior French civil servant, in an official report: "The barbarians are at the gates." In doing so he reinforced the nonsense that Australian wines are "industrial" whereas those from France are small-scale, *artisanale*. But in fact, until very recently, Bordeaux alone produced almost as much wine as the whole of Australia, often in giant cooperative wineries. In Australia, the majority of the country's 1,500 wineries are decidedly modest affairs. Calling Australians barbarians will not deter them. By definition they have always been outsiders, the bloody-minded minority confident enough to go their own way.

The strength of the Old World's reaction is a sign that there is more to the phenomenon than jealousy at the numerical challenge it represents. Despite Australia's surge in production and exports in the past decade, it remains in the middle rank of wine-producing countries, with less than one-third of the production of each of the big three – France, Italy, and Spain – and barely half of that of the United States. Its export figures are still far behind those of the big two, France and Italy, which together account for around half of world trade in wine. Nor are its vineyards all that productive – far less so, for example, than those of Germany, whose northern climate ought to reduce yields. Even the threat from that supposedly all-conquering variety, Australian Chardonnay, has been grossly exaggerated. Production is less than half of that in California, while the yield per hectare (ha) is comparable to that in the far less favourable climate of the Champagne region in northern France. No, the fearful reaction is not based on size or numbers but on the profound transformation in the winemakers' attitude to wine-drinkers.

The Australian revolution in wine stems from the perceived requirements of the customers rather than the ego of the winemakers – though God knows few Australian winemakers are noted for their modesty. It is an assertion of the democratic rights of drinkers of modest means to have access to decently made, fruity, reliable wines, rather than the rubbish on which they previously had to rely in a world in which there was a class divide between the lucky few who drank fine wines and the masses who didn't. This divide was, of course, partly financial; good wine is inevitably going to cost more, far more, than ordinary plonk. But, for the first time, Australian winemakers have offered drinkers a ladder of quality, up which they can climb as their taste for better wines grows with their financial situation. Whether the winemakers can continue to progress, to make more subtle, more distinctive wines in the twenty-first century remains to be seen.

This accessibility is profoundly Australian, and is perhaps more easily perceived by sympathetic outsiders than by the Australians themselves, for they tend to take this quality for granted. In a speech to a seminar on French wine, Mike Paul, then the managing director of Southcorp in Europe, said bluntly that one of the major reasons for the success of New World wines was simply "the will to win" fuelled by the growing domestic demand. He added that Australian winemakers speak that now quasi-universal language, English, and this, combined with their willingness to listen, their attention to labels and packaging, and their use of varietal names, make it easy for the buyer.

At a marketing conference, the English journalist Robert Joseph pinpointed the underlying psychological drive behind Australia's very diverse achievements in the last forty years of the twentieth century. "Cultural cringe," he said. "Having been told that you're only good at shearing sheep and playing rugby and cricket – maybe it does drive you to make better movies and make better wine and build better opera houses."

Indeed, the first sign of the new Australia was the construction of the Sydney Opera House, completed in the early 1970s. Then there has been the national focus on a continuing success in sport, beginning, perhaps, in 1983 with the triumph of the financier Alan Bond (universally known as "Bondy") in wresting the America's Cup from the USA, when every television screen in the country displayed two white triangles on a blue field. In 2000, the Sydney Olympics demonstrated to the world the Australian capacity for classiness as well as organizational competence – a stark contrast to the unappetizing haze of greed that had hung over the 1996 games in Atlanta.

Success has not been confined to areas in which Australia has been historically strong. I remember how, at the Cannes Film Festival in the mid-1970s, Canada and Australia were both neophytes in the industry, struggling for international recognition. Within a few years, the Canadians had returned to their previous obscurity. By contrast, the Australians were firing on all cylinders. Films like *Picnic at Hanging Rock* announced the arrival of a new force in world filmmaking while the *Crocodile Dundee* films were immensely popular (and what a lot of beer Paul Hogan sold in the USA!). Indeed, films such as *Gallipoli* expressed a knowledge of and pride in the past with fluency in a new medium. Similar characteristics were to feature prominently in the subsequent success of the wine industry.

The parallel between the film and wine industries is not of my making. In 1979, the Australian Film Board launched a campaign at Cannes under the slogan "A vintage year for Australian films". Both were signs of the emergence of a new and peculiarly Australian contribution to civilized living. But the success of Australian films is a warning: today, most Australian talent has been absorbed by Hollywood, wine remains one of the few successful locally owned industries, with firms able to compete on equal terms with even the biggest international groups. But even the biggest groups could be victims to the ambitions of major multinationals. A fact emphasized in early 2003 with the takeover of BRL Hardy, one of the Big Four Australian wine companies, by the American Winemakers Constellation.

Whoever owns the industry, wine will remain a product which distils, as does no other, most of the best qualities in the character of Australia and its people. The most obvious is the lack of fear when approaching a new challenge, a willingness to "have a go", to committing yourself without worrying too much about the outcome, let alone social norms. Such characteristics have provided Australia with a capacity, almost unique among New World winemaking countries, not to be abashed when competing with people like the French, with centuries and, indeed, sometimes over 1,000 years of experience. On the world market, only the Americans have the potential to compete effectively, and the vast majority of their winemakers, like the majority of their countrymen, are too insular, too wrapped up in their own (enormous) domestic market to provide effective competition. In addition, says Australian author and winemaker James Halliday, "There's this Australian assumption of self-help, the discipline of survival – 150 years ago you had to survive by yourself", and when you did work with other people "no attention was paid to status".

The atmosphere of mutual support created a strong ethos of "mateship" – that particularly Australian form of male bonding – but, so far as wine is concerned, the Australian tendency to cut any leanings to superiority down to size (the so-called "tall poppy" syndrome) has been counteracted by the show system. This has been a feature of Australian life since the early days. Shows are held in towns and cities throughout the country and bring together exhibits to find the "best of breed" for all the country's products – from knitting to cheese, from sheep to wine – and have proved an ideal means of "improving the breed" through what amount to major Australian sporting-cum-social events.

The early stages of the renaissance of Australian wines depended heavily on the Old Country, one of many manifestations of the complex relationship between Britain and Australia. Historically, Australian wine was designed for an English market that liked strong, uncomplicated, uninteresting wines, but this route led to a dead end after World War II as British tastes moved away from strong, fortified wines. Then came a desire to ape the French as the arbiters of taste. Fortunately, increasing success in a business that combines a traditional agricultural enterprise (growing the grapes) with the value-adding skills of making wine has diminished the need for Australian winemakers to seek approval from Old World arbiters of taste. As Ray King, one of the key figures in the industry in the 1980s and 1990s, put it: "We have created our own myth and magic about Australian wine and winemakers."

Curiously, the industry has not been considered economically significant; there is nothing about wine in *The Oxford Companion to Australian History,* published in 1998. The perceived lack of importance has had advantages since, as Lawrie Stanford of the Australian Wine and Brandy

Corporation (AWBC) points out, "It was too small an industry to be protected, so it was largely unaffected by government intervention. . . There's a contrast with wool, which was protected, and so there was no innovation." Wine also benefits because its producers were ineluctably in direct contact with their customers, whereas the boards that direct the country's more important agricultural products are far removed from the final buyer.

The way wine is treated as an agricultural rather than an industrial product is emphasized by the fact that, unlike the historical practice in more established winemaking countries, most of the grapes are not vinified by the growers, who form a community rather separate from the winemakers. As a result, it has always been natural to measure yields in tonnes per ha and not, as in other wine-producing countries, in terms of the amount of wine produced by a ha of vines.

But also, because wine has been regarded as an agricultural product, it has benefited from the guarantee of quality applied, through a strict inspection system, to any agricultural product being exported and therefore forming part of the world's image of Australian produce. Today the AWBC employs eighteen full-time tasters to ensure that all wine sold abroad conforms to stringently defined standards.

Good wine is the result of geology, geography, history – and the sheer bloody-mindedness of some key individuals. Wine has been made in Australia since the late 1790s and was always intended to be one of the continent's principal products. Yet for over a century, until after World War II, the country's winemakers were lulled into complacency by their ability to sell large quantities of (usually fortified and almost invariably rather inferior) wine in Britain. This imperial preference, combined with the local predilection for beer and fortified wines, made life difficult for the handful of enthusiasts who were trying to make fine wine.

Nevertheless, it is extraordinary how many of the themes that have contemporary resonance can be traced to the early years, whether it be the importance of doctors, the number of varieties in an individual vineyard, or the practice of mixed farming on an estate best-known for its wines. Historic echoes extend throughout Australian wine, not only in wineries and companies that have stayed the course since colonial times, but in winemakers and others in the industry whose family roots go back a century or more.

Australian wine regions are littered with abandoned wineries and wineries that have changed hands again and again over the decades, or have lived short butterfly lives, only to be revived sometimes nearly a century later. Happily, Australians have a strong sense of heritage – perhaps because they are not overburdened with it – and this shows through in the resurrection and continuing use of many of the oldest wineries. BRL Hardy, one of the big four that dominate the Australian industry, has its head office a few miles south of Adelaide at Chateau Reynella, which dates back to the 1840s. The firm has also restored the historic Houghton winery north of Perth. One of the first steps of the new management that took over the biggest company, Southcorp, in 2001 was to start making wine again at the historic Magill Estate on the outskirts of Adelaide and it is now restoring Seppeltsfield, most majestic of monuments to the glory of winemaking in Australia in Victorian times. The same feeling for heritage is shown at Chateau Tahbilk – now called Tahbilk Wines – in the Goulburn Valley north of Melbourne, where the Purbrick family has lovingly restored the nineteenth-century buildings and is still making a fine Shiraz from vines planted in the 1860s.

Another living and cherished piece of heritage is the estate at Angaston in the Barossa Valley, owned by the Hill-Smith family since 1849. Yalumba organizes regular "museum tastings" of historic wines made not only by the company but including many made (and donated) by its rivals. I was lucky enough to be invited to one held in London in 1998, the first outside Australia. These events provide proof of the quality achieved by Australian winemakers in the century before their renaissance in the 1970s, as well as a rare chance to taste wines made from the ungrafted vines grown in France and the Cape of Good Hope in the early nineteenth century, which have survived only in Australia. Everywhere else in the world, the depredation of the phylloxera louse at the end of the nineteenth century have meant that ungrafted vines have had to be replaced by new vines grafted onto USA rootstock unaffected by the louse. As a result, some parts of Australia, notably in South Australia, can claim to have vines older than those growing anywhere else in the world.

As Len Evans, the commentator at the 1998 tasting, put it, "The wines tell a lot about the character of the people at the time." "Almost every wine contains a story of some significance," added Robert Hill-Smith of Yalumba, "of the maker, the season, the region, the style or the variety."

He thus disposed of another myth: that all Australian wines conform to a certain pattern. Few, if any, were what you might call "bulldozer" wines.

Yet another myth (and one that the Australians themselves have done much to spread) comprehensively demolished by the tasting was that Australian wines do not reflect the region or site from which they come. Indeed, as is the case so often in vinous history, many of the best sites were discovered early on. A high portion of the best older wines of the tasting came from a handful of sub-regions such as the Clare, Eden, and Barossa Valleys in South Australia, settled in the mid-nineteenth century.

There were fine wines of every description. The 1962 Bin 60A from Penfolds was still fruity – it must have been overwhelming when young; the 1963 Chateau Reynella Cabernet Sauvignon was still showing some elegant fruit thirty-five years on, as was the 1969 Redman Claret from Coonawarra. These reds were some of the many wines called "claret" or "burgundy" without much regard to the grape varieties used or the style of the wine. A 1956 "claret" from Peter Lehmann, for instance, was sixty per cent Shiraz (or Syrah) and the rest Grenache and Mataro (the name sometimes used in Australia for Mourvèdre). In those days, the use of such fanciful names was the only way Australians could sell their better wines. There were also some startlingly good wines made from what was called Rhine Riesling. These included a 1982 Riesling from Brian Croser's vineyard in the Clare Valley with the sort of flinty butteriness characteristic of older European Rieslings, qualities echoed by a 1979 Heggies Riesling from the Eden Valley. Even more extraordinary were two fascinating, rather maderized but still delicious relics: Yalumba Rieslings from the Eden Valley dating back to 1944 and 1934.

Not surprisingly, it was the stronger, sweeter wines from Yalumba that stole the show. They included an Antique Tawny Port, which we agreed was the "nectar of the gods"; a Tokay made from the Muscadelle grape, which captured perfectly the overtones of late-summer flowers; and an 1889 Old Four Crown Port, which tasted like the distilled version of a nutty treacle tart. This was trumped by the 1894 Para Liqueur, one of a series of wines laid down by Benno Seppelt with instructions that it should not be touched until it had passed its centenary. One vintage of the Para Liqueur is put on the market every year. Apart from a handful of wines from Madeira, it is the oldest commercially available drink in the world. It had the most concentrated nose of any wine I have ever tasted, like an old-fashioned grocer's shop: "sugar and spice and all things nice" on the palate as well as on the nose. It was sweet but did not cloy because of the high acidity.

Unfortunately, stunning old wines such as these are now highly prized rarities. Nevertheless, there is a liqueur Muscat made by the Morris family of Rutherglen from a one-hundred-year-old *solera* (containing wines from a number of ancient vintages) that continues the tradition. The wine itself is balanced, with the deepest of Muscat noses, a subtle drink reminiscent of liquid fudge but without any of the cloying note so visible in lesser wines. The Morris family settled in Rutherglen in northeastern Victoria in 1891. In early 2002, Mick Morris, the founder's grandson, a small, stocky, stalwart septuagenarian, was still standing in his antique winery, as redolent of a glorious history of winemaking as the most devoutly worshipped winemaker in Burgundy. The corrugated iron roof of Morris's winery is susceptible to leaks, the presses are still of the old-fashioned basket design, its open concrete fermenting vats are surrounded by hundreds of casks of every possible age. When I casually remarked that one of the more ancient seemed to be leaking, Morris was indignant, "That cask came from a great cooper who went broke about a hundred years ago," he said. He explained the casks' longevity. "The cooper seasoned them so well. The thickness of the timber is greater than what you can get today. They were all hand-hewn rather than sawn, and the wood follows the line of the grain. You don't get the same degree of porousness as you do with modern casks."

Morris is by no means the only producer of divine fortified dessert wines. "Sometimes," Bill Chambers, a neighbour of Morris, told me, "the Muscat grapes won't go through the crusher" – because they're so densely concentrated. "They're certainly not accountants' wines," he added as he showed me round his vineyard, one part of which has been fenced off to allow sheep to graze on the foliage of vines which Chambers will then dig up. To him this is just another "paddick". The winemakers of Rutherglen tend to behave like agriculturalists, liable to infuriate pilgrims come to talk about wine, he says, who find that Chambers and Morris want to discuss sheep. Chambers's attitude is that of peasants the world over. "If you make a few bob, you buy a few paddicks."

An even purer relic of the past, if only because it remains virtually untouched, is at Yeringberg, an hour's drive from Melbourne above the

Yarra Valley, a large estate owned by Guill de Pury, the grandson of the founder. There the cooper's tools have been left undisturbed since they were last used for the 1921 vintage, after which winemaking ceased for nearly half a century. But it is not only the ambience that matters; it is the old-fashioned attitude of de Pury and his wife to their estate, most of which is still devoted to sheep and cattle. De Pury and his son David have planted only a couple of ha since 1969, nevertheless producing some of the best wines from the valley. Sales are strictly controlled, credit cards are not accepted, and the cellar door is open to the public only for a single weekend at the beginning of May.

One group of winemakers sums up the whole history. In 1848, Father Aloysius Kranewitter, a Jesuit, arrived in South Australia from Silesia. The Jesuits bought an estate in the Clare Valley called Sevenhill, originally to make only sacramental wine. Brother John, who has been making the wine since 1972, is only the eighth winemaker, and still devotes a quarter of today's 500-tonne crush to sacramental wines. The rest goes into a series of highly sophisticated wines ranging from dry reds to vintage ports. Blends of Chenin Blanc, Chardonnay, and Verdelho are used for the white wines, and Bordeaux varieties for the reds. Sevenhill wines win lots of trophies at the Clare Valley Wine Show. Need I give more examples to show that Australian wine has a distinguished history and does not consist solely, or even principally, of massive wine factories?

As an historian by training, I naturally responded warmly to the museum tastings, and to very lively "historical relics" such as Mick Morris. It was also natural for me to treat the story of Australian wine as an historian would, telling it in chronological fashion, and hoping that the reader will accompany me on a journey of discovery. Researching and writing this story has been one of the most fascinating adventures of a quarter of a century largely devoted to writing about wine.

2

In the Beginning

In a climate so favourable, the cultivation of the vines may doubtless be carried to any degree of perfection.

CAPTAIN ARTHUR PHILLIP

The story of wine in Australia starts with the First Fleet, the convoy of convict ships which brought the first British settlers to what is now Sydney in 1788. It carried vines, some of which were sent on to Norfolk Island, 1,600 kilometres (approximately ninety-nine miles) northeast of the settlement at Port Jackson. The wines these vines were expected to produce were among the essential items (like flax, hemp, spars, and masts) that, it was thought, the new colony could supply for the home country, replacing imports from "foreign countries." Indeed, Captain Phillip, the fleet's commander, hoped that Australian wines would "become an indispensable part of the luxury of European tables". This initial declaration of faith in the capacity of the new settlement to grow grapes and make wine – a belief for which there was no evidence, since no one knew much about the continent – ensured that settlers would at least try to plant vines and thus find the best regions for them. Without that element of belief, the grapevine would never have spread so quickly, if at all, throughout most of the Australian colonies.

Vines were originally planted in what is now the heart of downtown Sydney. According to John Beeston's *Concise History of Australian Wine*, Phillip was surprised to see "how the vines thrive and I am in hopes next year of having a vineyard of five or six acres [two or 2.5ha]". But a month later he was writing to the great botanist, Sir Joseph Banks, that the vines he had brought from Brazil and the Cape – not from Europe – had resulted in "two good bunches of grapes, the first this country has produced", yet "being neglected, they decayed on the vine". This was not surprising, given the more serious problems he faced on top of the dampness of the climate during the growing season. Nevertheless, before Phillip left Port Jackson in late 1792, only four years after he had first landed, he had, in John Beeston's words, "shown that grapes could flourish even in the hands of an invalid, botanically ignorant as he himself admitted, with the assistance of only a 'tolerably good' gardener". The speed with which the vine spread and, above all, that drinkable wine was produced formed a double miracle since the settlers had been chosen for the, often very minor, crimes they had committed and not their technical competence. There was virtually no qualified winegrower among the first settlers.

The next important figure in a story that, even today, revolves largely around a handful of key individual winemakers, businessmen, and opinion-formers was Lieutenant John Macarthur, a noted polymath, who, by 1793, had built a sturdy brick house with 1.2ha "given to grapes and other fruit." The idea of an estate devoted exclusively to vines took some time to develop and Macarthur was typical in planting grapes as just one of many other fruits. Indeed, it was not until the late twentieth century that winemakers abandoned their earlier preference for planting a wide range of varieties in a single vineyard. It never occurred to the early settlers (nor to many of their successors) that particular varieties of vines were "site-specific".

There soon appeared an early example of the "cultural cringe" that was to dog Australian life for 200 years when two French prisoners of war were encouraged to plant a total of 12,000 vine cuttings on the assumption that, being French, they would know all about vines and wines. There was no real reason why they should and, indeed, they didn't; their wine was undrinkable.

Macarthur was, among other roles, a "rum baron" at a time when rum formed New South Wales's most important currency. He was also an unlikely wine enthusiast, and unfortunately, the grape varieties he gathered during a two-year trip to Europe in 1815–16 proved largely useless. He brought back between six and twelve cuttings of up to thirty varieties of vines, but within a few years he made two unfortunate discoveries. Firstly, as his son William put it, "After several years careful cultivation, the only sorts which we obtained were those now known as the Gouais, Muscat Noir, Black Hamburgh, Little Black Cluster, Miller's Burgundy, and Sweet Water, all but the first three had been previously introduced to New South Wales." Worse, virtually all of them were either table grapes, or as with the Gouais and Chasselas, produced only mediocre wines.

It was Gregory Blaxland, one of the first explorers to cross the Blue Mountains in New South Wales and identify the potential of the rich lands to the west, who planted a vineyard close to the only possible market, near Parramatta, several kilometres west of Sydney. He carefully selected vines from the Cape of Good Hope that were resistant to anthracnose, a fungal disease often called black spot by growers, and in 1822 sent a sample of the wine he made to London. There it was judged "by no means of superior quality", but was nevertheless awarded a medal to encourage the winemaker in his efforts. In 1818, Sir John Jamison, one of the largest landowners in the colony, planted a vineyard, typically as part of an enormous estate. He was clearly an innovator, for the vineyard was irrigated and, according to John Beeston, he employed "a native of Madeira" to plant the vines and "a German immigrant of long experience" to make the wines.

These were small-scale, tentative, usually amateur gestures. The true father of Australian wine was James Busby, whom Beeston calls "the apostle of the vine". Like so many other pioneers, he was not the easiest of men. He had to be obsessive to achieve what he did and he was also self-righteous to the highest degree, his self-confidence precluding the possibility of being in the wrong. Thus, it was not surprising that his achievements were not immediately recognized and that he ended his life, in the words of the *Australian Dictionary of Biography*, a "tiresome conversationalist, a lone hand, crotchety, oversensitive, and embittered".

While Busby was still in his twenties, he provided Australian growers and winemakers with the two essential ingredients required to produce wine: manuals on how to make it and a wide range of (usually suitable) vine cuttings. Such a combination was unavailable to the winemakers of any other country or region for nearly a century. Through his combined activities, Busby towers over all other contributors to the theory and practice of winemaking in Australia to this day. Partly because Australia was one of the only two countries in the British Empire capable of producing wine (the other was its historic rival, South Africa), his books and those of Alexander Kelly were the only serious nineteenth-century works published in English on viticulture and winemaking.

Busby's aim was not only to propagate the vine, but also to use wine as a social improver. Like many other reformers and many early influential contributors to Australian winemaking, he crusaded for temperance against the spirits, above all rum, which so devastated the lives of early immigrants to Australia. He knew perfectly well what he was up against, how the convicts "brought with them their prejudice in favour of malty liquor and ardent spirits. . . the settler soaks over his keg of rum till he has drained it to the dregs, regardless of the squalid wretchedness of his family". Despite Busby's efforts, for a long time wine was, in Beeston's words, a mere "droplet in a sea of alcohol," a sea comprising mainly rum and gin.

Busby was twenty-three years old when he arrived in Sydney in 1824 as a sort of colonial civil servant. He already knew a lot about agriculture in general after a spell in Ireland and travels throughout France. He had lived for some time at Cadillac, up the Garonne from Bordeaux and across the river from the famous sweet white-wine regions of Sauternes and Barsac. On his arrival in Sydney he wrote *A Treatise on the Culture of the Vine* and started teaching at an orphan school at Liverpool, a small settlement to the southwest of Sydney. He planted vines on the estate of 5,000ha (12,355 acres), surrounding the school where he put into practice the theories he had described in his book. He was also given a personal land grant of over 300ha (741 acres), an estate called Kirkton, in the Hunter Valley, 160 kilometres (99.4 miles) northwest of Sydney. The Hunter was the first region to be extensively planted with grapes after it had been discovered that the region round Sydney itself was too wet for their cultivation. Although Busby himself probably never visited Kirkton, the property remained in his family for several generations and is an important part of the story of wine in Australia.

In *A Treatise on the Culture of the Vine,* Busby confirmed Phillip's hopes, claiming that the vine furnished "the strongest probability of its supplying the great *desideratum* [his italics] of a staple article of export". There was the distinct "probability the climate of New South Wales and many of its soils, at present useless for their sterility, would be favourable for the culture of the vine". It was clear from the beginning that Busby was aiming to reach French standards of winemaking. He absorbed a great deal from the work of Professor Chaptal, Napoleon's minister of agriculture, best-known as the pioneer of adding sugar to fermenting grape juice to increase its alcoholic strength, a process still used and known as chaptalization. Even more important for Busby was Chaptal's unprecedented work on the effect of climate, seasons, soil, exposure, and culture on the plant.

In the first of many encounters with the authorities, he was sacked in a rather shabby fashion from his job at the orphan school. Undaunted, in 1831 he wrote a second book, *A Manual of Plain Directions for Planting and Cultivating Vineyards and for Making Wine in New South Wales*, a work tactfully dedicated to Lieutenant General Ralph Darling, the governor of the colony. Support was boosted by Busby's statement that his work was guided by his "strong impression of the importance to the colony of any increase of its exportable commodities". Darling distributed the book throughout New South Wales and helped it to become a best-seller among an agricultural community, many of whose members were clearly interested in growing grapes and making wine.

Busby spent the last three months of 1831 in Britain discussing his prospects with the Colonial Office, his nominal employer, and then embarked on a long tour of southern Spain and France, starting in Cadiz and ending in Epernay, heart of the Champagne region. He compared himself with the famous late eighteenth century English traveller and agricultural expert, Arthur Young, who had noted that the grape was the most profitable agricultural product of any region he visited during his stay in France.

But his biggest contribution lay in the fabulous collections of cuttings carefully wrapped to withstand the long voyage Busby brought back to New South Wales. Among them he brought back 433 from the famous viticultural school in Montpellier in southwest France and a further 110 from the gardens of the Luxembourg Palace in Paris. Of these 543 vine varieties, 362 reached New South Wales safely – and, more importantly, were mostly still healthy.

Near Perpignan in southwest France, Busby came across the local red wines, made, as Beeston describes, from "the Grenache which gives sweetness, the Carignan which gives colour, and the Mataro [called Mourvèdre outside Australia] which gives quantity". In total there were "nine bundles, containing fifty each, of nine distinct varieties of vines". He then moved to the valley of the Rhône, where he noted that the local wine, made from the Syrah grape, was widely used to strengthen even the most distinguished wines of Bordeaux, for it was the Bordelais who first introduced that supposedly purely Australian blend, Cabernet/Shiraz. (For a long time, Australian winemakers gave Shiraz the name of Hermitage, after the most famous region in which that variety was grown.)

Busby aimed to propagate his treasures "in the most suitable soil and climate", noting, especially in Burgundy, the omnipresence of limestone in the best vineyards. In the journal of the tour, which he published in 1833, he wrote that the major lesson to be learned about fine wine was that "In all those districts which produce wines of fine reputation, some few individuals have the advantage of selecting a particular variety of grape and managing its culture so as to bring it into the highest state of perfection of which it is capable." These producers also seized on "the most favourable moment for the vintage by the rapidity with which the grapes are gathered and pressed, so that the whole contents of each vat may be exactly in the same state, and a simultaneous and equal fermentation be secured throughout". They sold only the best vintages, and then only after proper maturation. Here Busby was asserting that the wine's quality was due more to the winemakers' efforts than to the characteristics of the vineyard in which the grapes were grown. In doing so, as in so many of his other achievements, he was setting a pattern that was to be followed by Australian winemakers throughout the ages, although recently, as we shall see, the nature of the vineyard has come to assume much greater importance.

Even though Busby did not visit Bordeaux or the vineyards of the Loire or Alsace, his collection included most of the classic French varieties, with a few exceptions such as Merlot and Gewürztraminer. In addition he brought back a handful of varieties grown around Jerez in southern Spain, not only the dual-purpose Gordo Blanco and Doradillo, but the Black Muscat and Cornuchon, and whites such as Muscat of Alexandria, some of which should have been used exclusively for making dried fruit and not for wine. In Spain, the Gordo Blanco, which Busby described as the "large white Muscatel", was used primarily for drying. Unfortunately, in Australia it was responsible for too many inferior – and usually fortified – wines. This was a classic example of the curse of dual usage, which was to limit the quality of fine wine produced from suitable varieties in Australia for a century and a half. Yet Busby was aware of the importance of having an alternative use for the grapes and so was aiming to acquire "a competent quantity of the most valuable varieties cultivated in the best districts of Spain and France, both for wine and raisins".

Although Busby's travels were confined to France and southern Spain, winemakers could sometimes rely on receiving cuttings picked up by travellers *en route* to the new colonies. Indeed, to understand many of the varieties grown in the first century of Australian wine, you have to follow the route taken by the ships that carried the vines. From Madeira came the Verdelho, which produces the finest wines made on the island. The variety was immediately seized on as a suitable variety for Australian conditions, and is of increasing importance today, even though it has nearly died out in its original home. From the Cape came many varieties that were often called by their Cape Dutch names, such as Hanepoot, their name for Muscat of Alexandria.

In general, however, the Australians made do with Busby's collection. It took 150 years for Australia's winemakers even to start experimenting on a commercial scale with the many varieties from Italy, Portugal, and northern Spain, whose climates are so similar to Australia's grape-growing regions. Busby's influence was enormous – and, on the whole, enormously positive. But his successors were constrained by the severe quarantine restrictions governing the import of vines into Australia which drastically limited the number of varieties the country's wine-makers had to play with. To some extent this was inevitable since, until recently, Italian varieties, in particular, were virtually unknown outside the regions where they were grown.

Busby's early passion for wine seems to have faded after his three books, although he is believed to have been the first to make wine in New Zealand. At the age of thirty-three he became closely – but usually unsuc-cessfully – involved in the country's affairs, acting as a liaison between the Maoris and the settlers.

Not surprisingly, given his temperament, for a long time the credit for the introduction of his varieties was awarded to John Macarthur and his son William. Busby's collection was planted in Sydney's embryonic Botanic Gardens, where it was neglected. Duplicates were sent to Macarthur, to Melbourne, and to the new colony in South Australia. This was fortunate because, after languishing unnoticed in a corner of the Sydney Botanic Gardens for a quarter of a century, the plants were destroyed.

A nearly complete collection of 365 varieties was also sent to Kirkton, which passed into the ownership of Busby's sister Catherine and her husband WD Kelman. Their daughter married CF Lindeman, a member of the famous winemaking family, and the vines lived on for nearly a century until they produced their last crop of a hundred gallons (379 litres) each of Chablis and burgundy as late as 1924. But Busby's true legacy was nothing less than the foundation of the industry as we know it today.

3

Liquid Gold

One can only admire the knowledge and skill of the men who chose these lands a century or more ago, when the virgin country comprised stands of timber and grassland. Some followed a particular kind of tree (peppermint gums, box ridges) or grass as an indicator of certain soil qualities. It is impossible to believe that any of them just fluked the area which now produce such subtlety and complexity as our top wines show.

DR MAX LAKE, *CLASSIC WINES OF AUSTRALIA*

Within twenty-five years of Busby's departure for New Zealand in 1833, every one of the Australian colonies had developed vineyards in a first golden age for Australian wine. Many of the regions, and many of the names of the firms we know today, had already emerged as producers of fine wine. Within a few years of the first settlements in the Hunter Valley and then in Victoria and South Australia, these regions were producing wines of world-class quality. Their histories differed, but they were all based on the largely justified assumption that virtually every region of this, the newest of worlds, could produce at least decent wine. By 1860, the country was producing over 650,000 cases of wine, a figure that multiplied sixfold in the following decade.

The boom was concentrated in three colonies – New South Wales, Victoria, and above all South Australia – but there were attempts at vine growing even in Tasmania, most dismal of penal settlements. In the west, Thomas Waters, a botanist on the ship whose captain claimed the western third of the continent for Britain, planted vines and olives on his estate on the Swan River to the north of Perth. In 1829, a mere five years later, he dug the infant colony's first wine cellar, Olive Farm, which is still in use, and the State's first government planted a vine nursery in the garden of Government House, as Captain Phillip had done forty years earlier in Sydney.

For a long time, the winemaking tradition in Western Australia, like that in New Zealand, depended largely on immigrants from the Balkans. But the single most important initiative was taken in the name of an absentee landlord, Colonel Houghton, who is still commemorated on the label of one of Australia's best-selling white wines, Houghton White Burgundy. Unfortunately, although this name can be used in Australia, the wine had to be renamed HWB in the European Union to comply with the French insistence that a wine called "burgundy" must come from Burgundy. In 1859, Houghton's property was bought by Dr John Ferguson, the colonial surgeon. His son Charles spent fifty years on the estate and made it the finest wine-producing property in the west. It included a handsome, and now equally handsomely restored, homestead. Nevertheless, with the single exception of Houghton, it was the 1970s before Western Australia developed a major wine industry.

Ferguson was not the first of the many medical men in the history of Australian wine. That accolade should probably be awarded to Robert Townson, who made a naturally sweet Muscatel from vines at Bunbury Curran near Campbelltown, southwest of Sydney. The involvement was not surprising, for wine was regarded a "temperance drink" which, it was hoped (largely ineffectually) would convert the early settlers and their successors from their excessive thirst for spirits and fortified wines. Throughout the nineteenth century, wine of every description was con- sidered a medicine the world over. This attitude was ratified by an Australian royal commission, which claimed that the country's wines were splendid for the constitution.

Wine was widely prescribed especially for invalids, hence the term "invalid port", a nasty beverage designed to strengthen the constitutions of the frail and still sold in the mid-twentieth century. Since then, medi- cal opinion has changed. "If there is one way to put me off a wine," wrote Max Lake, a famous winemaking surgeon and author, "it is to tell me it is a remedy for anything." Nevertheless, as late as 1908, Angove's, a firm founded by yet another doctor, was guaranteeing not only that its wines were "Pure and Unadulterated" but also that its St Agnes Special Vintage Claret was "stimulating and recommended by experts for invalids". The firm was echoing Doctor Auguste Mueller, an earlier medical winemaker, who actually prescribed his own prize-winning burgundy for his patients.

Doctors weren't the only ones promoting wine as part of a temperance effort. Soon after the Reverend John Ignatius Bleasdale arrived in Melbourne in the mid-1840s, he was offered "half a pint of rum and white" by some "more or less drunk" bushmen in the street. "From that time," he wrote, "I turned my attention and all the knowledge I possessed then to forwarding wine-growing and -drinking as one efficient cure for spirit-drinking and drunkenness."

Even the destitute were entitled to their medicinal ration. One doctor tending to the poor of Adelaide used to prescribe gin. In 1857, his successor asked permission for a bottle of wine a week to be allocated to each of his charges. The only restriction was designed to ensure that the wine was domestically produced and not imported. Vineyards were even planted by the doctors in charge of lunatic asylums established to treat the many settlers suffering from what we would now call stress-related ailments.

Moreover, doctors were among the very few scientifically educated settlers and they were willing to read the best texts. They also had a broad range of interests and tremendous energy. As Max Lake points out, Dr William Angove, whose wines from his property in the west Tregrehan were well-known by the late nineteenth century, was equally famous for the many hobbies he successfully undertook, including photography, sailing, horticulture, and bird-watching. In the late 1880s, Dr Angove was reading the works of Louis Pasteur, the pioneering chemist and bacteriologist, as well as those of Dr Guyot, a pioneer of scientific pruning. Hence the doctors tended to embark on the whole process of wine-making with scientific precision. In Max Lake's words, Dr John Harris, one of the pioneers of winemaking in Rutherglen, "treated wine like a patient needing intense care". He added, "He kept it under constant watch to prevent the temperature from rising to dangerous heights. He had an almost surgical approach to cleanliness."

The spread of the vine did not depend solely on doctors. One still-famous estate in the Hunter Valley, north of Sydney, is that of a gentleman settler, George Wyndham, who bought 450ha (1,112 acres) in 1828, the year after he arrived in Sydney. The first vines he received from Busby had already died. Undeterred, he continued planting on his estate, which he called Dalwood after a family property in Britain. Troubles continued and his first vintage in 1836 proved suitable only for vinegar. Nevertheless, in the 1840s, when he had to sell his still-small vineyard, there were plenty of buyers.

In the last seven years of the 1840s the vineyard area in the Hunter doubled to 230ha (568 acres) and set the pace for Australian wines in the years up to 1850. The Hunter had a number of advantages, including a superb stock of cuttings, the duplicates of those planted in Sydney's Botanic Gardens, which had been sent by Busby to Kirkton. And, thanks to the *Hunter Packet*, the ship that sailed up the Hunter River from Newcastle a hundred kilometres (sixty-two miles) up the coast, it had relatively good transport links with Sydney. Unfortunately, the climate was totally unpredictable. Summer rains varied with each vintage, although the effect of excessive heat was much reduced by the cloud cover in the ripening period of January to March. Indeed, in terms of solar radiation, and thus the rate at which grapes ripened, the Hunter resembles Bordeaux or Burgundy.

One name that has endured as an advocate for Hunter wines is that of Henry John Lindemans. He was a surgeon – at the time a profession less highly regarded than that of a doctor – who made a small fortune tending goldminers in Victoria. By 1842 he had bought a property in the Hunter, and the following year he planted one of the most famous vineyards in the country at Cawarra[1] with a range of premium wine varieties such as Pinot Noir, Cabernet Sauvignon, and Shiraz. Like other wine doctors, he fought against the rum interest that dominated the politics of the colony. In 1854, when a bill unfavourable to wine passed through parliament, he thundered, "It clearly shows that the rum bottle interest is all-paramount, and the majority of the House are its abject slaves." He became an apostle of light table wines and by 1864 was lobbying for them.

Lindeman preferred to judge the ripeness of grapes on his palate rather than relying on a "saccharometer", an early piece of equipment for measuring the level of sugar in grapes. Noting that the Hunter had "a climate for the production of very rich wine", he suggested that its wines needed blending with lighter wines to be suitable for drinking during a

[1] In the local Aboriginal language, *Cawarra* means "running water". It was possibly the first time an Aboriginal name had been used for a settler's estate.

meal. Not surprisingly, his wines followed his palate. In 1860, one journalist wrote of a "pale, clear, light wine possessing bouquet and a very delicate flavour. . . it must be Dr Lindeman's wine". The medico-winemaking tradition continued, with the likes of Scottish-born Dr Otto Wein-Smith, who in 1894 founded the Stanley Wine Company, later famous for its Leasingham brand, and his medical partner Dr Bain, who also planted a vineyard. Like Lindeman and Angove, these men were hugely energetic all-rounders.

Busby's work in promoting the vine as an essential element in a gentleman's country estate bore fruit with John Macarthur's son William. William Macarthur was a quarrelsome fellow who refused to acknowledge the help he received from James King, the finest winemaker in the Hunter Valley, in resolving the problem of fermentation stopping prematurely by adding the juice of the Gouais, a thin white variety, and a frequently used remedy.

William Macarthur wrote extremely practical articles on his winemaking experiences, which were published in 1844 as a book. He also classified the known grape varieties and divided them into early ripeners, such as Traminer, which tended to be unsuitable for making a palatable wine because they did not develop enough acid; mid-season varieties, such as Riesling; and late ripeners, such as the reds Busby had brought back from the south of France. This was an extremely useful contribution since pioneering growers tended not to know that varieties ripened at different dates. The vineyards were a jumble of varieties, many of them of uncertain origin, for the winemakers could not afford to specialize in one variety.

James King was a prosperous merchant who realized that he had to learn winemaking and sought advice from a famous German chemist named von Liebig. As a result, his Semillon wine (called Shepherd's Riesling) became famous even in Germany. He also founded and was the first chairman of the Hunter River Vineyard Association, the first winemakers' organization in Australia, though, inevitably, it was dominated by doctors headed by Dr Lindeman. It was founded after a series of bitter arguments as to whether wine or wool was the more profitable crop in the region. It helped the cause of the vine that by then the yield in the Hunter was about 30 hl per ha, greater than in most European vineyards at the time. In 1848, the association conducted probably the first comparative tasting in the country's history when one of King's red wines (perhaps a blend of "Pineau Noire" (sic) and "Pineau Gris") was acclaimed as better than a wine from Chambertin.

Until the late 1970s, the names of the grape varieties in Australia were hopelessly confused, as were the labels attached to the wines themselves. Because most of the wine sold in Britain in the late eighteenth and early nineteenth centuries was either openly fortified or, as in the case of claret, strengthened with stronger wine or spirits, "Britons brought to Australia," wrote Oliver Mayo, held "odd views about what the wines of France were like. 'Claret' described wines which were almost undrinkable when young, on account of their acid and tannin content, and 'burgundy' described wines that were softer, richer in flavour, lower in acid, and much higher in alcohol. . . It was natural that the English should also use German names, Hock and Moselle, for white wines that were predominantly dry and firm or floral and softer."

William Macarthur didn't sort out these confusions but he made other major contributions, including the foundation of the New South Wales Vineyard Association – in obvious competition to King's similar group in the Hunter. Macarthur used this body to persuade a reluctant Colonial Office to allow skilled German families to come and work on his estate at Camden Park, thus opening the way for German immigrants, who were to have such a beneficial influence on Australian wine as a whole.

Macarthur's major coup was to introduce Australian wines to the world through exhibiting them at the Paris Universal Exhibition of 1855, the same one that produced the famous classification of the wines of Bordeaux which retains its authority 150 years later. At the closing ceremony of the exhibition, a sparkling wine made by James King was served to the Emperor Napoleon III and other distinguished guests. King was one of the first to realize that exports were vital to the success of Australian wine, and Macarthur followed suit. As early as 1849, King was lobbying for a reduction in duties, and was successful in getting parity with the producers from Australia's great imperial rival, the Cape of Good Hope.

Though it was the first, the Hunter did not remain the only vineyard region in New South Wales. By 1876, the year that marked a high-water mark for New South Wales's wine production, the Hunter had less than forty per cent of the colony's vines, ten per cent fewer than a decade earlier. There were, for instance, no fewer than thirty-three vineyards in the Hastings River area on the coast north of Sydney. Even what are now regarded as "new" regions, such as Mudgee on the western side of the Great Dividing Range, had been planted with vines. In 1858, three German families, Roth, Kurtz, and Buchholz, had established vines in Mudgee, which kept going for a century.

But relatively soon, New South Wales had been overtaken in wine production by both Victoria and South Australia. The reason for Victoria's importance is simple: the discovery of gold in the 1850s in Ballarat, Geelong, Bendigo, and later as far afield as Beechworth, northeast of Melbourne. Wealth from the mines enabled the population of Victoria to treble in the 1850s. Melbourne became one of the magic cities of the Victorian age, big and sophisticated enough to house larger numbers of wine connoisseurs than any other city in Australia, a distinction it maintained until the rise of Sydney in the 1960s. Yet the discovery was both a boon and a curse; on one hand, it engendered prosperity and thus much more a disposable income, but at the same time it became increasingly difficult to find labour to work in the vineyards and the cellars.

The two phenomena, gold and wine, were closely associated. In 1856, a mere four years after the discovery of gold nearby, a Mr Rochlitz planted the first vines at Beechworth in country regarded as wild bush. He had imported ninety-five varieties of vines from Adelaide "at great expense and trouble", according to local paper *The Ovens & Murray Advertiser*.

The story of wine in Victoria starts with Charles La Trobe, an Englishman of French extraction who arrived in Australia in 1839 to act as superintendent of the new town of Melbourne. He went on to become lieutenant-governor of the colony. When Victoria gained its independence from New South Wales in 1850, the toast was drunk in a wine made by one Monsieur Pelet, who had married La Trobe's housekeeper.

Melbourne's climate proved far more suitable than that of Sydney for the cultivation of the vine, which flourished in most of the city's private gardens. However, the biggest concentration was sixty kilometres (thirty-seven miles) to the north in the Yarra Valley, an idyllic region settled by the Ryrie brothers after they had travelled overland from New South Wales. William Ryrie had brought vines with him, which he planted on land where he had squatted. It helped that the slopes above the valley enjoyed much the same climatic conditions as those of Burgundy.

La Trobe was a typical man of parts, described by the American traveller and novelist Washington Irving as "a man of a thousand occupations; a botanist, a geologist, a hunter of beetles and butterflies, a musical amateur, a sketcher of no mean pretensions; in short, a complete virtuoso. . . never had a man more irons in the fire". He established a vineyard in the grounds of the governor's residence, but his greatest influence on the colony's wines came through his Swiss wife, a member of the de Montmollin family from Neuchâtel, one of the very few wine-growing regions in Switzerland. Hubert de Castella, another *émigré* from Neuchâtel, remembered the great sensation caused by "the departure for the Antipodes of a lady belonging to one of the oldest and richest families of the town". This was nothing compared to "the astonishment and awe of us little children when told how Mrs La Trobe would be six months on the big sea, how she was to take a wooden house with her in the ship to live in it in a country peopled by savages".

In the early 1840s, Mrs La Trobe's example was followed by over a hundred *vignerons* and labourers from the Neuchâtel region. These immigrants dominated winemaking not only in the Yarra, but also in Geelong, eighty kilometres (fifty miles) southwest of Melbourne. Extraordinary as it may seem to those who think of Switzerland as a uniformly prosperous society, at that time the Swiss rural regions were impoverished and thus a natural source of emigrants. Hubert de Castella's brother Paul had originally fled from Switzerland to London because of his involvement in the *Sonnerbond*, a league of Catholic cantons that had tried to break away from the Swiss Confederation. In 1849, Paul de Castella bought an estate in the Yarra on which vines had already been planted by William Ryrie. But de Castella went much further, buying 20,000 Cabernet Sauvignon vines from Château Lafite. Hubert saw how different regions could make "the light wines of France and Germany and also the rich wines of the warm latitudes, the latter being the rule". Technically, the combination of a cool climate and the presence of the much-prized "terra rossa"/limestone soil made it an ideal region for making the "cool-climate" wines that were to become so famous in the late twentieth century. Sensibly, his family's clients bought "the wine grown on the hill, and they do not like that grown on the flat".

Not surprisingly, de Castella waxed lyrical about this Elysian valley: "Hills after hills seem as if they had tumbled down from this last

[Dandenong] mountain, invaded the valley from the open end, and stopped just sufficiently away from the winding Yarra to display a succession of most romantic landscapes with a climate whose temperate moisture insures to the must the lightness so peculiar to the Yarra wines." The three hills that dominate the region are crowned with famous vineyards: Yering, St Hubert's, and Yeringberg. This last superb estate, one of the country's rare vineyards to be in the same family for over 150 years, was bought in 1870 by Guillaume de Pury, the aristocratic Swiss consul in Melbourne.[2] The quality of the Yarra Valley wines inspired their producers to fight what Hubert de Castella called the hard fight of good light wines against a population of beer- and spirit-drinkers. Not surprisingly, the valley reminded people of what Beeston calls a "vinous Camelot" in later, sadder days after World War I when the vines had been uprooted.

But the winemaker's life was not an easy one. De Castella was speaking for many other pioneers when he wrote, "We did not anticipate, when we began our plantations, the difficulties of all kinds which were awaiting us." Because of the cool climate, it took four years before a substantial crop was produced. The winemakers had to build cellars and buy increasing numbers of casks as stocks of unsold wines grew. As a result, de Castella continued, "To the vinegrower's enterprise each of us had to add that of the wine merchant, a difficult and ungrateful occupation to a country resident."

By the 1850s, wine was also being made in Geelong by Swiss and German growers, some of whom had acquired Pinot Noir vines from Dijon. We know about them through the letters sent home to Boudry, a few kilometres from Neuchâtel, by Charles Louis Tetaz, who had followed his uncle David Pettavel to the promised land.[3] He soon found that there were English syndicates buying a million young vines for a new vineyard in the Geelong region. According to Tetaz, "If things go on on this scale, this will be as much a wine-growing country as it is for pasture and agriculture." Tetaz soon found the best varieties: Hermitage, "very dark in colour and has a nice bouquet and a high alcohol content", and

---

[2] The existence of the consulate was a clear indication of the importance of Swiss immigrants in the colony.

[3] John Tetaz, *From Boudry to the Barrabool Hills*. In 2000, a new vineyard was named after Pettavel.

"Carignon": "one of the finest [varieties] there is". The Swiss and Germans remained rather aloof from the English and were relatively self-sufficient, asking when writing home only for a wine press, Swiss secateurs, and a recipe for "fortifying new wine with absinthe".

In 1862, when the gold boom showed signs of abating, the Victorian government began to encourage large-scale farming by allocating leases to newcomers outside known agricultural areas. The settlers found that the most profitable crops were tobacco and grapes. Immigrants could buy up to 260ha (640 acres) – one square mile – per person (the grant was halved later in the decade) for a mere £1 per 0.4ha, provided that they lived on the property for seven years. In a deliberate effort to encourage winemaking, the authorities also allowed immigration by non-British "vine dressers" who would tend and prune the vines.

Perhaps not surprisingly, these measures set off the first of so many mad rushes by non-winemakers to invest in vineyards. As de Castella put it: "Lawyers, doctors, and men of means, taking land under the new clauses, planted vineyards by proxies. Various syndicates were formed for a large extent of vines. In four years, over 2,000 acres [809ha] were planted. Speculation, fashion, public opinion, all were pointing to prosperity." Unfortunately, the rush concentrated on regions more suitable for stronger wines. "The light wines of the cooler districts, sold too young and cheaper on account of their lesser strength, mixed by amateur wine merchants with the former ones, developed their acidity", de Castella concluded.

In many cases, the investors and the owners of estates were not farmers or gold-miners but merchants and traders who had done well out of the gold boom. A typical family were the Trouettes, who had first settled in Beechworth and then set up a mixed farm in the Great Western region in 1863, relying on the knowledge brought by Jean Trouette from the Gers *departement* in Gascony, home of Armagnac. The Best family, founders of one of the region's best-known wineries, Great Western, in the region of the same name, had made their money as owners of a slaughterhouse and butchery business.

By the 1870s, they were employing former miners to dig the famous "drives", the tunnels originally used for maturing table wine. Later, in the hands of Hans Irvine, the Bests' successor, they proved crucial for maturing the region's famous sparkling wines. According to WS Benwell in *Journey to Wine in Victoria*, the miners "could use a pick like a precision tool, and their "signatures" are still there today by the million in the form of six-inch [fifteen-centimetre] stroke marks' on the walls.

To create fizzy wines, Irvine imported bottles from France because Australian manufacturers could not produce bottles of sufficient strength. Fortunately, Irvine found a firm supporter in Lord Hopetoun, the governor of Victoria. In 1901, he became the first governor-general of the Commonwealth of Australia after the previously independent colonies had – painfully, partially, and belatedly – formed themselves into a loose federation which left a great deal of power to the individual states. Hopetoun was a notably free-spending bon viveur and Irvine's "champagne" featured at most of his parties. Hopetoun stated publicly that Irvine's fizz would "satisfy the most exacting connoisseurs".

By 1860, northern Victoria had begun to attract organized capital, the result of the activities of Richard Horne, an entrepreneurial jack-of-all trades around Melbourne whose activities included being the Australian correspondent for the magazines edited by Charles Dickens. Horne organized the company that set up what is still one of Victoria's most famous properties: Chateau Tahbilk[4] by the banks of the Goulburn River in central Victoria. In a foretaste of the corporate jugglings of the second half of the twentieth century, the investment company was called, successively, the Tahbilk Vineyard Company, Australian Vineyards Proprietary Ltd, Tahbilk Vineyards Proprietary Ltd and Australian Freehold Land and Produce Company Ltd. Ludovic Marie, a Burgundian-born immigrant, first planted vines at the homestead, convinced that they would grow there after he had noticed that box trees flourished, because they, like vines, require deep, porous soil. By 1861, eighty ha (200 acres) had been planted with a number of wine varieties, some, like Riesling, still fashionable today; some, like Aucerot and Gouais, virtually unknown now. By 1870, the fabled Old Cellars, which are one hundred metres (328 feet) long, had been dug.

Tahbilk flourished under an outstanding viticulturalist, François de Coueslant, helped by a new cellar (still in use today) built in a mere ten weeks in early 1876 – crucially, the year after the railway from Melbourne

---

[4] *Tabilk* (the original spelling) means place of many waterholes in the local Aboriginal language. No one seems to know when the "h" was added.

arrived nearby. By 1886, Tahbilk had become the fourth largest estate in Victoria, producing 2,730hl a year. At the time, wrote de Castella, "Australian vignerons are imported from all countries and have methods each of his own province." De Couselant ensured that the vines were cultivated according to his ideas (he also, unsuccessfully, tried to breed silkworms and grow olives).

The biggest producing regions in Victoria were Rutherglen and Glenrowan, key points on the way to the gold-mines. Combined, they boasted 1,000ha (2,471 acres) producing mostly rich red wines – the biggest winemaking regions not only in Victoria, but also probably in the whole of Australia at the time. Together they represented a third of all the grapes grown in Victoria. Northeast Victoria was a region of large estates: five growers had estates of around eighty hl (198 acres), and together with nearly 150 other winemakers, they produced 3.5 million litres of wine a year.

A typical case is that of George Francis Morris. In 1859, after making money as a merchant supplying the miners, he bought an estate that started as a mixed farm. By the late 1870s, the vineyard had been connected to Melbourne by the all-important railway. By 1885, Morris had the largest acreage of vines in the region and won the first gold medal for Australian wine in Europe at the 1873 Vienna Exhibition. In a classic demonstration of the relationship between gold and wine, a vineyard was established in Rutherglen by a Dr Harkin to employ miners when the gold had run out. It was later bought by Peter Burgoyne, the famous British importer.

Even then, fine wines increased in value as they matured. One grower, Anthony Ruche, hoarded his wines for twenty years, selling the 310hl involved for over £1,680 to a merchant who managed to double the price within the day. Ruche's property became even more famous when it passed into the hands of the Chambers family, who today makes some of the world's finest dessert wines. Richard Bailey, a former storekeeper at Glenrowan, turned to the soil – and above all, vines – after he had made his fortune. Baileys of Glenrowan is still famous for its Muscat and Tokay.

The winemaking supremacy enjoyed by South Australia owed little to mining of gold, copper or silver-lead. More important was the fact that the colony had been settled by free men and women, and not by convicts. The high cost of land for free settlers in South Australia meant that their produce had to be of high value. In Max Lake's words, South Australia "was founded to substantiate a theory that if land were sold to men of substance, they would appreciate it, would have a stake in the country and use their best energy to develop it". This was only one factor in the colony's success. Such were South Australia's natural advantages that within thirty years, most of its best winemaking districts were already producing, and many of the names still familiar today were flourishing.

The wine culture of South Australia was born with the colony itself. In June 1836, the very first edition of the *South Australian Gazette and Colonial Register* wrote how the soil and climate of the newly founded colony offered "peculiar advantages for the cultivation of the grape". Yet it started with a number of disadvantages. Its "domestic" market was smaller than that available in the two other wine-producing colonies, for Adelaide was, and remains, far smaller than either Sydney or Melbourne. In addition, thanks to impenetrable import duties between the separate colonies, their markets were closed to South Australian winemakers until the colonies federated to form the Commonwealth of Australia in 1901.

It was Edward Gibbon Wakefield who created the idea behind the foundation of South Australia. Wakefield's plan was astute: land would not be given away, thus giving rise to speculation, but be sold at a fixed price. Money from land sales would be used only to help emigration by labourers, many of whom, he hoped (not without reason) would eventually buy land of their own. His ideas were put into practice by George Fife Angas, who became the chairman of the all-powerful South Australian Company. Angas's vision of large pastoral estates replaced that of Edward Wakefield, who had envisaged relatively small farms of thirty or so ha (seventy-four acres).

By 1839, a mere three years after the colony's first governor arrived, one AH Davis had planted the colony's first commercial vineyard, just west of the new town of Adelaide, from a large collection of cuttings he had obtained from the "mother lode" brought from Europe by James Busby. By the mid-1840s, Walter Duffield was well enough established to try to export wine to London – though arguments raged over whether it had been sent through "proper channels". At the time the local government clearly thought not, since Duffield was prosecuted for selling wine without a licence.

Vines were evidently going to be a major element in the economy of

South Australia. Edward Gleeson, the first mayor of the town of Clare, which he named after his birthplace, established a fund to obtain vines from the Cape – clearly considered the most reliable source of new varieties. Not surprisingly, Wakefield could state that Adelaide growers depended on their vines, either partially or solely, for their livelihood. Wine was seen as a potential source of great wealth to the colony, with climate and soil close to ideal. The government even encouraged the construction of the distilleries needed to produce the spirit for making the fortified wines that were always important in Australian wine production, and in 1858 passed the Wark Act which regularized their legal status.

In South Australia, as earlier in New South Wales, doctors played a major role in the wine business. Dr Christopher Rawson Penfold, one of the earliest South Australian winemakers, arrived in Adelaide in 1844. Like many other newcomers he had bought a large estate unseen – in his case that of Magill. He set up a medical practice that was soon highly successful on his property, which he called the Grange, a few miles east of the town. He had brought with him cuttings of Grenache he had obtained during a visit to the south of France which had been sealed in wax for the long journey before they were planted at Magill Estate. The wine Penfold produced, Grange Grenache, was at first available only on prescription as a (quite genuine) pick-me-up for immigrants. He felt that imported wines were no use, being inferior specimens "left over for the colonies" and that only the stronger wines he knew he could make would be of any use for anaemic patients. These included the majority of the immigrants who had been cooped up and deprived of adequate nourishment throughout the six-month voyage. His own preference was for port. After Penfold's death in 1870, his widow Mary and her son-in-law Thomas Hyland continued to expand the business.

The most amazing testimony to the rapid spread of the vine comes in a book by Ebenezer Ward, journalist, politician, and scallywag – for in 1880 he was forced to resign from his seat in the South Australian parliament, had been declared bankrupt and described as a "deceiver, a sot, and a debauchee". Even so, and like many journalists, Ward was a reliable observer. In early 1862, before his scandal, Ward toured many of the gentlemen's estates that were already well-established by what was termed the "squattocracy" in most of the major winemaking areas south to McLaren Vale and north to Tanunda in the Barossa Valley. From Ward's detailed, if obsequious, descriptions it is clear that wine was by no means the only crop but part of a balanced agricultural holding, hence the permanent Australian habit of referring to grapes simply as "fruit."

As Ward put it, the settlers were making "earnest persevering effort to make a *better*, and the *best* wine" (his italics). Not surprisingly, they were eager students of books on the subject. Ward was convinced that "South Australia will without doubt become one of the most important wine countries in the world" – the only problem, then as now, was "the large quantities of young, immature wines annually forced into the market". For within a mere quarter of a century after the first settlers had arrived in the mid-1830s, there were 1,287ha (3,180 acres) of vineyards in South Australia. Ward's survey covered only a third of the total, most of them vineyards on slopes rather than valley floors.

On average there were only 1,200 vines for every 0.4ha (acre) to make ploughing between the rows easier – a contrast with European habits that have lasted to this day – although a few owners preferred to crowd their vines to preserve their health and obtain a better quality of fruit. They often trailed their vines on trellises, using wire, a rarity in Europe at the time. Though average production seems to have been much the same as in the Hunter Valley, Ward also found examples of yields three times as high.

Typical was John Reynell's 182ha (450-acre) estate at Reynella, twenty kilometres (12.4 miles) south of Adelaide, which expanded into a town named after him. The cave cellar Reynell had dug is still preserved on the property, now the site of the head office of BRL Hardy. Originally, the estate was designed for a combination of vine-growing, grazing, and farming. Reynell had received cuttings of Pineau from William Macarthur, but they failed and he fell back on the reliable Spanish varieties, Palomino and Pedro Ximénez. Most of these estate owners grew a wide variety of fruits other than grapes: the Hon CG Everard had a dozen varieties of orange trees as well as "kumquat, Lisbon lemon, and citron trees", and Mr RR Torrens even managed to get banana trees to flourish. The aim was often commercial – at Wattleville, the Hon Thomas Reynolds MP was already making twenty-two tonnes of plum jam, a figure he was aiming to increase to sixty tonnes.

In most cases the South Australian winemakers planted a seemingly endless list of grape varieties, although Mr Patrick Auld had a "Verdelho Hill" planted exclusively with that variety. More typically, for his estate in

Clarendon a few kilometres southeast of Adelaide, Ward noted that Mr Edward John Peake had imported from Spain "Pedro Ximenes [sic], Palomino-blanco, Temprana, Doradilla, Mantua, Castellano, and some other white varieties whose names were lost in transition and have not been identified, while of the purple sorts there were the Molar Negro, and Ferastes Colora". He later planted the varieties found on most estates, "Shiraz, Malbec, Carbonet, Mataro, Carignan, Grenache, and Morastel, of the red varieties; and Verdelho, Gouais, Riesling, and Tokay of the white".

The names varied wildly. As Ward notes, the pioneering work of the French scientist Jules Guyot had established that "there are only forty known varieties worth cultivating, but these are called by no less than 300 different names". Of the most important varieties the Hermitage/Shiraz was often used for blending, while the Grenache flourished "no matter how the weather had been". And if the vines turned out to be of an inferior variety, like Sweetwater, they could be grafted with better varieties.

Both cultivation and, soon, winemaking were relatively sophisticated. The winemakers realized that they needed to induce the roots of the vines to grow downwards. While many of them didn't like irrigation, they recognized its necessity. They used ducks, which were let out at night to gobble up the "grubs". They already knew that the "first-quality" wine was that "drawn without pressure from the grapes". Some wineries – like that at Seppeltsfield in the Barossa Valley – were built on slopes so gravity fed the grapes into the vats in the absence of electric or petrol power. Large casks, often made out of American oak, which helped the rich, sweet style of wines from the Barossa, were used to provide balanced fermentation by allowing juices from a number of sources to blend. The winemakers knew that vats should be kept full to avoid oxidation through allowing too much air into the fermenting juice, while casks previously used for beer or spirits were avoided. But fine winemaking was not enough to ensure success in all cases. In 1862, Evandale, owned by Henry Evans, was the largest cellar in the colony. Ward signalled Evans's estate as a model; its owner "had an eye to the ornamental as well as the useful". He was a fanatic for cleanliness; his winemaker, Carl August Sobels, was a pioneer in barrel-fermentation and produced famously good wines. Nevertheless, in 1868 Evans died, and his widow converted the premises into a factory for dried fruit.

By 1850, vine-growing had spread eighty kilometres (fifty miles) north of Adelaide to the Barossa Valley. The pioneer of the region was one Joseph Gilbert. He planted what are now called premium varieties such as Riesling and Verdelho high above the valley in what were then known as the Barossa Ranges, now called Pewsey. The hills, at around 600 metres (1,968 feet), were cooler than the valley floor and have proved ideal for vines. Johann Christian Henschke, a builder and stonemason by trade, emigrated from Germany and set up at Keyneton, then called by the evocative name of North Rhine. But the Barossa[5] proper was dominated by settlers from Silesia, a region which then belonged to the king of Prussia but is now in southwest Poland. The trigger for the migration of so many Silesians in the late 1830s occurred in 1822, when King Frederick III of Prussia imposed a new liturgy that was too Calvinist in tone for many of his Lutheran subjects.

The Reverend Augustus Kavel of Klemzig, a Lutheran priest, led the way after a meeting in London with George Fife Angas. Angas had asked Johannes Menge, a German mineralogist, to explore the Barossa, and Menge had found it eminently suitable for all types of agriculture. In 1840, Menge had written to George Fife Angas: "I am quite certain that we shall see flourishing vineyards and orchards and immense fields of corn throughout new Silesia." The Barossa, he said, was "the cream, the whole cream, and nothing but the cream of South Australia, to skim from the milk". This creamy landscape could, of course, be used for grazing and general agriculture as well as viticulture, for the Barossa was not totally reliant on vines. As Beeston puts it, during the 1860s "three primary industries – mining, grazing, and viticulture – proceeded side by side". Nevertheless, over the years the vines took over. By 1861 they occupied 180ha (445 acres); by 1881, 560ha (1,384 acres). Ten years later, the figure had trebled and represented over half of all the vines in the whole state. By then the landscape of the valley had assumed the aspect it still bears today, complete not only with vines but also with small towns, each with their own German butchers, bakers, and Lutheran chapels.

By 1838, the first shipload of Silesians was on its way to Australia,

---

[5] There is some dispute about the name. The most authoritative version is that it was named by Colonel Light after a battle in the Peninsula War in which a friend of his had fought. Others say the name means a hill of roses. In both cases it should have been written *Barrosa*.

where most of them settled on land provided by Angas in and around Adelaide. The first twenty-eight German families in the Barossa created their own *Hufendorf*, or community, which they called Bethanien (now Bethany), while later ones included Langmeil (now called Tanunda).[6] From the beginning they were self-sufficient, for they were not all farmers. They included skilled artisans such as carpenters, cabinet-makers, wheelwrights, and tailors.

The Barossa Valley was always totally different from any other wine-growing area in Australia. As wine-writer Max Allen put it, the Barossa "was settled in an orderly manner. . . whole communities. . . the butcher, the baker, the priest all upped and shifted. And in this Brave New World, everybody had an orchard, a garden, a well, and, crucially, a small vineyard" – often planted with varieties the immigrants had brought with them. The cohesiveness of the community, marred only by squabbles between its churches, proved long-lasting, as did the families, even those not of Silesian origin, for the community's social fabric remains solid to this day. As George Bell and Geoffrey Bishop noted, "Families such as Atze, Boehm, Both, Burgemeister, Gerlach, Graetz, Gramp, Habermann, Hage, Hahn, Henschke, Hoffman, Hueppauff, John, Kies, Kleemann, Kreig, Lawes, Leirsch, Mader, Munzburg, Obst, Pech, Plush, Rohrlach, Schild, Schiller, Schliebs, Schmidt, Schrapel, Schulz, Schwartz, Semmler, Seppelt, Smith, Stiller and Waechter have been *vignerons* for over 120 years."

Many of the immigrants established wineries, some of which, such as Seppelt, Orlando, Henschke, and Yalumba remain famous to this day. But today the most famous name is that of William Jacob. He had been an assistant to Colonel Light when Light was surveying the district and had spotted the potential of the land round one rivulet in the south of the valley called Moorooroo. After Jacob bought the land and settled there, it was named after him: Jacob's Creek. The potential of the slopes above the little river were also spotted by a Bavarian immigrant, Johann Gramp. He had arrived on Kangaroo Island, off Adelaide, in 1837 and nine years later bought land on Jacob's Creek near Rowland Flat. He planted vines and, as was only natural, made a dry white Riesling, which he called a

[6] Named after the Aboriginal term for water-hole.

hock. He named both his business and the vineyard he had planted at Rowland Flat Orlando, which is still a famous name.

But the kings of the Barossa for over a hundred years were the Seppelt family. Joseph Ernest Seppelt was born in 1813, in a small town in Silesia, and was educated – largely through travels – to take over a family business, which he concentrated on snuff, tobacco, and the distilling and blending of liqueurs. In 1849, he gathered about him his family, then consisting of two sons and a daughter, as well as the families of thirteen neighbours and a group of young men from his factory, and took them all off to South Australia. In 1851, after an unsuccessful attempt to grow tobacco on an estate near Adelaide, he moved north to what was by then termed New Silesia. There he bought two estates and founded a settlement still known as Seppeltsfield.

At first, Seppelt planted wheat and tobacco, but soon, like so many of his fellow immigrants, he followed the advice Menge had given Angas. By then Menge lived in the wild, was thought of as a half-mad seer, and was nicknamed "Professor" Menge. Yet he was not truly insane; he was increasingly convinced that, "New Silesia will furnish the province with such a quantity of wine that we shall drink it as cheaply as in Cape Town." Seppelt made enough money selling wheat to the miners in Victoria to afford the wait while the vines grew. During the 1850s, he started to sell wine at the local market town of Gawler and to settlements along the Murray River. But he never forgot his native skill at making liqueurs – always a profitable business – and the increasingly imposing premises at Seppeltsfield were best-known as a distillery.

Joseph Ernst died in 1868, leaving Benno, the oldest of his sons (by then nine in number) to take over at the tender age of twenty-one. Over the next sixty-four years, right up to his death at the age of eighty-five in 1932, Benno became and remained one of the outstanding figures in the wine industry. Indeed, Benno was a real businessman. While most of the owners of individual estates relied exclusively on the grapes they grew themselves, he bought grapes from many growers to make wines in what the French would call an "agribusiness". Benno Seppelt was ever-restless. "Standing still is going back," he would say. He was a brilliant engineer – it was said that once he had seen any form of mechanical device he could return home and draw it to scale – and his talent ensured that all the mechanical equipment in Seppeltsfield was thoroughly modern. But

Seppelt was not the only technical innovator. At the Stanley winery in Clare, to the north of the Barossa, Alfred Basedow, a winemaker of German extraction working for the Knappstein family, had installed an early refrigerator that enabled him to cool 4,550 litres of wine by 5.5 °C (10 °F) in little over an hour.

Seppeltsfield, like most of the other estates in the late nineteenth century, was a business – not one of the gentlemen's estates Ward had described. Benno Seppelt started with the ambition of adding eight ha (twenty acres) to his estate every year. He grazed sheep on much of the land and added a major vinegar-making plant to the distillery and winery. His white vinegar was particularly prized. His wine won numerous awards and he was particularly good at making fortified wines – his sherries were sold (in lots of fifty dozen) in the Albert Hall in London.

By the 1880s, one of the many visitors to Seppeltsfield, still a handsome, dignified estate, could say that the winery was "quite a little town" complete with "the laboratory, the winery, the cellars, the distillery, the vinegar works, the cooperage, the blacksmith's shop, and the piggery".[7] The visitor was also impressed "with the methodical way in which everything is conducted". Benno was twenty years ahead in the use of the hydraulic press, years ahead also in "the use of the pasteurizer. . . there was a serpentine cooling device. . . a mobile poultry house, a butter cooler on the drip safe principle, gadgets in the chaff and corn rooms and stables. . . grape skins were stored in concrete sileage pits and subsequently fed to pigs. . . Seppeltsfield bacon fetched special prices", possibly because of "a delicate impregnation of wine". This diversification helped Benno Seppelt ride over the regular depressions in the economy – and the wine business – in the 1870s, and the even deeper one that occured twenty years later. By the end of the century, Seppelt accounted for one-third of all the 7.5 million bottles produced in the Barossa. To ensure that his sons were capable of following him, he sent them off to study in France.

There were a few non-Germans in and around the Barossa. One was Edward Salter, whose money came from a copper mine on his property Mamre Brook (later a famous brand). Salter dug cellars and experimented with different types of wine, experiments he recorded in his *vigneron's*

[7] *The House of Seppelt 1851–1951*, The Advertiser Printing Office, Adelaide, 1951.

journal. He was particularly happy when he made a port wine from Grenache at his famous cellars at Saltram. Yalumba, a firm and brand built up by another English immigrant, Samuel Smith, remains a strong force in the wine industry. Smith was a brewery worker from Wareham on the coast of Dorset. While he was not exactly a religious *émigré*, his Congregationalist fervour was certainly part of his decision to emigrate - not for nothing was South Australia as a whole known as a paradise of dissent. Smith was encouraged by the omnipresent George Fife Angas – and the promise of free passage. In December 1847, Smith, with his wife and four children, landed in Australia. Two years later they settled near the new town of Angaston, in the east of the Barossa.

Smith's talents as a horticulturalist fitted in with Angas's ideas and he enjoyed one early piece of luck when Angas entrusted him with some of James Busby's collection of vines. Four years after his arrival, Smith worked for a few months in the Victorian goldmines and earned £300: enough to buy thirty-two ha (eighty acres) of land. By 1862, Ward could report that his estate, called "Yealumba"[8] was planted mainly with Shiraz. In an echo of the eternal splits among the Silesians in the Barossa, Smith and a handful of other worthies walked out of the local church to found their own independent congregation, composed of believers in infant baptism, as against the orthodox belief in adult baptism.

From the start, Smith made wine good enough to win praise and medals. He specialized in what they then called "Albillo" (in fact, Chenin Blanc) which was eminently suitable for the sherries that remained best-sellers in Britain until some years after World War II and in Australia until the 1960s. By this time, Smith was running not just a vineyard but a business. In 1880, he owned over twenty-four ha (sixty acres) of vines and was buying grapes from another thirty-eight growers. In 1889, the year of his death, he was engaged in extending his cellars and setting up a factory to preserve fruit from his estate, which by then amounted to forty ha (one hundred acres).

The Clare Valley was also settled by Germans, in this case a group led by a wealthy farmer called Wiekert, who brought with him two Jesuit priests as well as cuttings of a vine that they naturally called Clare

[8] Ward's spelling is wrong. The estate was never called anything other than *Yalumba,* an Aboriginal term meaning "all the country around".

Riesling. This was later identified as Crouchen, although today the region is famous for the clean, aromatic wines made from "real" or, as it is called in Australia, "Rhine" Riesling.

At first the priests' vineyard produced only sacramental wines, but they then diversified into fine table wines which are still winning prizes today. The descendants of another German immigrant, JH Knappstein (who settled in the Clare in 1877 after making money selling produce to the mines) are still widely respected winemakers. One of the Clare's early *vignerons*, John Horrocks, was involved in what must surely be the most bizarre incident in Australian viticultural history when he was shot by his camel, said to be the first of its kind in Australia. According to Oliver Mayo in his book *The Wines of Australia,* the beast "kicked his gun as Horrocks handed it to his servant". The homicidal animal had already frightened the bullocks and was immediately shot.

Virtually all these settlers worked together, as was natural in a hard, pioneering, sparsely populated country. "Regular trips," wrote Aeuckens, "were made [by Edward Salter of Saltram] to Seppeltsfield and Yalumba to seek advice and discuss common problems." Advice was willingly given by Samuel Smith's son Sidney, Benno Seppelt, Thomas Hardy (who had a contract to purchase Salter's wines), and later by Professor Perkins. The same friendliness was, however, not forthcoming from one JC Gelly at Chateau Tanunda, of whom Salter said, "He was not very communicative" – a reputation gained by the Seppelts some decades later. "Gelly," Salter added, "was recognized as a fine winemaker and obviously did not intend to share that reputation."

Among the wine pioneers were a number of itinerant experts, what would now be called "flying" (or rather "galloping") winemakers. Possibly the most famous was Carl August Sobels, a native of Dresden, who had gained his spurs as advisor to the then-great Champagne house of Montebello near Ay, south of Reims. With his brother-in-law Hermann Buring, a former Seppelt employee, Sobels was part-owner of an estate in Clare that became famous for producing Quelltaler hock.[9] He also worked as winemaker or adviser to at least three other important estates, including that of Henry Evans. His recipe seems to have been simple. As

[9] They clearly thought that "Springvale," the English translation of the name of the wine and the estate, did not have enough charisma for the taste of the late-nineteenth-century drinker.

Ebenezer Ward noted, "The chief characteristics appear to be care and cleanliness. . . the addition of brandy, colouring matter, or flavourings of any kind he regards as altogether unnecessary except in wet or unfavourable vintages."

Wines were soon included in the products entered in Australia's many agricultural shows in capital cities and in wine-growing regions. The aim, with wine as with sheep, was to "improve the breed". The first show in which wine was exhibited was probably the Adelaide show as early as 1845. By 1850, there was a show in Sydney, precursor to the many such events that were to spread the fame of the best Australian wines in the following century and a half. Before 1860, local shows had sprung up in the Barossa Valley; entries jumped from a single wine in 1856 to forty-six three years later. Shows were always taken immensely seriously – Dr Angove entered as soon as he started to make wine.

The most surprising success story in South Australia – indeed, in the whole country – was that of Coonawarra. The region is the total opposite of the image of most of the world's fine vineyards, including the Yarra and Barossa valleys. It is a bleak nothingness, 350 kilometres (217 miles) south of Adelaide in the middle of nowhere. Notably unlike most other great vineyard regions in Australia – or indeed, in the world – it is not attractive. "It's a God-forsaken corner of Australia," wrote Oz Clarke, "so flat that you begin to think that perhaps the world isn't round after all. Lashed by wind and rain in its dismal winters. . . at best it is a dull nonentity of a place, at worst an Antipodean Siberia. There's got to be a saving grace." There is – and not just because Clarke was exaggerating (in fact the climate is a little warmer than that of Bordeaux). At Coonawarra's heart is a long, slim streak of terra rossa soil over a well-watered and well-drained limestone subsoil, which has produced some of Australia's greatest red wines – above all a uniquely elegant and leafy Cabernet Sauvignon.

Fortunately, Coonawarra had John Riddoch. By 1880, he had made enough money supplying the necessities of life to the gold-miners to own a run of 700 square kilometres (270 square miles), capable of sustaining 160,000 sheep. By 1881, this self-made man had moved far enough up the social ladder to be able to entertain George and Albert, grandsons of Queen Victoria (George was to ascend the throne as George V).

In 1891, Riddoch decided to subdivide over 460ha (1,137 acres) of his estate. Within a few years seventy-three ha (180 acres) of vines had been planted, mostly of Cabernet Sauvignon, Malbec, and Pinot Noir – a specialization unusual in Australia at the time. In 1897, W Catton Grasby, a local writer, summed up the reasons for the region's chances for success: "My belief is that the future of Coonawarra will depend mainly on its wines and apples. . . the nights are always cool. . . the water supply. . . is so good and cool that the operation of fermenting wine is a comparatively simple one. . . Coonawarra claret promises to have a very high and wide reputation – indeed, there is no doubt but that it will be a beautiful wine of good body, fine color, delicate bouquet, and low alcoholic strength." This remains as good a description of the region's wines as it was then.

Alexander Kelly was the twelfth doctor to be registered in South Australia, and like many of his fellows, he was a passionate believer in the medicinal qualities of wine. Of Scottish extraction, he probably planted his first vineyard in the early 1840s, and a trip to Britain in the late 1850s to bring his recently widowed mother to Australia enabled him to visit some of Europe's vineyards. In 1862, he brought together one of the earliest syndicates to invest in vineyards. As Philip White puts it, Kelly convinced "the moneyed captains of the colony – Elder, Hughes, Cleland, Stirling, Barr-Smith – to buy shares in the Tintara Vineyard company." Despite an overproduction of wine and uncertain markets, Kelly remained optimistic and bought Tintara, a rather inaccessible property near McLaren Vale, some miles further south than Reynella, in a region in which the soil had been impoverished by over-intensive farming. At Tintara he made the heavy "burgundy" wines that he favoured for his patients, but in the late 1860s he was hit by the depression.

Kelly had advanced ideas. His vineyard was contour-planted to prevent soil erosion, and he published two books, *The Vine in Australia* and *Wine Growing in Australia*, which continued the educational efforts started a generation earlier by James Busby. As Valmai Hankel put it, in his books Kelly "assembled and translated extracts from the leading European oenographers of the day, adding his own comments and those of other Australian practitioners".[10] *The Vine in Australia* sold well, requiring a second printing of 1,000 copies – evidence of Kelly's expertise and the general interest in wine in the colony at the time.

Kelly was one of the first winemakers to preach the gospel of exports.

[10] Valmai Hankel, *Wine Industry Journal*, January–February 2002.

In 1871 he met one Peter Bond Burgoyne while on an urgent sales mission to London and together they set up an association to run the vineyards at Tintara. Yet Burgoyne alleged that he could not sell the wines at a profit; indeed, he returned one pipe (a cask holding 550 litres, usually used for storing port) of burgundy as unsaleable. This was surprising because he made a fortune in the trade in the subsequent thirty years with wines such as "Burgoyne's Red Tree Burgundy".

Kelly was undeterred. As he pointed out, most of the earliest shipments had been "raw and new, and unfit for so long a voyage". He rejoiced when a later trial shipment arrived in a drinkable condition, claiming, "That they reached their destination without being utterly spoilt speaks well for their soundness and keeping quality, for many of them were not fortified with spirit."

Nevertheless, Kelly could not escape the economic problems that resulted in a reduction of the hectarage of vines in the colony from 2,685ha (6,630 acres) in 1865 to 1,758ha (4,340 acres) twenty years later. The bubble had burst, thanks, as Beeston puts it, to "overproduction, uneven quality and lack of markets". According to Kelly, "None are so depressed at the present time as wine-growers. The prospects of the wine-grower appear at this moment the reverse of encouraging or hopeful; for of all our productions, wine is the most difficult to sell." He had to put Tintara on the market, and Thomas Hardy boldly snapped it up.

For all the future success of Coonawarra, and of Orlando, Seppelt, and Yalumba, the biggest single success story is that of Thomas Hardy, the man who first set the pattern for the growth of major wine businesses in Australia. He was a Devonshire farmer's son, who arrived in South Australia in 1850 and went to work for John Reynell before he left for the gold-fields. Within eighteen months, his butchery business in the Victorian gold-fields provided him with the means to return to Adelaide, marry a cousin and buy a riverside property (which they naturally called Bankside) on the Torrens at Thebarton, close to the city. Hardy's first aim was to grow grapes for dried fruit and olives on a commercial scale. His marmalade and dried lemon peel were still winning prizes in the 1890s. Nevertheless, by 1859 he was confident enough to return to Britain to sell the 1858 vintage of his wine, which, "had it been fortified properly", he declared later, "would have been a splendid wine".

Hardy was among the first to rely on blending fruit and wines from many different districts; he also bought grapes from as many as forty growers on the plains and in the foothills – two practices that continue to dominate the Australian wine industry today. He was prepared to pay more for premium varieties such as Cabernet, Shiraz, and Malbec, an unusual practice at the time, and one based on the (correct) assumption that he could sell varietal wines at a higher price.

After he bought Tintara, Hardy managed to sell the wine Burgoyne had rejected, and replanted the estate with vines for making lighter wines. A heartbroken Kelly died just one month after the sale of his beloved estate. One of his sons remained as Hardy's manager, and in 1887 established the famous Tatachilla vineyard. Alexander Kelly's grandson won the gold medal when Roseworthy, then the country's only viticultural college, introduced an oenology course in 1938.

Hardy was ever the opportunist, "always having an eye open", in the words of a local journalist, "for anything novel, treasuring it up and being able to put it to good use". As early as 1904 he prophesied that "in another five years we shall see motors employed in agriculture". No detail was too small; the dam at the back of his winery was covered with vine cuttings that kept it cool during the summer, and a mobile furnace was towed between the rows of vines to burn the cuttings. Hardy was always a fanatic about quality, winning numerous medals at shows, including a gold medal at the 1889 Paris Exhibition. His method was simple and the model of modern brand creation and management: "Planting good kinds [of vines] in the soil to which they are suited, that is the greatest part of the business. That of the winemaker is to handle the grapes in the best possible way and to mature wines and to produce uniform samples of as few types as possible."[11]

By the mid-1890s, Hardy was the colony's biggest winemaker, producing the equivalent of over two million bottles and accounting for over four-fifths of the production of McLaren Vale. He had even opened a bar in Adelaide, Hardy's Bankside Cellars, where a light lunch of a ham or tongue sandwich was served with iced claret or claret punch. Hardy's energy was amazing, and, like so many of the country's early winemakers, his tally of non-remunerative jobs scarcely less so, for he was active not only in every conceivable wine-related body but also as a firm proponent

[11] *The Hardy Tradition*, Hardy, Adelaide, 1953.

of federation. In his seventies he undertook a long trip round Europe with his son and successor Robert.

By then winemaking was no longer an amateur affair. Indeed, the wine industry, strictly speaking, started when winemakers such as Hardy and Seppelt started to buy grapes from growers, no longer relying exclusively on their own produce. As Hardy put it, "The manufacture of wine is now almost wholly gone into the hands of those who make a business of it, and do not follow it merely as a secondary pursuit. The wines are better grown, better made, and proper attention paid to their after-management. Many firms and individuals also have grown to be the proper medium between the grower and the consumer, and large stocks of superior wines have accumulated in their hands. . . thus surely laying the foundation of a future export trade in the article."

Well before these words were written, there was a real Australian wine "industry" dominated by businessmen like Hardy and Benno Seppelt, followed a long way behind by hordes of the "gentlemen amateurs", who are still an abundant presence in the industry. It had helped, of course, that so many doctors, an influential breed, were so keen on wine, and that the pioneers had been able to rely on the money generated by the mining booms of the 1840s and 1850s and by the middle-class the booms had created, above all in Melbourne. Moreover, and crucially, the wine, as we shall see, was good enough to compete in the all-important European – and especially British – market.

4

An Imperial Bevy

Gather his rays by his rays fondly nurtured
And send them out sunshine imprisoned in Wine.

WINE & SPIRIT GAZETTE

The qualities that were to constitute "Brand Australia" in the last decade of the twentieth century were quick to emerge, as the *Wine & Spirit Gazette's* poem on wine from "the land of the warm southern sunshine" clearly demonstrates. By 1863, Charles Louis Tetaz could claim that he was exporting wine, and that "if we had four times as much as we did, we could have sold it all" – even though the next decades were to bring a series of ups and downs for winemakers. He, like all the bigger Australian winemakers, always needed new outlets for his wine because the local market was inevitably small, and customs duties prevented sales outside the winemaker's own colony.

As Alexander Kelly put it: "The public have complained, with good cause, that they cannot procure the native wines. Neither from the wine merchant nor the publican can a bottle of colonial wine be had.". In Sydney, Kelly noted, not one of the 421 public houses sold "colonial" wine. Surely, he wrote, "Instead of sending Australian wine to England and importing thence European wine, it would be more profitable to consume our own wine and save the expense of double freight."

Matters became worse in the 1870s, when the government of Victoria repeatedly raised duties on imports from other colonies. By 1879, the duty was six shillings a gallon (thirty pence per 3.8 litres) – six times the value of even the best wine from Rutherglen, a region which made some of Victoria's finest wines. These prohibitory duties were particularly important because Melbourne was far and away the biggest market in

Australia for wine and so bore particularly hard on the winemakers of South Australia with their very limited "local" market.

Fortunately for the winemakers around Adelaide, the British statesman William Gladstone came to their rescue. In 1860, he abolished the preferential duty on wines from the Cape of Good Hope, which opened the door to wines from Australia (and from France through the Free Trade Treaty he concluded the same year). Even more importantly, his 1860 budget distinguished between ordinary table and fortified wines, the latter paying more duty than the former. The wine trade was further encouraged the following year by the Single Bottle Act, which allowed licensed grocers to sell wine, a new possibility exploited especially by the Gilbey family.

These measures triggered a boom in the sale of table wines that, unfortunately, lasted only twenty years until older habits returned. From the 1880s until well after 1945, the British turned back to their old favourites, port and sherry, as well as Champagne and the new blended Scotch whiskies, made from (infinitely) cheaper grain spirit, as well as the traditional, and far more expensive, malt whiskies.

Nevertheless, in the last forty years of the nineteenth century Australians took full advantage of the changes. The first figures for British imports of Australian wine are for 1854, when 500 cases had been imported, and in the following ten years only 20,000 cases entered the country. In 1885–6, the first year in which figures were officially recorded in Australia, sales had leapt to 87,000 cases. A decade later they rose to over 300,000 cases, which became a rough annual average until the mid-1920s, amounting to just under one-fifth of Australia's total production. The popularity – particularly once fortified wines had made their comeback – was not surprising, as the two countries shared a predilection for wines that were either naturally strong or fortified, a taste exported to Australia by British colonists. According to WS Benwell, George Smith, a famous winemaker at All Saints in Rutherglen, put it bluntly: "If offered a wine that tasted like Château Margaux, they say it's too acid."

From the first, Australian wine had the great advantage over those from the Cape of being branded "sold as they were", in the words of HE Laffer, "under proprietary labels". By contrast, most wines from the Cape were "presented as blends under time-honoured regional names" – usually French – or as port or sherry. To their disadvantage, Australians suffered from what Geoffrey Blainey so memorably described as "the tyranny of distance". Wool, the country's major export, "was valuable enough to pay its own way across the world" – and of course did not risk much spoilage on the voyage. But wine was volatile, living stuff, which had to endure a journey measured in months rather than weeks, although times were cut by a month or more in the 1870s with the introduction of the compound steam engine and the opening of the Suez Canal.

Consequently, quality could vary wildly – especially when sales suddenly accelerated. In the 1860s, for the first but by no means the last time, Britain was flooded with raw, young wine made by inexperienced winemakers. They ensured that members of at least one generation were, in Bleasdale's words, "for ever afterwards abominators of colonial wines". The obvious solution was to beef up the wines with brandy, which not only strengthened but also coarsened them. To make matters worse, Australians themselves did not appreciate locally produced wine. As Alexander Kelly put it, "Although the native wines are getting into more general use, it cannot be denied that, generally speaking, they have been decidedly unpopular. Like everything else produced in the colony, with the exception of wheat, wine has suffered the detraction which has fallen to the share of all things colonial."

The long-lasting English snobbery toward Australian wines was already raising its patrician head. While on a visit to Australia in 1870, novelist Anthony Trollope found a wine from a large-scale Victorian wine-grower "certainly superior both in flavour and body to the ordinary wine drunk by Parisians". "It is wholesome and nutritious," he added, "and is the pure juice of the grape." This was no accident. Three years later he drank "the best *vin ordinaire* that I ever drank" – in Melbourne at a mere three pence a half-pint glass (one penny per 0.25 litres). "It is a white wine made at Yerring [*sic*], a vineyard on the Upper Yarra, and is both wholesome and nutritive." But, alas, he continued, "The workmen of Melbourne, when they drink, prefer to swallow the most horrible poison which the skill of man ever concocted." Moreover, as was the case, for English drinkers for over a century, Trollope didn't like any of the "fine" wines he drank in South Australia. "I did not much relish them," he admitted. "I thought them to be heady, having a taste of earth, and an after-flavour which was disagreeable. This may have been prejudice on my part." Nevertheless, another of his criticisms is now a staple accusation: "The South Australian wines had a heaviness about them, which made me afraid of them." Trollope displayed to the full the generally supercilious tone adopted by British commentators for another century when he asserted that, "I am bound to say that Queensland wine was not to my taste. I am delighted to acknowledge that their pineapples are perfect."

For nearly a century the British market in Australian wines was dominated by two companies, both with well-known brand names. The first was Emu. In 1861, Patrick Auld, whose estate (which he named Auldana) created the South Auldana Vineyard Association, in partnership with a retired excise officer, Mr Burton, formed a London company called Auld, Burton. The next year the name Emu was registered. The company subsequently declined into bankruptcy, and in 1885 was bought by Aylwin Whately Pownall, in whose hands it flourished enough to allow him to employ an agent in Australia, Walter Bagenal, to look after the business. By then the name Emu was probably the most important single wine brand in Britain. Its wines ranged from one made from the "Carbinet" grape at thirteen shillings (£0.65) a dozen to a "Carbinet Sauvignon" at thirty-two shillings (£1.60) – the same price as a Muscat of Alexandria. The wines were sold not only in ordinary-sized bottles but also in imperial quart flagons (1.1 litres) with screwtops at eighteen shillings (ninety pence) for both the "burgundy" and the "chablis".

Until 1973 and Britain's entry into the European Economic Community, labelling was haphazard. Muscatelles were described as like superior hock; Espanoir (a name seemingly unknown to viticulturalists) as between a claret, burgundy, and Hungarian wine. This reflected the confusion in categories in Australia, even within the major shows. At Sydney in 1903, there were different classes for "light dry red, claret-type" and "full-bodied dry red", which was also called "claret-type."

But for a whole generation the dominant individual in the business in both countries was Peter Bond Burgoyne, who sold wines under his own name after founding his import business in 1872. Burgoyne bought Hardy's Tintara claret in bulk – up to 250 hogsheads, or 75,000 bottles, a month. He was the sharpest of operators. According to John Beeston in his book *A Concise History of Australian Wine*, "In the late 1880s, when on a business visit to Adelaide, he caused a furore when he reproached some South Australian winemakers for 'making inferior grapes into poor, vapid characterless liquids'." Having thus forced down prices, he proceeded to buy "substantial quantities of wine and always forecast a promising future for the Australian industry". In 1889, Burgoyne was rich and important enough to offer a prize of fifty guineas at the Centenary Exhibition in Melbourne for a "light, claret-style wine suitable for the export market to the UK." This was a typically shrewd and commercial idea, since to win the prize, 2,500 gallons (over 1,250 cases) of the wine had to be available for immediate shipment.

The Centenary Exhibition was proof of the capacity of Australian wines to compete in the international marketplace. They had started slowly. At the London Intercolonial Exhibition as late as 1865 there were only nineteen Australian exhibitors entering a mere thirty-five wines. According to de Castella, the 1867 Paris Exhibition gave wines from South Australia "the first signalised [signalled] approbation". Nevertheless, some commentators still doubted the honesty of the (unusually strong) Australian table wines. In 1872, the splendidly named Dr JLW Thudichum, a medical doctor and all-round self-styled expert on drink and diet, together with Monsieur Auguste Dupré, a chemist colleague, claimed roundly that wine from South Australia had been adulterated and fortified. To them it was unthinkable, if not actually impossible, for wines to reach fourteen or fifteen per cent alcohol naturally without a spiritual boost. In fact, government research showed that the colony was "capable of producing full-bodied, natural wines of a high order. . . South Australian wines naturally excelled in alcoholic strength".

Thudichum and Dupré's biggest mistake came later, when they claimed that the Australians obtained only one award at the Vienna Exhibition of 1873, when in fact they had been awarded a round dozen: a feat much lauded in the British press. Indeed, in 1874, the eminently respectable *Morning Post* remarked that "Australia promises ere long to become as celebrated for its wines as it is already for its wool and gold." At the same exhibition the judges were "surprised at the quality of the brandy from South Australia and could hardly believe that it was colonial". Even the French judges had praised some wines made from "Hermitage", only to withdraw in protest when they discovered that they had actually come from Bendigo.

In 1881, as de Castella put it, the Melbourne International Exhibition, by "displaying an unsuspected and general amelioration, again brought the wine industry to the fore". He was in a good position to pronounce.

An exceptional, and exceptionally valuable, prize of over £800 offered by the emperor of Germany, no less, for the best product manufactured in Australia went to a wine from St Hubert's, de Castella's own estate. At the Bordeaux Exhibition in 1883, the Australians were out in force with thirty-three exhibitors and 190 exhibits winning sixteen gold and twenty-nine silver medals, a more-than-respectable tally. But, according to de Castella anyway, it was the Colonial and Indian Exhibition in London three years later which provided "the great educational opportunity for Australian wines" to demonstrate their qualities to the whole world.

Unfortunately, by then disaster had hit Victoria. There, as in the world's other winemaking regions, the woes of the last quarter of the nineteenth century, with results that prevailed until well after World War II, are generally attributed to the devastation caused by the phylloxera louse. It forced growers – except those growing grapes on sandy soils in which phylloxera did not flourish – to uproot their vineyards and replant with vines grafted onto immune rootstocks imported from the United States. But in Victoria as in Bordeaux, which suffered almost as badly, phylloxera was only partly to blame. The economic problems of the 1870s – and in the case of Victoria, the slump of the 1890s that included a collapse in the property market in Melbourne – badly affected demand for what was still a luxury product. Even before 1877, when the bug reached Australia from Europe, the market was demanding strong, cheap wines – what Hubert de Castella describes as, "wine at a minimum of price in order to affect manipulations afterward". "Alcohol," he concluded, "is the virtue, or rather the vice, which the growers are advised to secure." Even show judges were influenced, awarding prizes to "sweet-bodied red and sweet-bodied white – abomination of desolation".

For a few years before the bug arrived, the wine-growers in Victoria were living in a fool's paradise, for they could supply wines to France, where phylloxera had struck rather earlier. In 1873, Sir Charles Gavan Duffy, the premier of Victoria, had predicted that the wine trade would become as important to the state as wool or gold – both products which, like wine, were subject to cycles of boom and bust. But his hopes were decidedly premature. The phylloxera bug first hit the Geelong region in the mid-1870s and then moved slowly through the state, reaching the Murray River twenty years later: a rate of a mere eighteen metres (twenty yards) a day.

The Victorian government panicked and organized repeated vine-pull schemes, unaccompanied by the obvious corollary, the subsidizing of grafted rootstocks. By 1876, Tetaz was in despair: "I wish I'd never planted vines. . . in the last five years I've planted nearly 2,000 apple trees; they'll pay better than the damn vines, at least I hope so." It did not help that the government had not originally been sufficiently systematic. In 1886, wrote Tetaz, "The Department of Agriculture ploughed my twenty-five acres [ten ha] with a tremendous great plough drawn by ten strong horses. They ploughed to a depth of twenty inches [fifty centimetres] and fourteen men uprooted all the roots, big and small, and burned them, and then put carbon bisulphate [the standard insecticide in the fight against the bug] on each of the furrows left by the plough. . . if only they'd done the job properly in the first place!" Not surprisingly, by the end of the century there were few, if any, vines left in the region.

In the 1890s, the state government tried to make amends by giving a bonus for replanting, but not of grafted vines. This merely compounded the problem. In 1900, a royal commission of enquiry found that "For the most part, wrong and too many varieties of vines were planted, and the bonus was generally distributed without knowledge or foresight to guide the grower, or to ensure the production of distinct types of wine." To make matters worse, the new plantings carried the louse to the rest of the state. When the government reversed its policy in 1906, it was too late.

By 1898, the louse had reached one of Victoria's biggest vineyard regions, Rutherglen, in the far northeast, although it was not until 1905 that the vines died in any great numbers. It did not reach Milawa, to the west of Rutherglen, until toward the end of World War I. Indeed, the veteran winemaker John Charles Brown remembers his family's original vineyard being uprooted as late as 1920.

In the event, Rutherglen (and to a much lesser extent Milawa) survived, largely because, once they had been replanted with grafted stock, they could supply the British market with the strong, rich, red wines it demanded. Many other historic regions, above all in Victoria, had to wait until the last thirty years of the twentieth century before they were revived.

Rutherglen growers used the delay in the arrival of the louse to good purpose. The area under vines grew five times to 1,400ha (3,459 acres) in the first half of the 1880s and much more in the remaining years of the century. The charge was led by a leading local figure (and Mick Morris's great grandfather), George Francis Morris, the wine commissioner at the 1886 Colonial and Indian Exhibition, and a leading supplier to both Emu and Burgoyne. In 1892, the latter established a vineyard of his own at Mount Ophir on the outskirts of Rutherglen. Burgoyne's 250ha (618 acres) soon became a showplace for the whole region.

In 1906, when Morris brought back a stock of phylloxera-resistant vines from Europe, they were confiscated by the customs authorities of the new Commonwealth government. This had been formed in 1901 at the behest of the government of South Australia, wishing to continue to escape the pest – and indeed, South Australia remains phylloxera-free to this day. The plague was not confined to Victoria. Although the Hunter Valley escaped, most of the vineyards of Mudgee were sold or simply abandoned because of the lack of demand for the relatively light wines they produced.

Never was there a better case of an ill wind blowing someone good than phylloxera, which firmly established the supremacy of South Australia in the country's wine industry. Until then, progress there had been uneven because of the ravages of oidium (better known in Australia as powdery mildew) and the problems of small growers. Nevertheless, partly thanks to official help, the area under vines had more than doubled during the decade, reaching 3,800ha (9,390 acres) by the end of the decade producing over four million litres of wine. The general economic crisis of the 1890s even led the state government to offer up to two million cuttings to anyone who wanted them in an effort to encourage the production of so exportable a product.

South Australia escaped the phylloxera plague thanks to draconian measures: all vineyards of more than 0.4ha (one acre) had to be registered, and the Phylloxera Act of 1899 aimed to keep South Australia phylloxera-free through a government-appointed Phylloxera Board. The measures placed responsibilities on both the state and the wine industry, and, symbolically, the act was signed at Penfolds' Magill Estate. The board, complete with an "outbreak-response management plan", carried out a triumphantly successful policy of quarantine and isolation, ensuring that, to this day, no possibly infected vines or grapes have ever entered South Australia. In 1999, the board, now part of the state's Grape Industry Board, celebrated its centenary.

The government of South Australia had always been aware of the value of wine. In 1875, already conscious of a need to improve the quality of wine to help exports, it appointed a four-man commission to investigate agricultural education. Six years later Roseworthy College was founded in the small town of the same name to the west of the Barossa Valley. Originally intended to improve wheat yields, the college soon became, and for nearly a century remained, the country's only educational establishment to train viticulturalists and, later, oenologists. For several generations most winemaking families sent their (male) scions to specialize in viticulture as part of the Diploma of Agriculture course offered by the college; indeed, for a long time these youngsters formed the majority of the students. Some of the more serious went onto study in Europe, either at Geisenheim in Germany or at the Ecole Nationale d'Agriculture at Montpellier in southern France. The latter, then as now, is probably the world's leading viticultural academic institution, and one that for over a century formed a sort of postgraduate institution for a handful of influential Australian winemakers.

Part of South Australia's campaign against the phylloxera bug involved the introduction of the scientific study of vines and vinification in the person of Professor Arthur Perkins, a government viticulturalist and oenologist. Born in Egypt and educated in the Middle East and Britain, Perkins went on to study at Montpellier. In 1892, when he was only twenty-one, the government of South Australia managed to lure him away from Tunisia, where he was working at the time. As Rob Linn, a leading academic expert on the history of Australian wine, puts it, through "his teaching at the fledgling Roseworthy College" – where he became principal in 1904 – he "spread ideas about scientific agriculture, viticulture, horticulture, and winemaking through the community", above all at Yalumba, thanks to his friendship with Fred Smith, son of Samuel. Fred, a leader in preaching the need for research in the wine industry, had satisfied himself and many others that irrigation "will materially add to [the industry's] profitability".

Perkins' overall aim was that wines should exhibit both "soundness and purity". In an article he published in 1900, he listed four main reasons why wines were diseased: "poor hygiene, poor handling, poor fermentation, and poor wine composition". He was less prescient in an 1895–6 report he made to the government: "Today the grower should be the winemaker, his perishable crop should not be under the whip-hand of the winemaker." Unfortunately over the next half-century, only a few winemakers tackled any, let alone all, of these problems.

5

Riverland and After

Plant a six-inch nail in this soil and in a year you will have a crowbar.
JOHN JAMES MCWILLIAM, WINEMAKER

In 1987, in Renmark, on the banks of the Murray River, Ralph Chaffey unveiled a plaque to the memory of his grandfather William. The plaque commemorates William as "the co-founder of the Renmark irrigation settlement", initiated a hundred years earlier. The plaque stands by one of the original pumps used for the irrigation scheme on the Murray in the northeastern corner of South Australia. To Europeans and North Americans, the river may not seem impressive, but it is the major water-way in the east of this, the driest of continents. Today the Murray is the source of the water required for the – invariably irrigated – vineyards that produce over two-thirds of the grapes used by the country's winemakers.

The region's potential was first understood in 1885 by Alfred Deakin, a future Commonwealth prime minister. After several drought years in Australia he visited California to look at irrigation, returning a convert. "Water is the richness of land," he declared. "Water spells wealth." In California he met the Chaffey brothers, George and William, described as "big in stature, big in vision, and big in enterprise".

The Canadian-born brothers had already made a fortune by buying property and water rights on newly irrigated land wholesale and reselling in four-ha (ten-acre) lots at a considerable profit. Deakin, and a number of rather hyperbolic Australians, induced George to come to Australia to repeat the California success, even though, in the words of Peter Westcott in the *Australian Dictionary of Biography*, the brothers had been warned by government officials that they "would have little chance of obtaining a land grant on terms similar to those in California". They also failed to appreciate that Australians preferred their large-scale agricultural projects to be cooperative, government-controlled schemes rather than purely free-enterprise ventures. Nevertheless, George found a suitable site for an irrigation scheme at Mildura Station on the Murray River in northern Victoria, 150 kilometres (ninety-three miles) east of Renmark. He made his brother William sell up in California. But the brothers grew impatient with local opposition, as well as with the obstacles that the government of Victoria appeared to put in their path; they moved downriver to Renmark because the South Australians appeared to be more welcoming. By 1887, a trial scheme was underway and they had been joined by their younger brother Charles.

The Chaffeys moved fast. The South Australian government allocated £250,000 for the first irrigated settlement in Australia, and within a year the Chaffeys were offering land for orchard blocks in what was described as a "hissing desert", over 250 kilometres (155 miles) from the nearest railhead. By September 1888, 700 four-ha (ten-acre) blocks and one hundred kilometres (sixty-two miles) of drains had been surveyed, thirty-eight blocks had been sold, and six ha (fifteen acres) of vines and two ha (five acres) of peaches had been planted. In 1913, the transport problems of the Riverland, as it came to be called, were greatly eased by the extension of the railway to Paringa, just across the Murray from Renmark. By 1913, a steam-powered ferry joined the wineries to the railway, and fifteen years later a railway bridge was built across the river.

Unfortunately, the Chaffeys had used "associates and salesmen", in Westcott's words, "who were indeed deficient in truth and honesty" and they were thus open to charges of being "cute Yankee land-grabbers". Moreover, although the towns they created were impressive, the settlers were furious at the rate at which water leaked. Moreover, they had been told by a retired government official that they were entitled to free water.

By 1893, the government-owned Renmark Irrigation Trust had taken over one of the Chaffeys' schemes and a similar trust took over in Mildura two years later, despite George's frantic efforts to find fresh financing. In the event, it was South Australia, rather than Victoria, that gained the most from the development of irrigated land. South Australia has always been the bigger producer of the grapes, which eventually became one of the state's most important crops. George Chaffey was so disgusted that he returned to the United States, but William remained and became mayor of Mildura, where he was known affectionately as "the boss". Charles disappeared from sight. Although William established the Mildura (later Mildara) Winery, he was best-known as a proponent and marketer for local fruit – which, of course, included raisins and sultanas.

Carl Angove was the major pioneer of winemaking in the Renmark region; indeed, he was one of the few established winemakers to set up in the Riverland. He was the son of Dr William Angove, a member of a Cornish mining family who had migrated to Adelaide in 1886, and Carl was interested in buying fresh and dried grapes for his distillery at Adelaide. He was told that he would never do anything on the river, although later his achievements were recognized – as one local put it, "It was a godsend Angove coming to Renmark." By 1911, Carl – universally known as "the skipper" because of his love of yachting – was building his own distillery at Renmark to make spirit to fortify the sweet Muscat Gordo Blanco as the base wine for his sherries.

Carl Angove also started the trend away from fruit farming to viticulture. In 1925, the Angoves pulled up two ha (five acres) of peaches to plant Shiraz. Later Carl turned to making brandy, developing the St Agnes brand, which now has two-fifths of an (admittedly shrinking) market. It was, says his son Tom, "getting away from medicinal brandy". Nevertheless, Carl's heart remained at the family's original property at Tea Tree Gully on the outskirts of Adelaide, where his pride and joy were his sherries.

The Angoves made a considerable – if involuntary – contribution to the Riverland region by employing Ron Haselgrove, who also worked at the Chaffeys' backward and floundering Mildura Winery. In the words of Bishop's official history of Angove's: "Ron was using experience in part gained at Angove's to put a potential competitor on its feet." After Haselgrove resigned from Angove's in 1938, he rebuilt Mildura Winery and transformed it into a supplier of better wines. Despite the arrival of both Penfold and Hardy, the Riverland region became dominated by cooperatives, which were to become one of the major driving forces behind the expansion of the region's winemaking business, and which were also strong enough to buy up defunct companies such as the Adelaide Wine Company at Renmark.

The Murrumbidgee Irrigation Area, round Griffith in the extreme southwest of New South Wales, the third irrigated region, was even further upriver – and even hotter. At first the vines had to be watered by hand as the irrigation works had not been completed. This did not deter John James McWilliam, who arrived in 1912. Carl was one of the few established winemakers to set up in the Riverland, but John James McWilliam's father, Samuel McWilliam, had settled in Corowa near Rutherglen where he produced his first wines in 1877 from a winery called Sunnyside. In 1913, John James applied for two leases of irrigated farmland, bringing in 40,000 cuttings and producing his first wine in 1916. He established a nursery and later a winery and distillery at Hanwood, near Griffith, that was so successful that by 1922 he had also built a second facility at Yenda a few kilometres to the east. Ninety years later the family is still the biggest producer in the region

In theory, McWilliam could buy only one twenty-ha (forty-nine-acre) vineyard, for corporate buyers were not allowed until the 1980s. The scheme was highly paternalistic; even the price of grapes was set by the Irrigation Commission, a typical example of Australian corporatism. To avoid the restrictions, further purchases had to be made in the name of members of the family; the McWilliams ended up with five farms.

The region's other major wine business, De Bortoli, has only sixty ha (148 acres) of its own grapes. Vittorio De Bortoli, its founder, was a former employee of McWilliam's who had arrived from his family's small farm in northern Italy in 1924. Within three years he had saved enough money to buy a fruit farm just outside Griffith. The next year his fiancée, Giuseppina – a determined woman known as the *bossa* – arrived (via France, where she had been working as a maid to earn the fare), and Vittorio started to make table wine, initially for his own consumption. He attracted other Italian families to the area, and they soon found them-selves confronted by a surplus of fruit. Fortunately, Italians working as cane-cutters in Queensland were looking for table wine and vermouth, which the De Bortolis sold (as claret or hock) in barrels and flagons, while they sold their fortified wines to Lindemans.

The limitation of all three irrigated regions was the quality of the fruit and thus of the wine they could produce. In 1923, Carl Angove pointed out an alternative possibility, which unfortunately was to be largely neglected for over half a century. The growers, he said in a speech, "could undoubtedly make a better wine from Shiraz than from the currant. . . The first steps to success were to plant the better kind of vines and let the grapes mature properly." Nevertheless, until 1962 when Angove's bought

800ha (1,979 acres) of land east of Renmark, the firm depended totally on bought-in grapes, which were inevitably from inferior, dual-purpose varieties.

The introduction of irrigation and the development of the vineyards along the Murray basin may have made Australian wine increasingly competitive in the crucial British market, but it also created a case of Gresham's Law: the (cheaper and almost entirely fortified) bad drove out the good wines that were made before the louse's arrival, and which were no longer in demand in Britain or Australia. They also, not coincidentally, established South Australia as by far the largest wine supplier in the country, as vineyards elsewhere could not compete on price even when they had been replanted. In the early years of the twentieth century, there was a selection of regions to meet the demands of both the British and the domestic market for strong, generally fortified wines.

These consumption patterns were an additional blow to Victoria, and even to a number of other winemaking regions in South Australia, which were suitable only for producing light table wines. According to Aeuckens in *Vineyard of the Empire*, by the late 1920s, when wine production in Victoria had largely been abandoned with the single exception of Rutherglen and Mildara," the level of production in the Riverland threatened the viability of the entire wine industry in South Australia", because so few of the state's other winemaking regions could grow grapes so cheaply.

Until the early years of the twentieth century South Australia's vineyards were not noticeably more productive than those of other states, but by the end of World War I, the state was producing three-quarters of the country's wine from less than half the area planted with grapes. Moreover, productivity leapt four times in the course of the century to reach an average of 8,000 litres per ha (2.47 acres). The Murray River irrigated regions were particularly productive, 1,430ha (3,534 acres) producing twenty-five million litres, nearly three million cases, of wine.

The importance of South Australia was due not only to the increased area under vines but also to the higher yields from the rich soils of the sandy alluvial flats and the higher ground above them. It also helped that on these irrigated vineyards, the vines could be cropped after a couple of years. Yields from non-irrigated vineyards were inevitably lower, and cropping could start only after five years.

In fact, in the sixty years after the triple whammy of repeated slumps, phylloxera, and federation, only South Australia, especially the Riverland, the Barossa, and, to a much lesser extent, the Clare Valley and McLaren Vale – the source of much of the wine sold under the Emu label – could keep their wine-producing heads above financial water. In the Clare, the winemakers Hermann Buring and Sobels, Carl August and their successors set the pace with their hock and, above all, Granfiesta, a sherry that continued to be a best-seller for nearly half a century as a staple for parties in place of the normal beers or much heavier ports.

South Australia's grip on the whole country's wine production had been greatly boosted by federation. Before 1901, sales outside the state were effectively non-existent. In November 1901, just after federation, the *Australian Vigneron* reported that "Not one man in 500 in Sydney has ever tasted any of the higher class of the wines of South Australia, and so. . . probably not one man in 1,000 in Adelaide could as much tell one of the chief brands of New South Wales wines." By then, more South Australian wine was sold in Britain than wine from Victoria, the other major supplier. The gap was already large – by 1899 it was 1.9 million litres as against 1.3 million from Victoria.

Not surprisingly, South Australians fought hard for federation and none more so than the winemaking community. The delegates to the convention leading up to federation were royally entertained by leading winemakers such as Thomas Hardy. He was particularly confident of the future. "South Australia," he declared, "is better adapted than any other colony for producing a variety of wines. . . in fact, within our colony we can produce all the different types of wine grown in Europe." Over eighty-six per cent of the population voted for federation in the state's major wine-growing regions (Barossa, McLaren Vale, and Clare) as against around two-thirds in the state as a whole.

Federation's major effect on the wine industry was to introduce free trade. In every other respect so far as wine was concerned, the states were left in charge. As Section 113 of the Australian constitution puts it: "All fermented, distilled, or other intoxicating liquids passing into any state or remaining therein for use, consumption, sale or storage, shall be subject to the laws of the state as if such liquids had been produced in the state."

Free trade was what the South Australians needed, especially at a time of ever-increasing production. "There would have been a crisis in the wine trade this year if it had not been for federation," the manager of Chateau Tanunda told journalist Ernest Whitington. "They realized that interstate free trade would give them splendid markets to exploit." Within a year, Seppelt and Hardy had established branches in Sydney and Melbourne, and Penfolds had bought two major estates in the Hunter, Dalwood, and Minchinbury, probably the first example of cross-state investment. In Valmai Hankel's words, "Australia's national wine industry had begun." By then only a handful of major concerns had the wines to supply the markets in Western Australia – where little wine was produced – and in effectively vine-free Queensland.

Fortunately, the South Australian winemakers had, literally, cleaned up their act. "New clean and up-to-date appliances have taken the place of old-fashioned and dirty methods," noted Whitington approvingly, and the wines *had* improved. As one French winemaker, Edmond Mazure, told him, "A few glasses of the old colonial wine would give you a headache that would last you a week." Most of the vineyards were planted in proper rows, albeit without any trellising or supports (a photograph in Whitington's book shows that the vines at Magill straggled all over the place). By 1914, interstate "exports" from South Australia, as they were still called, amounted to 2.5 million bottles, twenty times their pre-federation levels. South Australian dominance extended to brandy. Within the four years 1904–07 the amount of brandy exported by South Australia jumped nearly fivefold to 550,000 litres. The most prominent "exporter" was Benno Seppelt. He deployed his nine sons not only at Seppeltsfield but also throughout the continent to ensure that his wines were effectively marketed from Perth to Brisbane.

One of Benno Seppelt's greatest coups came through his friendship with Hans Irvine, who had transformed the immense "drives" – the caves at the Great Western winery, in the Grampian region 150 kilometres (ninety-three miles) northwest of Melbourne – into proper cellars. They housed thousands of bottles of Australia's leading brand of sparkling wine which had been made from an estate founded by two Swiss pioneers who had failed to find gold. After Irvine took over in 1887, he extended the drives to house the maturing wines and set the standard for sparkling wines using largely Ondenc, which was even renamed "Irvine's White". Being childless, Irvine was happy to sell his enterprise to his friend Seppelt, who also took advantage of the depressed conditions in northern Victoria and bought Clydesdale, a leading estate in Rutherglen. By 1912, Seppelt was unquestionably the leading wine business in the whole country.

In 1916, Oscar Seppelt, Benno's eldest son, bought Chateau Tanunda, the only rival to Seppeltsfield in the Barossa. It had been founded in the late nineteenth century by a group of investors, and produced wine as well as a highly respected brandy, named after the winery and matured for ten years in French oak. In 1910, the owners had bought the Riddoch cellars in Coonawarra and built a new winery next to the railway station at Lyndoch in the Barossa Valley. A disastrous drought in 1914 proved a fatal blow to the already rocky finances of the Tanunda venture, and Oscar snapped it up, thus making Seppelt the strongest single force in the brandy market throughout the British Empire.

The family's appetite for expansion seemed insatiable. Benno bought up a cooperative winery at Nuriootpa in the Barossa and established a nursery near Rutherglen to propagate phylloxera-resistant stocks in case South Australia's defences against the plague proved inadequate.

But Seppelt was not the only one to benefit from other people's troubles; so did the Gramps, descendants of Gustav, who had arrived in Australia in 1837 and established himself at Rowland's Creek. When the Adelaide Wine Company folded in 1920, he bought William Jacob's old property, which was already planted with Riesling vines.

By then Seppelt was producing 2.6 million bottles of wine, more than Chateau Tanunda with just under two million, Yalumba with just over a million and Hardy's in fourth place at just under the million mark. Penfolds, by far the biggest producer in the region a round Adelaide, was producing only 600,000 bottles. Nevertheless, by the 1890s it was growing rapidly, thanks to Frank Penfold Hyland, the son of the founder's daughter. She had married Thomas Hyland, and their son had added his mother's surname by deed poll. But even South Australia, Australia's star producer, was not a major player in international terms. It was making only fifteen million bottles (about the same as the Cape of Good Hope) out of the Australian total of thirty-three million. This national total was less even than Madeira, and less than one per cent of the Italian total, while the French produced a total of 9,000 million bottles, almost 300 times the Australian total.

By the time Seppelt's major rival, Thomas Hardy, died in 1912, he was convinced that "much was due to Mr Seppelt", but believed, incorrectly, that Hardy & Sons came next. Hardy was lamented as "the father of the wine industry in South Australia" and the firm was run by his only surviving son, Robert, together with a number of nephews. They took early advantage of the irrigation schemes on the Murray-Darling and by the 1930s were running one of the most regionally diversified wine businesses in Australia. Inevitably, all the major companies depended greatly on the British market, which in the early years of the twentieth century was absorbing at least a fifth of their production, although the exact proportion is difficult to judge since so much of the wine was destined for distillation.

In Britain, the big producers attempted to create "Brand Australia" through the establishment in London of a central warehouse for receiving Australian wines. The warehouse was seen as, and indeed became, a competitor to Burgoyne and the Emu brands, with regular auctions as well as a new brand, Orion. Although it helped increase the South Australian share of the market, the importers were furious, the redoubtable Burgoyne launching an especially vicious campaign against the depot's manager. Burgoyne – and political opponents in South Australia – ensured that the warehouse was sold off in 1904, after only a few years in business. This removal of a major competitor helped to ensure that Burgoyne could impose his views, and, crucially, he bought only wines made according to his own view of the British market.

Burgoyne lorded it over his suppliers with the same ruthlessness as the merchants of the Quai des Chartrons in Bordeaux terrorized even the most distinguished estates in the Médoc for two centuries until the 1970s. At a dinner in 1902, John Christison, then part-owner with JH Knappstein of the Stanley wine company (Knappstein bought out his partner two years later), said, "Burgoyne can go to Timbuctoo." The local newspaper declared bluntly: "There was not a man who had the pluck to come forward and speak a word against this man," although one grower did refer to him in a letter as "that skunk Burgoyne." Nevertheless, generally speaking, Burgoyne and his buyers were fêted because they were such key players and because Australian producers feared competition from South Africa where land was cheaper.

Even so, Burgoyne often had cause for complaint. When the wines arrived in Britain, they were often out of condition because they were not well enough made to stand the long journey to the UK. At the worst, they would simply turn into vinegar, and if, as was so often the case, the casks were mouldy, they infected the wine. Even when they were sound they fetched low prices because, as strong, young wines, they were used for what the French would call "medicinal" purposes. In Britain, they were called "bonesetters" – used to strengthen weedier wines from older, established suppliers such as France. According to one local veteran, these wines "were needed so that they could be diluted with the weaker wines from Cyprus". Naturally, the producers were not proud of the wine they exported, the better stuff being sold locally. "They only sent wine to England when things were desperate," says one veteran in Rutherglen.

Still, Burgoyne was never satisfied. In a letter written to Benno Seppelt, he complained that "The prevailing flavour in South Australian wines is 'oak', due of course to insufficient seasoning of the casks. The majority of winemakers seldom keep a stock of casks in hand, but buy from hand to mouth, just as they require them." He also objected to white-wine casks being repaired using staves from casks previously used to house red wine "so that the white wine when it arrives is pink".

Not surprisingly, the vendors often indulged in that standard trick of the wine trade throughout the ages (one still not unknown today) of sending a sample from their best cask and hiding defective casks in a load of others. But, as Burgoyne pointed out, "A cask of indifferent or diseased wine inoculates the whole and the disease develops through the heat of the Red Sea." As a result he would buy wine only when it had arrived in bonded warehouses in London. The wines also tended to become "scuddy" during the journey, which meant they remained cloudy even after the scum had been removed. As the depot's former manager pointed out, there was one infallible, and thus much-employed recipe to help wines in bad condition: "A good dose of strong spirit. I need scarcely say that we prefer the less drastic method of rest and racking."

It helped that the Australians could call their wines almost anything they liked. In 1907, when the French objected to the use of the words "claret" and "Keystone burgundy" made from a hotchpotch of varieties, an English court ruled that such terms could be used legitimately, provided that they were preceded with the name of the country of origin.

Nevertheless, as I have already noted, much of the Australian sales effort was designed to satisfy the British thirst for fortified wines – not for nothing was the winery at Yalumba called the "Oporto of Australia." Unfortunately this left exponents of light winemaking, notably Professor Perkins, crying in the wilderness. Perkins was preaching a doctrine of avoidance of the "coarser, fuller, heavier" types of wine so successfully promoted, both in principle and in practice, by Burgoyne, and a return to more delicate, lighter styles. It was, of course, to no avail. As François de Coueslant of Chateau Tahbilk put it: "English people, accustomed to port and sherry, like strong wine. Although, probably, with time they will come to know better, for the present they do not care for light stuff." Alas, the time required turned out to be three-quarters of a century.

Most Australians accepted the inevitable. "The demand for the English market must be respected," wrote Ernest Whitington. Such tastes also left in the lurch vineyards, like that of Dr Kelly's son John at Tatachilla, "planted [in the 1880s] when Mr Burgoyne advocated the shipping of light red wines and complained that South Australian wines were too high in alcoholic strength and colour. The cry is now [1903] all the other way" – with even the normally light clarets for which Coonawarra was already famous having to be doctored for the London market.

With the outbreak of World War I, many winemakers went away to the front, affecting the quality but not the quantity of production. The war also led to a wave of anti-German feeling; the name of the Seppelt region was changed from Dorrien and Kaiserstuhl to Mount Kitchener after the South Australian government had stipulated all names with Germanic associations should be changed, though the old names returned after the war.

The war did not greatly affect the shipment of wines to Britain except in the last year, when shipping was not available. Indeed, some of its effects were positive – and not only because supplies of wines from continental Europe, above all Germany, were disrupted. As the *Wine and Spirit News* put it in 1917: "The brave deeds of the gallant heroes of Gallipoli. . . appealed to the imagination of the people of Britain" and "brought everything Australian into prominence and popularity". Unfortunately, the war also led to the increasing political power of the temperance movement. In Australia, as in Britain, it proclaimed itself as "patriotic", taking its cue from the idea put forward by David Lloyd George, the British prime minister, that alcohol was an even greater menace than the Germans. To fight such a threat, the Vinegrowers'

Association of South Australia immediately imposed a levy on its members. They were supported by the state government, aware of the industry's economic importance. In fact, it was the temperance threat that brought the Australian wine industry together for the first time in 1916 in the form of the Federal Viticultural Council.

In 1916, in an attempt to enlist the Portuguese in the British war cause, Britain signed a treaty with Portugal. This ensured that only Portuguese wines could carry the labels "port" and, later, "Madeira". So, until 1924, Australian wines were largely confined to the category of table wines, virtually all of the heavy "burgundy" type. The sweet red Australian "ports" – neither tawny nor vintage – made from Grenache and Mataro (Mourvèdre) had to be labelled "port type." The name, with all its implications of an inferior imitation of the real thing, was naturally a deterrent to sales, and in the long run condemned such drinks to the bottom of the quality ladder in British eyes. Indeed, the stuff could be pretty vile. In Anthony Powell's novel, *Casanova's Chinese Restaurant*, set in Bohemian London in the 1930s, the narrator describes how he "had bought the bottle labelled Tawny Wine (Port Flavour) which even Moreland [a musician and notoriously undiscriminating drinker] had been later unwilling to drink. . . Following a preliminary tasting we poured the residue of the bottle down the lavatory."

Despite such views, Australia's export position was greatly strengthened during the 1920s because of (and partly in spite of) government interference. In 1924, the Australian government passed the Wine Export Bounty Act, intended to help the many ex-servicemen who had planted vineyards after World War I by subsidizing above all fortified wines (made from the dual-purpose varieties the soldier-settlers would naturally have planted). These grapes could be used for dried fruit as well as wine, and so never made decent table, or unfortified, wine. In the event, most of the ex-servicemen gave up after a few years, thus benefiting entrepreneurial winemakers such as John Tulloch, who bought up six twelve-ha (thirty-acre) blocks. The increased area under vines inevitably resulted in a glut of grapes, particularly of the Doradillo, a variety used for making brandy, whose price fell by two-thirds in 1924.

The following year the British government introduced Empire Preference, a system of preferential tariffs with a ten-year, fifty per cent margin of preference for empire produce. In 1927, the Australian government announced that, partly because of the boost given by Empire Preference, it was reducing the bounty – but only in six months time.

The six-month notice led to what HE Laffer describes as "excessive zeal displayed by both shippers and merchants in order to get as much wine as possible away in the interim. . . unfortunately also a deal of the wine was in the hands of people who were not really in the wine trade and knew very little about their handling and care. . . the fact that these baby wines were lying on their lees for long periods was a very grave disadvantage. . . in bond, stored in hogsheads, regular attention was an impossibility". Worse, they included many from the 1927 vintage, by then only a few months old. As a result, exports quadrupled in two years. "Poor little wines," wrote Rosemary Burden in *A Family Tradition of Fine Winemaking*, "lying around in their hogsheads, unracked after maturation, pushed around from pillar to post by people who did not love them or care what was happening to them. All they wanted was the money." Many of the wines caught a mysterious "disease" in transit and proved undrinkable. It did not help the Australian cause that what HE Laffer calls "a section of the old Wine Trade" encouraged a French offensive, arguing that "winemaking was an art which. . . was the God-given prerogative of the Continent of Europe".

The government's response to the problems it had largely created itself through the six-month delay in ending the bounty was typically confused. In 1929, a Wine Overseas Marketing Board was set up, designed to improve the quality of Australian wines and brandy. It also established a London agency, together with money for wine exports, funded by a proportion of the excise charges on the spirit used to fortify wines. Originally these were to be paid only for three years but, as is the way with such measures, some of them have lasted to this day, through the renamed Australian Wine Export Council. The intention was to stabilize prices and a minimum export price was established. Unfortunately, the British merchants succeeded in treating the minimum price as a maximum by playing off the producers against each other; thus British buyers avoided having to pay premium prices for the better wines. The Australians were also penalized when the importers cut the prices they paid as a result of a twenty-five-per-cent devaluation of the Australian pound. In 1930, the Australian government introduced the country's first sales tax on wine – albeit of a mere 2.5 per cent. Thanks to pressure from the industry, even this impost was hastily withdrawn a year later.

The "disease" that had afflicted the wines and had so lowered their reputation in Britain did, however, trigger the federal government's first systematic attempt to help the industry – seven years after the Commonwealth Scientific and Industrial Research Organization (CSIRO) had established its first viticultural research laboratory at Merbein, near Mildura. In 1934, John Fornachon, a graduate of Roseworthy and the University of Adelaide, was appointed as the Wine Board's first research officer and emerged as a key pioneer in Australian scientific research into all aspects of viticulture and winemaking. In 1936, largely thanks to his backing, Roseworthy introduced a separate Diploma in Oenology, promoting it from being an optional subject in the general course on agriculture. As always with Roseworthy, the industry backed the new initiative: winemakers not only sent their offspring to be educated at Roseworthy (until the 1960s, few – if any – outsiders took the diploma), but the industry also offered prizes for outstanding students.

Fornachon was described by that perceptive observer, Valmai Hankel, as "very tall, thin, with a distinctive craggy face, curly hair and glasses, a shy quiet man with a ready sense of humour". He established that the disease in spoilage was caused by lactic acid. After nine years of research, he published his epoch-making paper, "Bacterial Spoilage of Fortified Wine." As one observer put it: "If the Wine Board had done nothing but the investigation into the spoilage of wine, it would have more than justified its existence."

Unfortunately, Fornachon's remedy for the problem involved substantial doses of sulphur dioxide, whose aromas lingered in far too many Australian wines for far too long. In 1955, the money from the bounty scheme was redirected to the Australian Wine Research Institute (AWRI) based at the University of Adelaide, with Fornachon as its first director. This proved very useful. As James Halliday says, "In contrast to Davis" – the university in northern California, which has dominated winemaking in the state for fifty years – "the AWRI has balanced research and industrial requirements," whereas Davis has tended to impose its ideas on the industry. In 2002 the AWRI received the supreme accolade of the Australian wine industry when it was awarded the Maurice O'Shea Award.

The poor quality of the wines hurriedly shipped to the UK in 1927 may have left a lingering aftertaste on the British palate, but during the 1930s, the Australian presence was considerable, largely because fortified wines remained favourites with the vast majority of the British wine-drinking public. By the outbreak of World War II, port dominated the market with nearly one-third of the total. The Australians had twenty-two per cent of the market, just ahead of "Spanish whites" (mostly sherry) while the French, selling purely table wines, had a mere six per cent. Australia also dominated the market within the British Empire. Malaya took the bulk of the exports of Australian brandy, replacing the previously dominant French suppliers, and some table grapes were even being shipped under cool storage to Britain and Ceylon. Yet consumption within Australia was a mere 5.1 litres (nine pints) per person a year – the only instance, apart from the United States, of an important wine-producing country having inhabitants who were not habitual wine drinkers. Not surprisingly, in 1939, a quarter of Australia's wine production was exported, a level not to be exceeded until 1993-4, and then only just. As a result, any fall in British imports would have a severe effect on the Australian industry.

The immense pressure to mass-produce wines for distillation, for fortifying from Doradillo or dual-purpose varieties like Gordo, or to produce strong wines suited to the English taste inevitably took its toll on many famous regions, especially in Victoria and New South Wales. The balance sheet of the interwar years was grim. Some vineyard owners turned to other agribusinesses; in the Yarra Valley they raised cattle, which could easily be driven to market in Melbourne. As the locals put it: "Rumination supplants fermentation." In 1930, in Pewsey Vale, above the Barossa, the long-established Gilbert family gave up grape-growing to concentrate on sheep, cattle, and horses. In the same region, the Henschkes had to concentrate their efforts on fortified wines. In Coonawarrat the area under vines dropped by two-thirds, partly as a result of a vine-pull scheme initiated by the South Australian government in 1936.

By the outbreak of World War II, "Cheap fortified wine", in John Beeston's words, "seemed well on the way to impoverishing our wine industry both financially and perhaps more importantly, in self-esteem." As Sir James Hardy told me, "In the 1930s the family drank most of the dry wine we made," for table wine was now drunk only in a tiny proportion of households.

The Hunter, always the bellwether for production in New South Wales, was ruined by the swing to fortified wines. In the 1920s, there were unsuccessful attempts to settle returned soldiers, but the young men went off to work in the local coalmines, which were by far the largest source of employment in the region. A long strike in the mines at the end of the 1920s finally ruined the wine business in the Hunter. An attack of downy mildew earlier in the decade had reduced the vineyard area by three-quarters. By 1947, it was down to five ha as against 1,000 in 1922. The only firm to try to expand was Lindemans. Lindemans, which bought a number of estates. Charles Frederick died in 1916 and in 1923 his son Eric was forced to accept a manager appointed by Lindeman's bankers to run the company.

Even the Riverland suffered throughout the interwar years. The biggest cooperative, at Berri west of Renmark, began producing fruit and then, after 1918, extended to wine, brandy, and fortifying spirit. A distillery was a normal adjunct to any major winery to provide fortifying spirit. In the Depression years, cooperatives could survive, and then only with difficulty, by selling fortified wines cheaply. In 1934, Hardys bought all the surplus wine from its growers for distillation as a way of reducing surplus stocks, thus draining what we would now call the local wine lake.

By the early 1920s, the previously overwhelming influence of the Burgoyne family had started to decline because Peter Burgoyne's son Cuthbert misread the market. In 1920, he told the Australian Viticultural Congress that the policy of the British government was to "control strong drink and to create an increased demand for light wines and beers". If this was indeed the intended policy, it failed, although Cuthbert Burgoyne continued to be of considerable importance. When he visited Rutherglen in 1932, he was naturally fêted by the growers and, going back on his earlier forecasts, was buying enormous quantities of fortified wine. In 1933, John Francis Brown at Milawa sold him 270hl of tawny port.

In 1924, Burgoyne's great rival, the Emu brand, had come into the hands of WH Chaplin & Co, though Walter Bagenal remained as their local Australian representative. In 1930, Chaplin & Co bought a major vineyard in Morphett in McLaren Vale, which was also used as a centre for buying wines – and for making good ones under a young winemaker called Colin Haselgrove. Sales, above all of the firm's Keystone Burgundy, soon climbed above those of the Burgoyne family and, for better or worse, Emu remained the emblematic brand of Australian wine until well after World War II.

A handful of producers managed to escape the duopoly of Emu and Burgoyne. Angove's had established a healthy partnership with an English agent to form the Dominion Wine Company. Yates, a chain of wine bars concentrated in the north of England, sold a sweet sherry from Hardys (made from Muscatel, Palomino, and Pedro Ximénez) and designed to be stronger than port. "We wanted the people in Yates to know they've had a drink," was how Sir James Hardy put it. But the trade was never very profitable; the buyers, in the words of Tom Angove, "thought we had a constantly compressible waist-line".

There were warnings aplenty of the dangers of overproduction. Herbert Kay, the chairman of the Wine Board, warned growers of the "dangerous position arising from overproduction". "Growers," he added, "are warned against any further planting of wine grapes." And as François de Castella put it: "Grape prices can be fixed, but people cannot be forced to buy." In 1931, the growers in the Barossa banded together in a cooperative, and a couple of years later started to market their own wine, which they called Nurivin. In October 1938, the whole industry was greatly weakened by a tragic accident. That month, the federal government convened a meeting in Canberra of the leaders of the wine industry. Three of them, Hugo Gramp of Orlando, Sidney Hill Smith of Yalumba, and Tom Mayfield Hardy, were killed when their aircraft crashed.

Fortunately Gramp's son and heir, Colin, proved to be a major force for good, while Hardy's widow, Eileen, maintained the business, supporting Hardys for several more decades. She is commemorated in the firm's finest wine, the Eileen Hardy. Sidney Hill-Smith's younger brother Wyndham, universally known as "Windy", was recalled from Perth where he was selling wine, but also generally enjoying himself and playing cricket, with some notable innings for Western Australia in interstate matches.[1] Fortunately he rose to the challenge of running Yalumba. In the words of Rob Linn, Windy was a "gracious host, hospitable *vigneron*. . .

---

[1] Far and away the most distinguished cricketer associated with any Australian winemaking family was his uncle – his mother's brother – Clem Hill, one of the greatest batsmen in Australian cricketing history.

caring father, enthusiastic sportsman, larrikin, and artist were all rolled into one".

Windy inherited the business in a very depressed condition and, to make matters worse, he did not get on at all well with his uncle Percy, a distinguished viticulturalist. After persuading the banks not to close down the business, he deployed his considerable talents as a showman and salesman, as well as using his not-inconsiderable shrewdness. Norman Hanckel, one of his key associates, recalled an occasion when Windy baited two of his competitors by saying they knew nothing about sherry and thus they didn't sell a drop. They immediately told him at length of their successes. The next day Windy told Hanckel: "Gee, they were fools last night. I now know their total export and their total sales of each area."

It also helped that Rudi Kronberger, a great Austrian-born winemaker, worked at Yalumba at the time. He was one of the first to use brandy spirit rather than rectified, and thus characterless, spirit for making ports. In this way he greatly improved their quality, especially when he used really ripe Shiraz from the Eden Valley as the base wine.

Ironically, Windy, like many of his brethren, was saved by the war. Although it was responsible for the deaths of thousands of Australian soldiers, it had a very positive (if short-term) effect on the wine industry's fortunes, even though exports to Britain were soon stopped and the alternative market in Asia did not survive the Japanese invasions of late 1941 and early 1942. Servicemen, USA as well as Australian, were especially good customers. USA servicemen, in particular, fell for Yalumba's Galway Pipe Port. Rationing produced an interesting result. As HE Laffer points out, "Wine was difficult to obtain, owing to a rationing or quota system imposed, and, as is always the case, there came the incentive for most people to battle for their quota and thus – albeit only temporarily – increased domestic consumption." An appalling-sounding red port called Fourpenny Dark was especially popular – at least until beer became freely available again.

On the home front, many locals of Italian or German stock were interned in prison camps throughout the war or, like the De Bortolis, had their movements severely restricted. Worst affected were the Silesians in the Barossa. Even though they had been living there since the 1840s, they had retained their language and they paid a price for this. Only one of their pastors – the father of Peter Lehmann – could even preach in English. Peter himself never learned German because his mother had been pitched into an English-speaking school before she spoke a word of English. She was not going to allow her son to suffer the same trauma.

Wartime profitability helped to cushion the industry from the slowness of the recovery of the British market, where imports of such luxuries as wine were severely restricted. Even by 1950, sales had recovered to a mere quarter of the pre-war level, a severe blow to the industry. In 1950, Burgoyne shut down its operation in Rutherglen and was forced to sell it piecemeal. Six years later, Emu bought what remained of the Burgoyne business.

In Australia, tastes had started to change. Mildara Chestnut Teal was first produced in 1950, from Palomino grapes, and became a popular sweet sherry style. The general pattern of sales was largely unaffected by the war. In 1950, over four-fifths of the wine produced was fortified. Rationing, above all of beer, continued, and the brewers retained their iron grip on the sale of all types of alcoholic drinks, for, historically, sales had been confined to the pubs and other outlets they controlled. Moreover, the brewers bought wines only from members of the Wine and Brandy Producers Association, thus effectively barring the road to newcomers.

There was a shortage of everything from corks (which were often cut in half) to bottles, which were generally reused, often more than once. Colin Gramp made a point of emphasizing that his famous Barossa Pearl, launched in 1956, used only new bottles, of a special shape. Until the 1960s, Browns bought mixed twenty-dozen lots of bottles from the local bottle dealer. Just as used and overused were the oak casks in which the wines and brandies were matured – and exported. In general, Australian society returned to its pre-war habits, so sales were not greatly helped by the prosperity of the 1950s, a boom due largely to the high price of wool, Australia's major export. The best hope for the winemakers was to take on agencies for popular imported spirits as Yalumba did with Gordon's Gin and White Horse Scotch.

Typically, the federal government was both helpful and unhelpful. In 1951, there was an increase in excise duty on the spirit used for fortifying wine, and at the same time a tax was imposed on maturing wine, but two years later the depression in sales of wine triggered a rare tax concession. For taxation purposes the wine in the makers' cellars would be valued at only a nominal amount until it was actually sold. This measure had two effects: it delayed the tax burden on the industry and encouraged winemakers to mature their stock and not sell wine as soon as possible to pay the tax. Moreover, the Wine Overseas Marketing Act of 1954 allowed the Wine Board to undertake promotion at home, whereas its activities had previously been confined to exports.

The next year saw the foundation of the Australian Wine Research Institute, funded by the money left over from the export bounty which had been abolished in 1947. It was modelled on the research bodies founded a few years earlier for the bread and sugar businesses, other agricultural-based industries. But any renewal had to overcome a host of obstacles. The market, at home and abroad, was still dominated by fortified wines, or by table wines that were at best rough and undistinguished. Apart from a handful of connoisseurs in Melbourne and, to a lesser extent, in Sydney, the home market was hopelessly insular and ignorant, unaware of the existence of decent, let alone fine, table wines. The industry itself was composed of small family-owned businesses, dependent on the talents of the individual in charge, and unable to mount effective brands.

As a result, any initiative, above all outside Australia, involved the whole industry acting in the same sort of corporatist fashion as was usual in other Australian agricultural industries at the time. Most obvious was the abortive attempt to create what would have been literally a "Brand Australia" in the form of a cooperative brand of wine. In 1960, the same spirit led to the foundation of the Australian Wine Centre in Soho (UK), designed to sell all the country's different – and mostly pretty basic – wines. Fortunately for the reputation of the wine business, the previous quarter of a century had witnessed the gradual foundation of modern types of table wine.

6

The Long, Hard Road to Quality

A population which had been used to drinking fortified wines naturally moved to partially or fully sweet wines as the entry point for table-wine consumption.

JAMES HALLIDAY

Even in the depths of the bad years, which by my reckoning lasted for the first two-thirds of the twentieth century, there were signs of quality peeping through. Nevertheless the general taste for fortified wines meant that the handful of winemakers trying to produce superior table wines had a hard time of it. As Max Lake records in *Mines, Wines and People*, in the Hunter Valley although he could have been writing about any other wine-making region in the country – in the 1930s, "Great wine was sold cheaply if at all. Women in the district, working at vineyards, would cut onion hessian bags into foot-sized [thirty-centimetre] squares at night and soak them in water. In the morning they pulled them to shreds, using the fibre for tying vine arms to the wire. It was nothing to walk the fifteen miles [twenty-four kilometres] to Maitland with a can of cream, to obtain a few extra shillings from the townspeople." This sort of suffering was endured at the time by the inhabitants of other famous wine regions such as Bordeaux. Nevertheless, by the 1950s there were many signs that ever better and better wines could be made, and that the popular taste was slowly turning toward table wines, giving rise to the belief, justified by experience, that once drinkers have been exposed to table wines they are likely to move up-market, albeit slowly.

In Victoria, virtually the only light in the darkness was François de Castella, the son of Hubert. In the absence of any books, "He was the only authority," according to a veteran grower. François had been educated at

Montpellier and in his father's native Switzerland. He spent years trying to prevent the state government from achieving its apparent ambition of uprooting every vine in the state. The government's only response was to remove him from the Department of Agriculture where he worked. Then, in 1907, in an effort to make amends for its disastrous anti-phylloxera policy, de Castella was appointed government viticulturalist, and a research station at Wahgunyah was set up under his supervision to provide growers with grafted stock to supplement the research station set up in Rutherglen. François de Castella was not universally popular. "Another bloody Frenchman," grumbled one veteran, "but he made his presence felt."

On two later journeys to Europe, de Castella performed a notable service to the whole industry by bringing back *flor* (sherry yeasts) from Jerez to make proper sherry. The first to use it was Dr (later Sir) John Harris, one of whose sherries was named after the famous racehorse, Phar Lap. Even today the best Australian finos and amontillados are delicious, although, as so often with Australian wines, rather richer than their European equivalents. Unfortunately, the reputation of Australian sherries, like that of the ports, was permanently damaged by the inferior quality of the cheaper brands – most Australian sherries were, and in most cases remain, cloying cream-style drinks made from Muscat Gordo Blanco. Nevertheless, drinks such as the Montilla Sweet Sherry produced at the Berri cooperative for Lindemans (which had finally emerged from receivership in 1947) did attract many respectable women drinkers for the first time.

Although de Castella could do little to help the Victorians sell their better wines, in Rutherglen he developed techniques for grafting vines in the vineyard itself and introduced dozens of new varieties – Durif, Mondeuse, Grand Noir, Alicante Bouchet, Trebbiano, Müller-Thurgau, Fetyaska – and offered them to anyone who would plant them. Probably the most interested was his friend John Francis Brown at Milawa, who, fortunately, was also a friend of Peter Burgoyne. John Francis's father, George Brown, had emigrated from Scotland in 1853, attracted, like so many others, by the gold rush at Bendigo. He and five friends pooled their resources to buy an estate and George ended up with thirty-eight ha (ninety-four acres) when the syndicate split up in 1865.

John Francis Brown settled in Milawa, the very heart of the Ned Kelly bushranger country, full of horse thieves who would drive their herds across state borders to escape capture. In 1902, he built a distillery but soon ventured into the wine business, selling table wine, mostly to the Italian growers who supplied him with grapes. His family, however, still did not drink table wine during meals. The first time John Francis's son John Charles Brown remembers drinking table wine with a meal was in 1933 at a banquet (for Cuthbert Burgoyne) when he was already eighteen years old.

Life was hard. John Francis was too busy with municipal affairs to help the young John Charles (a late arrival in the family, a decade after three daughters) run the business. Indeed, John Francis was on the point of giving up when he was joined in the business by John Charles, who, at the age of twenty-eight, took over the business on his father's death in 1943. John Francis had made some good wines, but on a relatively small scale. By the 1950s, John Charles was making wines described by one expert as "very distinctive, very clean". He had been forced up-market when the Italian growers who had bought his wine in bulk found they could get cheaper wine from makers in Griffith.

Brown faced the full gamut of the many disasters (grasshoppers, tornadoes, even a great frost in November 1967) that are seemingly inevitable in rural Australia. He survived, thanks largely to a capacity, which he shares with the De Bortolis to forecast which varieties would be in demand ten years ahead. He was even able to take advantage of accidents such as the one when fermentation stuck in 1962 and he ended up with some superb dessert Riesling.

In 1950 John Charles bought Everton Hills, a forty-seven-ha (116-acre) property at a higher altitude than Milawa, from an Italian family. Typically, it was a mixed estate with cherry trees, passion fruit, and a mere two ha (five acres) of vines of dozens of varieties, some unidentifiable. The investment didn't pan out. He was ahead of his time, the yield was low, and the property would have been viable only if he could have charged today's prices. He then bought Mystic Park, an historic property, to plant more prolific varieties such as Grenache and Carignan from which he could make cheaper wine. He found water by drilling bore holes on the property, which enabled him to produce seventeen tonnes a ha (2.5 acres) every year. He ploughed all the profits back into the business and was eventually joined by all four of his sons as soon as they had finished school or college.

De Castella was also instrumental in helping Eric Purbrick, the owner of Chateau Tahbilk, to restore the finest property in the Goulburn Valley. Purbrick showed his commitment in 1931, when, after graduating from Cambridge, he forsook a career as a barrister in London to live at Tahbilk. He arrived six years after his father Reginald had bought the rundown property, one of only a handful in Victoria (outside Rutherglen and Milawa) still planted with vines. For over half a century, Chateau Tahbilk had been in the hands of the Bear family, who had initially helped build up the estate's reputation. After the death of Mrs John Pinney Bear, the ninety-two-year-old widow of the previous owner, Tahbilk was put on the market.

After buying the estate, Reginald Purbrick immediately hustled Tahbilk's surplus stocks of wine round Melbourne from the back of a truck. The Purbricks were lucky. Much of their vineyard was either on sandy soil, where the phylloxera bug did not flourish, or by the river, which was easy to flood. So they were, if only partially, spared the phylloxera blight – though a recurrence in the late 1970s meant that some of the vineyard had to be replanted with grafted stock.

Eric Purbrick not only saved the estate, he also initiated a number of new practices. He started selling kegs of wine to local hoteliers throughout the Goulburn Valley and appointed agents in other Australian states. This was an unheard-of step for a relatively small estate, as were his postwar journeyings to the Middle East and parts of Asia. He stayed faithful to a concentration on table wines – including, remarkably, a Marsanne served to the young Queen Elizabeth II when she visited Australia in 1954 (on a subsequent visit in 1970 she was served a Tahbilk Cabernet Sauvignon).

In the Hunter, the star of the 1930s was Maurice O'Shea, a winemaker more influential than Purbrick, whose name is immortalized in the most coveted prize awarded by the industry every year. Normally the prize, for an outstanding contribution to the industry, is awarded to a winemaker but it has also gone to a wine (Jacob's Creek) and to Hazel Murphy, a prime mover of Australia's export efforts to Britain in the 1980s and 1990s. O'Shea was born in Australia in 1897. At seventeen he went to study in France, his mother's homeland. When he returned to Australia seven years later, he persuaded his by now widowed mother to buy him a small vineyard near Pokolbin in the Hunter. He renamed the estate Mount Pleasant and remained there until his death in 1956, exploiting the potential of the property's red loam soil, a rarity in the Hunter and exceptionally suitable for fine grapes.

O'Shea very much went his own way. He was a pioneer in making single-varietal wines and calling them after relatives, friends, and the vineyards where they were produced. He also blended different varieties and wines from different regions to achieve consistent results. He was one of the first to appreciate the ageing capacity of the Semillon from the Hunter, a success commemorated today in Mount Pleasant, a marvellously deep and oily aged Semillon. In John Beeston's words: "He was both conservative, relying on Semillon, white Hermitage, and Shiraz as major varieties, and innovative, incorporating rare varietals such as Montils, Picpoul, and Aucerot into his blends."

After 1932, when the McWilliam family began to back him, O'Shea had even greater scope for his talents. As a result, according to Max Lake, his importance "was many-fold". "He introduced contemporary French winemaking techniques to the area. He had the pick of other makers' wines in the district, so that the Mount Pleasants of his day frequently represented the best wines of other vineyards and thus enhanced the reputation of the Hunter." The Hunter-oriented Lake inevitably exaggerated by claiming that O'Shea was second only to Busby in his influence of wine in Australia – although he did greatly influence Roger Warren, the widely respected head winemaker at Hardy's. Unfortunately, after his death, the McWilliams pulled out every second row of his closely planted vines to make the vineyard easier to cultivate, thus eliminating one of the factors that had contributed to the quality of his wines.

O'Shea was an excellent cook and gave memorable dinners. He and a group of his friends founded the Wine and Food Association of Australia, associated with Johnny Walker, a leading wine merchant. In Max Lake's words, O'Shea's "stewardship and great matching wines for their food" were vital. In the 1930s he brought together as never before (and rarely since) winemakers with a select band of wine-lovers, generally through clubs.

Decent restaurants were few and far between, and virtually confined to Melbourne. John Charles Brown remembers that in the 1930s there "were only a handful of licensed restaurants". "Virtually all were Italian with names like Romano's, The Ritz, Mario's, The Italian Society restaurant, Triaca's Italian Restaurant, and the Florentino," he recalls. So the only real meeting places for wine-lovers until well into the 1960s were the clubs, which brought together wine-lovers – many of them doctors – and wine merchants in regular sessions to drink, judge, and discuss wines. Typical was Max Lake's description of the "august Friday table at the Masonic Club in Melbourne. . . frequented by many wine-loving doctors".

Possibly the most famous institution was not a club but the wine bar and restaurant owned by Jimmy Watson at 333 Lygon Street, Carlton, which benefited from its proximity to the university. Watson had worked as a flautist in cinema orchestras, but the coming of sound put paid to that ambition. He brought a strict independence to his business; he had no ties to the wine companies and would not sell by the flagon. By the 1960s many tourists thought his premises a more important landmark than the Melbourne Town Hall. After Jimmy Watson's death, his contribution was recognized by the institution of the trophy named after him, awarded to the best red wine less than a year old exhibited at the Royal Melbourne Show.

Watson was not the only star in the Melbourne firmament. Dan Murphy, a third-generation restaurateur from South Yarra, had cellar claret (which became cellar Shiraz), cellar hock, and cellar "chablis" on his wine list. Then there was Tom Seabrook of the old firm of WJ Seabrook & Sons. He had the reputation of being able to recognize every table wine in Australia – partly, it has to be said, because there were so few distinguished ones. An even classier self-named establishment was started in 1951 by Douglas Lamb, a Cambridge-educated barrister known as "Old Velvet Balls". When Lamb died, one of the obituaries said that "It is not fair to say that had it not been for Douglas Lamb, Australians would still be drinking whisky with dinner, but it is not far from the truth."

In contrast to the bars and restaurants, the clubs were certainly not intended to appeal to the general public. The Beefsteak and Burgundy (B & B) clubs were started in Adelaide in 1954 because the longer-established Bacchus club seemed to be getting too big. By the mid-1960s there were seven different B & B clubs, one as far as away as Brisbane. In the far west, the Port Wine club was so called not after the wine, but because it was based in faraway Fremantle, a port on the Indian Ocean a few miles from Perth.

For all their exclusiveness, members of these clubs did create institutions that spread the word. These included "societies", pioneer mail-order groups. Dr Gilbert Phillips, a world-famous neurologist, founded the Australian Wine Consumers Cooperative Society (modelled on the Wine Society in Britain) and the Wine and Food Society of New South Wales (also modelled on the English society of the same name). According to Max Lake, Phillips was one of the pioneers in attacking the "tyranny of European wine names being attached to our own native wines". "This claret and burgundy business," he said, "has caused more downgrading of Australian wines than many realize" – by forcing people to think in terms of French wines and preventing Australian wines from establishing their own separate identities. Lake cites the award of gold medals in both claret and burgundy classes at a show in Sydney as late as 1954 to a "magnificent private bin red" from Tullochs. Both Sydney and Melbourne had wine-and-food societies, while Melbourne was host to the long-established Viticultural Society of Victoria founded by François de Castella.

As usual, Sydney was generally considered less respectable than Melbourne. In 1925, when he was only nineteen, Johnny Walker took over the Lord Roberts Hotel in Woolloomooloo – an establishment which had the reputation of being the hangout of the Razor Gangs, a collection of Sydney's leading crime figures, and could never have been considered an ideal launchpad for selling fine wine. Walker went into partnership with McWilliams, who, like Lindemans, the other major producer in the Hunter, normally sold only through its head office in Sydney. Until well into the 1960s, the McWilliams and Hector Tulloch of Tulloch and Elliot – who had a wine shop in Cessnock – were among the few makers in the Hunter selling under their own names. Another was well-known wine-maker Leo Buring, who also owned the Ye Olde Crusty cellars, where he held regular tastings.

Leo Buring was the son of Hermann, who had been responsible for the Quelltaler wines. Leo was a major figure in the transition from fortified to table wines. Sent by his father to Roseworthy and then to Montpellier and Geisenheim as a twenty-six-year-old in 1902, he joined Penfolds and made its first bottle-fermented sparkling wine at the company's Minchinbury estate on the Hawkesbury River. It provided the only real competition for the "Champagnes" made by Hans Irvine in far-off Bendigo.

In 1919, Buring left Minchinbury to work – like his father's partner, Carl Sobels – as a consultant. During the 1920s he spent seven years, vainly trying to rescue Lindemans, which had been placed in receivership in 1923. For the next thirty years he became famous for his Rieslings and for his best-selling Rinegolde, a sweet table wine made from Hunter Semillon, which was not a run-of-the-mill wine. Years later, Max Lake tasted a 1945 "of surprising quality and ageing gracefully".

Even after Leo Buring died and his company had been sold to Lindemans, he left a legacy. In the 1960s, John Vickery, a young wine-maker trained by Buring at Quelltaler, made some superb Rieslings from Eden Valley grapes; in the 1950s so did Rudi Kronberger, the young Austrian winemaker at Yalumba. Vickery has now been going his own way for nearly fifty years, and as Phil Laffer, his (nominal) superior puts it, "He's a single-minded perfectionist. He doesn't make the cheapest wines." These attitudes ensure that, not surprisingly, "assistants come and go".

After World War II, winemakers started to become involved with the tasting of fine wines. In the late 1940s, a small group of winemakers formed the Barossa Club. They included Colin Gramp, who was already a member of the Adelaide equivalent where the wines were tasted blind. Gramp had spent the war hunting for enemy submarines in the North Atlantic. He then visited California where he inspected the most modern winemaking techniques. In 1947, he produced his first table wine: a Special Reserve Claret made from Shiraz blended with some Cabernet Sauvignon. It was a signal to the world that the Barossa Valley was capable of returning to its Victorian glory.

Until well after the war, most Australian winemakers were more used to making fortified wines and had little or no experience of the very different techniques required to produce fresh, clean, dry, white table wine. In making fortified wines the production process is largely oxidative, with no temperature control. The wines were deliberately exposed to the air – which is the very opposite of the conditions for making table wine, above all from white grapes. In 1953, Colin Gramp made his break-through. He managed to obtain a precious import licence to buy the first German closed-pressure fermentation tanks for white wine, which he had seen when the company's German manufacturers visited Australia the previous year. These tanks prevented the escape of carbon dioxide while the wine was fermenting and thus slowed it down, crucially enabling the winemaker to control the process and produce far fresher and more aromatic wines. Until then, as Gramp wrote, temperature control was nearly impossible, and after fermentation "The wine was usually aged in large, old wood [casks] for a least a year before bottling." The result was a heavily oxidized beverage without any fruity freshness. Not surprisingly, this type of wine, typical at the time, was normally "consumed as a long drink with soda, lemonade or ice" and rarely, if ever, drunk neat or with meals. By contrast Gramp's wine was cold-fermented and cold-stabilized.

The first (1953) vintage of Gramp's Barossa Riesling was a sensation. It was only six months old when it gained first place in the hock-chablis class at the 1953 Melbourne Wine Show, although the drinking public was rather bewildered by the novel fruitiness of the wine. Gramp had problems with oxidation, which he solved during a visit to Germany in 1954. The 1955 vintage confirmed the wine's potential, sweeping the board at wine shows. Gramp's techniques also avoided the problem of "haze" (a cloudiness which the French call *casse*). This is due to fermentation in metal vessels, above all those made of copper, as opposed to wood or the chemically neutral cement vats widely used in France.

Nevertheless, later commentators could be critical. In 1985, a party of masters of wine noted that the "method gave too much of an aldehydic/herbaceous character to the wines". But more prevalent is the opinion of Philip White, who calls Gramp's Barossa Riesling an "impossibly fresh" wine. Gramp had just pipped Yalumba, the only other winery prepared to try the new machinery. When Yalumba had installed its closed-pressure fermentation tank in time for the 1954 vintage, the two wineries compared notes. Indeed, in a typical example of camaraderie, Gramp invited the whole industry to see his new machinery in action.

At a time when the refrigerator was becoming a normal household appliance, it was not surprising that white wines became all the rage. Following his 1954 visit to Germany, Gramp grew ever more ambitious. He decided to produce the Australian equivalent of one of the sparkling *perl* wines, made by the *charmat* process, which were so popular in Germany. Gramp's wine was to be made from Tokay and Hunter River Riesling (generally known as Muscadelle and Semillon, respectively). The wine needed to be produced in conditions even more strictly controlled, but fortunately Gramp had bought the necessary filtering and bottling equipment while in Europe. He could use the pressure tanks to produce the "fizz" generated by the carbon dioxide.

The result, Barossa Pearl, proved a real winner. Gramp had hoped to introduce the wine to coincide with the 1956 Melbourne Olympic Games, which, combined with the postwar influx of immigrants from southern Europe (especially Greece), transformed Melbourne into a far more cosmospolitanity. But there were problems with closing the bottles until a local glass manufacturer came up with a special plastic stopper on top of a bottle that had a marked and deliberate resemblance to the bulbous shape of a Perrier bottle – although Gramp himself preferred to call it the shape a bowling pin. Barossa Pearl was launched a couple of months late to mark Guy Fawkes Day on November 5. It was the first alternative for women drinkers to Ringolde or the sweet sherry that had been their normal tipple, and indeed, it made wine-drinking respectable for properly brought-up Australian women. It was also, importantly, a wine promoted as being made from fruit from a single region.

The success of Barossa Pearl meant that Gramp had to find bottling equipment capable of handling up to 400,000 cases of the wine every year, and it soon replaced Ringolde as the country's favourite non-fortified wine. It is easy to mock such wines today, but they were certainly far cleaner and less cloying than most of the wines being sold on a large scale anywhere else in the world at the time. Gramp's Riesling and Barossa Pearl were key events in the history of Australian wines, for his techniques could be replicated with many different varieties and regions.

Gramp had brought a young winemaker called Gunther Prass over from Germany to help him make the wines, and one of his competitors, Ian Hickinbotham, did something similar, attracting Wolf Blass, another young winemaker who, like Prass, was destined to make a major contribution to the industry. According to Blass, Hickinbotham had a "theoretical mind like Einstein". The son of Alan Hickinbotham, who had initiated the oenology course at Roseworthy, Ian Hickinbotham had been appointed chief winemaker at a virtually bankrupt concern in the Barossa, the South Australian Grapegrowers Cooperative, which in the past had been reduced to canning fruit. His first step was to change the name of the winery from Nurivin to Kaiser Stuhl, after the tallest of the three hills overlooking the Barossa. The hill's name had been changed to the more patriotic Kitchener for a time, during and after World War I.

Hickinbotham echoed Gramp's initiative with the wine's name, Pineapple Pearl, but could afford only the most primitive equipment: three pressure tanks bought secondhand from a brewery for a mere £71 each and a filling machine bought from Schweppes for £93. But then, as Blass says admiringly, the Australians have always been good at improvisation: "They could have built a tank out of a sardine tin." Both Pineapple and the less successful Cherry Pearl were sickly beverages, sold in bottles of the same shape as the fruits which were genuinely used in their production for. As Wolf Blass says, "Hickinbotham was stoutly opposed to artificial flavourings."

The Pearls helped to spread the word about non-fortified wine. For example, a lad called Chris Hatcher was raised in a strictly Methodist household where alcohol was regarded as a sin. When he was twelve, his sister won a bottle of Barossa Pearl in a raffle. The wine became an icon to him, and his first act of teenage rebellion was to go out and try it. From there it seems to have been a natural progress to his present position as chief winemaker of Beringer Blass.

The new wines appeared at a time when tastes were changing. Lindemans produced one of the long-lived postwar sensations, Ben Ean. Its name had first become famous between the wars as a rich red made from Lindemans' vineyard of that name in the Hunter. In its postwar form, it held over one-fifth of the sales in bottled wine within Australia. It was not, it has to be said, a distinguished beverage, produced mostly from Sultana, with some Trebbiano and Muscat added to beef up the fruitiness. In its day it competed with the drier, frankly more acceptable Houghton White Burgundy, which was introduced in 1937 by Jack Mann, the fabled winemaker at the Houghton Winery north of Perth, then part of Chaplins, owner of the Emu brand. Houghton White Burgundy was made from Chenin Blanc; the grapes were allowed to ripen longer than usual and then left on their skins for twenty-four hours with the addition of some extra acid if the wine was too soft. The result was a delicious, flavourful wine that remains a best-seller today, although called HWB outside Australia to avoid clashing with the French monopoly of "burgundy".

While Colin Gramp expounded the virtues of wines made from grapes from the Barossa, the region that emerged during the first sixty years of the twentieth century as the country's most reliable source of fine wine was Coonawarra. In 1901, a fourteen-year-old Bill Redman arrived at John Riddoch's vineyard there. But, typically of individual quality initiatives before the 1960s, Riddoch's venture lasted only his lifetime. The market was simply not ready to accept fine-wine brands and needed an individual's impetus. Without it, even the most promising vineyards reverted to type, producing wines destined for fortification or even the ultimate brand of shame: distillation. Inevitably, but unfortunately, after Riddoch's death in 1901, the immense stocks of wine he had accumulated had to be distilled – and for a further fifty years, the estate continued to distil its whole production. After several hard years at the vineyard, Redman concluded that the only commercially viable solution was to make his own wine. Riddoch's executors were so desperate they sold him a sixteen-ha (forty-acre) block on easy terms. He was lucky to find a buyer for the wine he made in the person of a well-known merchant, Douglas Tolley, who owned an estate near Adelaide. Unfortunately, in the early 1920s, Tolley refused to buy any more of Redman's "burgundy", claiming that it was so good his English customers wouldn't buy any of his other wines.

Luckily, Redman found another partner: a retired army officer, Lieutenant Colonel Fulton, who owned a well-known Adelaide wine-merchant business, Woodleys, and whose own vineyards had been swallowed up by the growth of the city. Together they evolved the first wine in a style that has remained famous through the years: light in alcohol, high in acidity, leafy without being grassy, and of a delicacy unequalled at the time in any Australian wine. For the past half century it has been known as Coonawarra Cabernet, but when it won the first prize in an exhibition of Empire wines in London in 1936, it was called simply St Adèle, without any mention of its region of origin or, for that matter, the winemaker responsible for its quality.

After the war, Woodleys bought another Coonawarra estate, Chateau Comaum, as well as the historic cellars dug by John Riddoch, and between the 1949 and 1956 vintages called the wine the Treasure Chest series. As the best-known winemaker in Coonawarra, Bill Redman naturally made the wine (also called Chateau Comaum), but the first year saw a devastating and unprecedented outbreak of downy mildew. The venture folded and Redman returned to his own vineyard.

The region was relaunched by David Wynn, son of Samuel Wynn, a

Jewish immigrant who had arrived from Poland in 1913 and changed his name from Schlomo Weintraub (the surname means "wine-group" grape). Samuel Wynn's first great success was as a restaurateur and wine merchant. His initial investment in winemaking was a disaster, but he rescued the business with the help of exports and a sparkling wine called Romalo, which proved a favourite with servicemen – especially the well-heeled Americans – during World War II.

Samuel, David, and Samuel's grandson, Adam Wynn, were crucial in the development of table wine in Australia. After the war, David continued his father's good work, emphasizing the (at the time novel) idea of drinking wine with food. For Roseworthy students, dinners at the Wynn family's Italian restaurant, Café Florentino, was one of the highlights of their excursions. In 1951, while his father was in Europe, David bought the run-down Chateau Comaum estate. When informed by telegram, his father replied succinctly, "Admiring your courage" – a not-surprising reaction given the region's reputation as being liable to frost and downy mildew, and too far from civilization to find enough labour.

David Wynn was just in time, the estate had nearly been sold to the Department of Lands and Forests. He set about making the first modern red wine in South Australia, proudly flaunting the name of Coonawarra on its elegant labels and employing Ian Hickinbotham, the first wine-maker seen in the district who was actually a trained viticulturalist. The Wynns were unique in combining fine winemaking with marketing flair. Their basic idea, as David Wynn's advertisements put it, was "The luxury of wine at little expense". They also captured a substantial share of the wine market in Victoria with a major innovation, Wynvale, the two-litre reusable glass flagon. David Wynn employed the same skill in marketing Wynns Coonawarra Claret, probably the first time that a regional identity had been attached to a table wine, because he reckoned, rightly, that even in a depression – for wine, anyway – people would still buy a wine of such quality.

Previously, growers like Bill Redman had sold their wines to a number of merchants who all wanted rather different styles of wine, and Redman was only too happy to oblige. The Wynns initiative encouraged the Redman family to sell its own wine for the first time, calling it Rouge Homme. Within a few years the example had been followed by Mildara, which, under the aegis of Ron Haselgrove, bought twelve ha (thirty acres) of the precious Coonawarra terra rossa. Penfolds soon joined in, and when John Beeston tasted the Cabernet Sauvignon from the great 1959 vintage twenty years later, he found that by then it "had matured into a brick-red, minty magnificence".

Coonawarra was not the only region on the move. In 1959, Glen McWilliam planted the first Cabernet Sauvignon in the qualitatively much humbler Murrumbidgee Irrigation Area where his family was the most important producer. He went on to plant Riesling and Traminer the next year. McWilliam was a gifted engineer and designed his own form of stainless-steel tanks to help make fresher, fruitier white wines.

Other winemakers in the 1950s were also trying, often successfully, to "improve the breed". There was Colin Preece, a former *dux*, (top student) of his year, at Roseworthy who had been appointed chief wine-maker by Seppelt in 1932 and couldn't do much before the war because of the lack of demand for even half-decent table wine. Later, WS Benwell found him "a taciturn, rather donnish person who would be just as much at home in the science masters, common room as at the wine-judging tables". He was adept at using wines from a number of regions (he was a great blender) and maturing them in small oak casks. They soon became famous and won awards after 1952, when the Seppelt family allowed him to enter them in shows. Previously, Preece had been confined to entering his sparkling wines from Hans Irvine's former cellars at Great Western which remain famous today. Occasionally they were even labelled with the date of the vintage.

Another innovator, Roger Warren, the chief winemaker at Hardy's, employed the same techniques as Preece, even buying in wine from his competitors. After Warren's early death in 1959, the wines made by his successor, Dick Heath, were of the same style and quality. Not surprisingly, Warren, Preece, and Maurice O'Shea were friends and often worked informally together. Even in the Riverland, things were improving. There the Berri Cooperative installed better equipment in the 1950s, including refrigeration, and in 1959 started to make a red table wine. Unfortunately these efforts have been overshadowed by the reputation of a single, albeit remarkable wine: Grange. Most histories give the impression that Grange was a solitary peak rising suddenly from a desert plain, whereas in fact it was a peak in a whole range of mountains – although admittedly by far the highest one. The renaissance of Australian wines is generally dated from 1951, the year Max Schubert produced the first vintage of Grange Hermitage, then, as now, unquestionably the finest wine in Australia. A more relevant date, perhaps, is 1960, the year the board of Penfolds, Schubert's employers, allowed him to make the wine on a regular basis.

Schubert had worked for Penfolds since 1931 and was appointed chief winemaker in 1948. The fourth generation of the Penfold-Hyland family decided there might be a future for red table wine, and this hunch led to Schubert's historic journey to Europe in 1951, primarily to study fortified winemaking in Spain and Portugal. But he was also allowed to visit Bordeaux where he was royally entertained by Christian Cruse, the most gentlemanly member of a family that was to be destroyed by a scandal in 1973, when the family firm was found to be labelling wine from the south of France as claret.

The wines Cruse offered Schubert gave the Australian the idea of producing a wine which, like those he had drunk in Bordeaux, would last a couple of decades or more. As he remarked, "It would not be impossible to produce a wine which could stand on its own feet throughout the world and would be capable of improvement year by year for a minimum of twenty years." It was an idea that seemed ridiculously arrogant not only in the 1950s, but for a decade or more after that.

Schubert's first happy accident on the road to achieving his ambition was that he was forced to use Hermitage (Shiraz) because the varieties used in Bordeaux were either (like Cabernet Sauvignon or Merlot) available only in tiny quantities or, like Cabernet Franc, simply unobtainable. So Shiraz it was – with a little Cabernet or Malbec. The Cabernet came from choice fruit grown by the Redmans on terra rossa soil at the north end of Coonawarra. Schubert had an eye for a fine vineyard site, notably Kalimna[1] in the Barossa, where Penfold had bought 145ha (358 acres) in 1945. But most of the fruit came, then as now, from growers' groups he encouraged, such as the Shiraz Club in the Barossa, whose members were able to produce fine fruit regularly each year that could be used either in Grange or other premium wines.

From the start, Schubert's objective was clear: "to produce a big, full-bodied wine containing maximum extraction of all the components in the grape material used". This involved "a much longer period of fer-

---

[1] "Pleasant view" in the local Aboriginal language.

mentation and skin contact. . . necessitating strict fermentation control" with an even rate of fermentation ensured by using a heat exchanger (itself a novelty) and continual monitoring of the process. In the vats he used header boards, which ensured that the cap of skins and solids was totally immersed all the time during a fermentation period of up to twelve days – four times that of the three days normal in Australia at the time. The wine – a mere 11.5–12 degrees Baumé, and thus relatively unalcoholic by Australian standards – was matured for up to twenty months in small, new 300-litre American oak casks, possibly because Schubert couldn't get the French oak used in Bordeaux. During that time, the wine was frequently racked to intensify its richness.

Grange Hermitage[2] was named after the Grange cottage built in 1845 by Dr Christopher Rawson Penfold at Magill, where, three years later, he had also planted a vineyard of the same name. The estate shrank to only seven ha (seventeen acres) during the 1960s and 1970s, when Penfolds, then strapped for cash, sold most of the land for housing. There was great opposition to the sale from wine-lovers but most of the land did not produce great grapes.

The key to Grange was allying Shiraz to small casks of well-seasoned American oak – "A marriage," as James Halliday put it, "arranged in heaven" – and a style that had also been favoured by Dr Penfold himself. Its very special style was a matter of winemaking and maturation techniques rather than the precise variety or source of the grapes. Schubert ranked the pure Cabernet from Kalimna, produced in 1953, "as one of the best Grange-style wines we ever made", thus rather deflating the idea that its quality was based on Shiraz.

The result was a wine so powerful as to be virtually impossible to taste in its first year – "knife-and-fork stuff", in the words of Robert Joseph. "I wouldn't put it in my fountain pen," said Gerald Boyd. "It would clog it up." Not surprisingly, when Grange was first tasted it was profoundly misunderstood because the wine was too young, given that its maker intended it to mature for at least twenty years. Indeed, it was so different from any existing Australian red that the first vintages were hated by virtually everyone. It was famously described by one contemporary

---

[2] Since the 1995 vintage it has been called, simply, "Grange".

expert as "a very good, dry port which no one in their right mind will buy, let alone drink".

In Grange's first decade, virtually its only supporters were two Penfolds directors: Jeffrey Penfold Hyland and Melbourne restaurateur Douglas Lamb. Other supporters included Max Lake, who bought or drank, most of the 1953 vintage himself. In 1956, Schubert was officially forbidden from continuing the experiment by the Penfolds board – though Hyland privately encouraged him to continue. For the next four years he had to make the wine in secret, unable to use the small, new-oak casks which were crucial elements in the wine's quality; using old oak made all the difference between a good and a great wine because the new American oak provided much of the concentration, depth, and richness that were such crucial elements in the style of Grange.

It was partly the passage of time that altered the Penfolds board's opinion because, over the years, the early vintages became much more approachable. Ideas were changing, and in 1960 Schubert was given official permission to start making the wine again after a decade that he described as one of "discovery, faith, doubt, humiliation, and triumph". Two years later the wine was officially brought within the pale when the 1955 Grange was awarded a gold medal at the Sydney Wine Show. Today, the earliest vintages in particular are collectors' items. Sensibly, Penfolds has jealously guarded the wine's quality. Although production in a normal year is between 5,000 and 10,000 cases, in the difficult 2000 vintage it dropped to 2,500 cases because of lack of fruit of an acceptable quality.

The casks used for Grange were sent to make other, inevitably lesser, wines, a usual practice in all major winemaking regions. Schubert's aim, as he put it, was to create and establish "a dynasty of wines". "These may differ in character year by year," he said, "but all. . . bear an unmistakable resemblance and relationship to each other and the original ancestral starter-member of the dynasty." Halliday defined the hallmarks of the Penfolds style, then as now, as "rich, sweet fruit, almost always at the riper end of the spectrum; number two is oak influence, manifesting itself in the structure and flavour of the wines; number three is pronounced and rounded tannins". The most distinguished of Penfolds' "lesser" wines was Bin 389, originally known as "the poor man's Grange", even though it was deliberately different, described as a multi-district, "supple and fleshy" wine.

The term "bin" came from the sections of the underground storage areas, holding up to fifty cases, used for wines that were originally experimental. If they were marketed commercially they took the number of the first bin that housed them. In the 1950s, the numbering was rather casual; the early Granges had four or five bin numbers.

The Cabernet equivalent of Grange was Bin 707, named by a marketing executive who had previously been employed by Qantas. It was made using Cabernet from Coonawarra (much of it from Penfolds' own vineyards) and from the Barossa. Although it was discontinued for a few years in the early 1970s because the still-limited supplies of Cabernet were needed for other wines, today it is the Cabernet flagship of the Penfolds fleet.

Some of the best bins, such as 84A and 95A, were experiments, never put on the market even though they kept winning trophies. Other outstanding bins fondly remembered by the winemakers include the 80A and 820. They were usually produced in quantities of under 1,000 cases – showing that Penfolds could make boutique wines. Virtually all of them were blends of Shiraz and Cabernet Sauvignon, though Bin 2, a wine deliberately aimed at the export market, was a blend of Shiraz and Mourvèdre. Even further from the pattern was the Clare Estate Red that was dominated by Merlot – another example of a single sub-region wine, its grapes from a site selected by Max Schubert. It took ten years to convince Schubert that the wine would never be satisfactory because it was simply not rich enough for the Schubert treatment.

Over the years the (inevitably modified) versions of the techniques employed by Schubert when making Grange have been successfully applied to an ever-widening range of wines. Bin 407, for instance, was deliberately different: leafy, minty, much more Coonawarra-ish, showing that the Penfolds style is not monolithic and can be adapted to make "regional" wines. Koonunga Hill (originally made from grapes grown in Koonunga, northeast of Kalimna) and Rawson's Retreat, a deliberately "commercial" style, were at the cheaper end of Penfolds wines. The whole range was, generally successfully, designed to show how, as an official Penfolds leaflet put it at the time, "a combination of winemaking skills and resources can bring quality wine to the average consumer".

Schubert's winemaking abilities – and the technical back-up he enjoyed above all from Ray Beckwith, a brilliant chemist – ensured that, for the first time (in the twentieth century, anyway) the Australian industry showed that it was capable of producing a world-class wine. The success of Grange facilitated the slow dissolution of a lack of confidence that had hung over the industry since the beginning. Schubert's declaration of independence from the French was far more profound than is sometimes realized. From Christian Cruse he gleaned the idea of producing a long-lasting wine, matured in small oak casks. But the variety he used, the type of oak – indeed, the whole style of the wine – were all alien to the Bordeaux tradition.

There was a downside. The glorification of Schubert, and of Grange and the style it represented, typecast the idea of fine Australian wine and tended to overshadow two other initiatives. The first was the style of the St Henri Claret produced by John Davoren, another distinguished winemaker in the Penfolds stable. He was a meticulous craftsman. "He would taste the fermenting wine three or four times a day," remembers Bruce Tyrrell. "His aim was fine, sweet tannins and not overly extracted wines." Davoren took precisely the opposite tack to Schubert with his St Henri Claret. Davoren looked for varietal characteristics. The wine was matured in large oak casks so it had little oak character with much more vintage variation. The 1998 vintage, tasted in 2002, was a smooth, spicy, elegant drink with fleshier fruit than Grange.

The other alternative to Grange was Hill of Grace, still the supreme example of a distinguished site in the whole of Australia. The first vintage of this wine was made in 1958 by Cyril Henschke, great-grandson of Johann Christian, one of the many Silesians who had arrived in the Barossa in the 1840s. Henschke's estate is not in the Barossa but on the hills above, in the Barossa Ranges to the east of the valley. Gnadenberg – German for "hill of grace" – is the name of the lovely little church across the road from the vineyard.

During the 1950s, Cyril and his brother Louis, a brilliant viticulturalist, started to phase out the use of their wine for fortification. In 1956 they produced one of Australia's first wines from a truly distinguished single vineyard, Mount Edelstone (German for "gemstone"). The wine instantly began to win prizes. In 1958, the Henschke brothers came up with an even greater single-vineyard wine, which is now an icon second only to Grange: Hill of Grace, which, like Mount Edelstone, is almost pure Shiraz from a eight-ha (twenty-acre) vineyard that also has a few vines of other varieties. The key to the wine lies with the old vines, the oldest, the "grandfather plot" planted in the 1860s by Nicolaus Stanitzki, son of Carl August Stanitzki, the original owner; were others planted between 1910 and 1965. In 1989, Prue Henschke started to replant a plot with vines selected from the sturdiest of the older plants.

The wine is rich but spicy, herby, comparable only to the finest wines from the Rhône: not woody, not as impossible as Grange in its youth. In a vertical tasting in early 2002, I found the 1990 the most outstanding, with all the spiciness and fruit of a great Rhône, rich and powerful but not overly heavy, like a big man dancing lightly. The 1996 showed what the wine is like in its relative youth: still tannic but with an extraordinary depth from a great mass of acid and ripe fruit.

The deification of all these wines, even of Grange, was for the future, for it was undreamed of at the end of the 1950s. That decade ended with a surplus of grapes and flat exports – the traditional English market was clearly dying, while the social conservatism characteristic of an era dominated by conservative, ultra-Anglophile Prime Minister Sir Robert Menzies ensured that domestic sales of table wine were still below the level of the early 1950s. Not surprisingly, 110 million litres of the 1962 vintage were distilled, fifty million fortified – mostly into sweet sherry – and a mere thirty-two million used for table or sparkling wines. The general public was still unaware of the goodies on offer, still less of those to come. As John Fornachon had put it, the limiting factor in the production of wine in Australia was not land but markets. It took another decade for the country's inhabitants to sit up and take notice of Australian wines.

7

The Voice of the Bard

To enjoy what Australia can do, you need two lifetimes.

LEN EVANS

The 1960s saw the first wave of a popular swing toward table wines as opposed to the fortified variety that had reigned supreme for so long. The swing was largely generational, as better-educated, more sophisticated, well-travelled drinkers reached maturity. The arrival of the first Boeing 707 at Sydney in 1962 showed that, in future, a trip to the old country need no longer be a once-in-a-lifetime experience. The growing predilection of young Australians for travel (at times Earl's Court in West London resembled an Australian ghetto) enabled them to pick up the customs of the countries they visited at a time when wine-drinking was growing apace in Britain. Licensing laws in Australia were finally relaxed in 1967, bringing an end to the infamous six o'clock swill and encouraging people to eat out. The 1959–60 sales of table wine – including sparkling – were a mere third of fortified types. Six years later, sales of fortified wines had declined a little, but sales of "dry" (that is unfortified), reds and whites had risen by more than half. In the last five years of the decade, sales of red wine went up two-and-a-half times, and by 1970, table wine sales were – just – greater than those of fortified.

The swing was also influenced by the nature of postwar immigration to Australia. Many previous immigrants had come from Ireland, the only non-wine-drinking country dominated by the Catholic Church, or from the non-wine-drinking classes of England and Scotland. The Italians lived mostly away from major cities. At first they bought their table wines from Browns in Milawa, but then realized that they could buy it cheaper from Italian-born winemakers in Griffith, suggesting that, before the

1960s, the influence of immigrants from southern Europe was largely confined to the lower end of the market.

But the story changed with the opening of hundreds of restaurants, above all in Melbourne, home to hundreds of thousands of post-war immigrants from wine-drinking countries such as Greece and Hungary. The new restaurants provided an outlet for the handful of adventurous firms, like Browns, that were already making substantial quantities of "dry" red wines. The Browns were lucky. Whereas, as John Charles Brown puts it, "The red wines of the period were big, full-bodied wines made from very ripe grapes and carrying heavy tannin and generally rather lacking in acid, Milawa reds tended to be lighter in style than those of Rutherglen – again because of a rather different climate." This advantage was to prove of inestimable value to the Browns in subsequent decades.

As is often the case in the story of wine in Australia, one man made a huge difference, in this instance to the trend toward civilized wine-drinking. Len Evans, a Welsh immigrant with a golden tongue and a great palate, took the tradition personified by the Jimmy Watsons and their like and introduced their idea of fine wine to a far wider public. I don't think it is too much to say that his ideas, and those of his disciples, have done more to shape the industry than any other single influence. Evans is what the Welsh would call a "boyo": large, enthusiastic, and per-suasive, with a manner that closely resembles another Welsh performer, Sir Harry Secombe (although Evans only lived in Wales for three years as a young boy). As Jeremy Oliver, his official biographer, puts it: "The Evans flair is known to stretch reality. It is instantaneous, spontaneous, Elizabethan, grandiose." In the words of one friend, he is a "cocky Welsh bastard".

Evans's whole life has been one long wake-up call to Australians to appreciate their own wines, as well as a crusade in favour of wine in gen-eral. He has been a major figure in bringing the appreciation of fine wine out of the closet, away from the private clubs and dinner parties to which it had previously been confined and into the mainstream of Australian life. By wine he meant table wine, not just Australian but the finest from all over the world. He ensured that Australian winemakers and -drinkers realized what they were up against by opening thousands of bottles of superb French wines to teach and delight them.[1] This was not as far-fetched as it sounds, for in the 1960s and 1970s, the value of the Australian dollar was much higher. It also helped greatly that the price even of the finest clarets and burgundies were ridiculously lower than they are today. Evans also steered drinkers away from fortified wines, which are barely mentioned in his voluminous writings. Moreover, he and his friend, the financier Peter Fox, brought in the outside investors who have provided finance for much of the industry's expansion over the past thirty years.

The son of a former RAF officer turned peripatetic businessman, Evans refused a place at Cambridge to study architecture, which nevertheless remained a passion of his, with results including a remarkable house of his own design. Instead, he chose to become a golf professional. He enjoyed the experience, but soon discovered "the world of difference", as he put it, "between being a professional golfer and a golf professional" – in other words, he would only have continued if he had thought he was a potential champion. So off he went to New Zealand, where he started work felling trees and culling deer before he completed the two-year apprenticeship required of immigrants by working in a factory making golf carts and exhaust mufflers. There he showed the first sign of his organizational skills, one of his most surprising qualities.

After a row with a boss, he left for Australia and worked at a dozen varied jobs (mostly simultaneously) at Mount Isa in Queensland, where he met and wooed the local beauty queen, Patricia Hayton, invariably called Trish. She agreed to marry him only when he had graduated from glass washer to stock manager (that organizational streak again) at the Ship Inn in Sydney. While he was at Mount Isa, he had been spotted by Mark Hill-Smith of Yalumba, and this helped when he was looking for a wine-related job in Sydney.

His real apprenticeship in wine started when he wandered into a newly opened art gallery owned by a Czech-born wine-lover, Rudy Komon. Komon was aggressive and totally sure of himself. Characteristically, in 1955, when he was served a glass of Coonawarra red on a visit to Adelaide, he asked, "Vere is this Coonavarra?" before racing off to the

---

[1] He was not alone in learning from the French. In 1971 John Charles Brown dispatched his three eldest sons on a world tour. In particular they admired the public relations and customer relations of the French; there was even an Australian flag to greet them at Chapoutier's winery in the Rhône Valley.

region of which virtually no one outside South Australia was aware at the time. He then made its wine famous in Sydney. Komon was seemingly generous with his artists – save that he cheated them mercilessly. He was famous for his bluntness; when he was charged A$9 (£3.20) for a bottle of wine; he accused the restaurant owner of being a crook. When he was told that the wine had cost A$7 (£2.50) a bottle, he exclaimed, "Then you should be in the asylum."

Komon became Evans's acknowledged guru, though he was not an easygoing one. When he asked Evans about his favourite wine at a wine-appreciation course, Evans said, "I rather like Gewürztraminer." "Don't worry," snapped Komon. "You'll grow out of it." Komon introduced the young Evans to the then tight-knit world of wine-lovers, but Evans's life work really began during his three years at the Chevron Hilton in Sydney, which had catering facilities for thousands but only 220 bedrooms. Given a free hand by the hotel's manager, Frank Christie, Evans dreamed up innumerable ideas, including the Friday Lunch, an event that echoed other club-like festivities. More serious was the First Thursday Club, which brought together wine professionals and merchants to discuss the world of wine, and to analyze and appreciate the best Australian wines.

Evans was always ready to absorb influences, such as the style of Eric Purbrick of Chateau Tahbilk, Rudy Komon's knowledge of wine, and the judging ability of George Fairbrother, king of the Australian show scene and a hero of Evans's. Until the 1960s, wine shows had copied the agricultural-based system. Medals were awarded only for the first-, second-, and third-placed entrants, but then judges started to award gold, silver, and bronze medals, sometimes in profusion. The first such awards were in 1960 at the Adelaide Show, which was usually the innovator. The wine shows remained an inherent and increasingly important – element within the overall Australian agricultural show scene, serving as a major bridge and forum for mutual education between the winemakers, commentators, and those few journalists considered serious enough to be judges.

Evans became a notable show chairman. The chair can be more or less authoritarian (Len Evans was surprisingly democratic) in his attitude toward fellow judges and to the "associates", the young trainees who all too often had only to wait until the death or retirement of one of their seniors. Evans still defends the system. "If a public-relations company came up with the idea of the show system," he says, "they would be regarded as bloody geniuses. It has terrific clout in the market and a huge power for publicity."

Evans, as well as other outsiders, including officials from the Department of Agriculture, were an essential leaven to the usual ranks of judges from the wine industry itself, who tended to be too inward-looking, unable to judge by standards other than those they applied to their own wines. Evans exploited his position to introduce the previously parochial judges to foreign wines and to campaign for purer wines. He understood the nature of his crusade only too well, as he put it: "I had to make the industry make the right wine." As one wine-writer explained, "The technical networking involved in discussion of the wines is the reason why the show system has played such an important role in the improvement of Australian wines."[2]

The move into a larger arena, toward converting a wider public to the joys of wine, started with Evans's newspaper columns under the pseudonym "Cellarmaster" though he used a number of other names. The columns were chatty, blokey, informative, never condescending, and always enthusiastic; he hated modern "technical" writers. Evans introduced his readers to great wines from non-Australian as well as local sources. George Fairbrother performed the same function by opening bottles of the finest French wines for the benefit of his students at Roseworthy. Evans was the country's first regular wine columnist. His predecessors, like Walter James, did not have a regular weekly column. Indeed, Evans was moving into a desert; when James published *Barrel and Book: a Winemaker's Diary* in 1949, it was the first non-technical book on wine published in Australia for half a century. Evans's influence didn't stop at wine; his habit of calling his nearest and dearest by their surnames was much imitated. As Max Allen put it, "I can still remember the first time Len called me 'Allen'. I couldn't sleep, I was so excited."

Crucially, as James Halliday noted, Evans appealed to three classes of readers: "People who didn't really want to learn about wine but were amused by his stories and the way he presented them; others were occasional drinkers who suddenly had their attention caught; and finally the complete wine experts who used him as a yardstick for their own

[2] Huon Hooke, *Online Report*, in August 2001.

opinions." Evans's has always been restless ("been there, done that" has been his – unspoken – motto throughout his life), and in 1965 he joined the Australian Wine Board as its national promotions executive. There he discovered that he had written fourteen of the seventeen articles on wine published the previous year. He disregarded the findings of market research, which showed that Australian drinking was heavily weighted toward port, vermouth, and sherry, and claimed he had been hired to promote table wines. This was not entirely true. Ian Seppelt, the chairman of the AWB, had told him that his main job was to promote fortified wine, but typically, Evans took no notice and no one seems to have protested. Otherwise, his taste covered every type of wine, still or sparkling, dry or sweet, red or white.

Before Len Evans, the wine industry's promotion efforts had been almost entirely reactive. Seeing that his budget was too small for effective advertising, Evans went the educational route, organizing more accessible wine tastings, and hiring writers and broadcasters to spread the good word. All this was part of a policy that inspired a standard of wine-writing at least as good as that prevailing anywhere else in the world – and, crucially, ensured that, today, every serious newspaper and magazine has a regular and usually well-written and informative column. By the time Evans left the AWB, articles were running at a rate of over 500 a year.

The culmination of what might be called Evans's private promotional efforts came when he bought and restored premises at Bulletin Place in the heart of Sydney to create a restaurant, tasting room, and wine shop. The reconstruction allowed him to indulge his lifelong love of architecture and decoration. From the start, the Tasting Room sold wine – inspiring the single most Len-ish announcement ever: "Len Evans Wines, Bulletin Place, regrets to announce that it has sold out of 1928 Pichon-Longueville." I rather doubt if he ever did stock any of that fabled claret. Nevertheless, his stock of fine wines, lavishly distributed among his guests, had the desired effect in motivating young winemakers to emulate, rather than copy, the French example. Bill Pannell, founder of Moss Wood, one of the finest wineries in Western Australia, claimed that his life "was changed forever after drinking a Clos de Bèze in 1980". After this experience he started visiting Burgundy on a regular basis and used John Gladstone's recommendations to pinpoint Pemberton as a place to grow Pinot Noir (see Chapter Eleven).

Evans opened Bulletin Place in October 1969, at the height of one of Australia's most expansive mining booms. For the next decade it was the most extraordinary venture in educating drinkers Australia has ever known. It, and more particularly, Evans's fabulous lunches – the Monday Table and their like – were the single most effective promotional and educational tool in the history of fine Australian wines if only because they were systematically presented to a large circle of drinkers.

Evans frequently went well over the top, wildly ordering expensive wine for the events, which frequently became uncouth, very noisy, and very expensive, not only for Evans himself. Nevertheless, he was always generous, selfless, and sharing, and a superb taster, a man for whom the motto "the bottle does not quench the thirst" could have been coined. His enthusiasm for particular wines sometimes led to gross overstocking and the occasional sale of wines from his own cellar to repair the financial damage. "It's either the family, the business or the wine. So it has to be the wine. I can always replace it," he would say. The adventure also reflected his lifelong belief that people, especially but not exclusively himself, were put on earth to enjoy themselves, and not necessarily to make money, an attitude that has led to consistent disappointment for most of those who have invested in his many ventures.

Evans was not only operating at the right time but also in the right city. By character he is a pure – albeit Welsh-born – Sydneysider, never at home in Melbourne, which he found stuffy. As a result, he naturally became a symbol of the rise of Sydney. He was greatly helped by the rise of what the sniffier Melburnians would call the new rich in Sydney. Because Melbourne had always been the more sophisticated market, the change in the balance of vinous power was difficult for its inhabitants to understand. It was assumed, for instance, that his Cellarmaster columns were written by someone from Melbourne. The hostility and the snobbery were palpable and long-lasting. When Evans judged at the Melbourne Show, Doug Seabrook, the chairman, didn't agree with anything he said and he wasn't invited back. There are still many Melburnians who refuse to admit the extent of Evans's influence.

Bulletin Place provided a magnificent apprenticeship for dozens of future merchants, writers and winemakers, one of whom was told by Evans, "You will work very hard, you'll get paid nothing, but I'll teach you wine." One of the most attractive aspects of Evans's complex character is his joy in teaching, his appreciation of potential young stars whom a lesser guru might have slighted or kept down as potential rivals. And they don't come more famous than Brian Croser, an introvert whose character was totally unlike that of the exuberant Evans, a brilliant, highly intelligent, winemaker who became a star in the firmament in the 1970s. They did have something in common: the jealousy they aroused. Evans describes Croser as "another poppy that continually gets criticized". Less arrogant, albeit influential in a way similar to Evans, is his other outstanding disciple, James Halliday.

Halliday's father had been a physician and heart specialist who had got the taste for fine wine while studying in Britain during the 1930s and through an introduction to Lindemans. The young James learned about wine from his father, who had a cellar well-stocked with wines, not only from Lindemans but also from other producers. While studying law at the University of Sydney, Halliday dominated the wine club and took full advantage of the ability to bring wine into the college hall for two dinners a week. For twenty years after qualifying, he combined an increasingly successful career as a corporate lawyer with what for anyone else, would have been a full-time job, for he did not leave the law firm where he had become managing partner until 1988. All the time he was writing numerous articles and books, including the pioneering *Wine Atlas of Australia and New Zealand*. Through his sheer energy and depth of knowledge of the whole of Australia, he became Len Evans's natural successor as a publicist for Australian wines – albeit in a much less charismatic style. According to Michael Hill-Smith, "He is the complete man of wine." But unfortunately, both Croser and Halliday shared, to a lesser extent, Evans's inadequacies in business, though this was not apparent until rather later.

Evans was always ready to applaud and encourage the efforts of the handful of winemakers, old and new, who were trying to push the envelope of Australian winemaking, the most obvious being his old friend and drinking companion, Dr Max Lake. In the 1960s, Lake was a young surgeon obsessed by wine who had already written extensively about wine in Australia. He had been inspired not only by Len Evans but also, and perhaps more importantly, by Graham Gregory of the NSW Department of Agriculture. At the time there were other professionals, usually doctors, in Sydney, Melbourne or even distant Perth who could have taken the plunge, but Lake was the first. In doing so he was returning in some respects to the innocent times described by Ebenezer Ward in which wines were made by people who did not depend on them for their living, before the arrival of professionals like the Hardys, the Seppelts, and the Gramps.

Max Lake's estate, appropriately named Lake's Folly, was the result of a process of scientific selection based on his realization that the best wines in the Hunter were grown on volcanic soil. After some years of searching, his choice fell on twenty-five ha (sixty-two acres) near a paddock owned by the McWilliams, which had already produced some wonderful wines. Despite the fact that there were virtually no Cabernet Sauvignon vines in the Hunter – and precious few in the rest of Australia – Lake plumped for that variety. In the late 1960s, thanks partly to what he called – in an a typical fit of modesty – "Lake's luck", he made some lovely Cabernets.

Lake's most important legacy was pinpointed by John Beeston: "This confidence in small wineries was surely the lasting contribution made by Lake's Folly to the Hunter boom of the 1960s." Lake himself felt that he had "not so much rubbed Aladdin's Lamp as opened Pandora's Box", as hundreds of "weekend farmers" went out and established vineyards, in what James Halliday calls "diversion therapy". This form of treatment cost the patients (the weekend farmers, though not Lake) millions of dollars in the following decades and created some wondrous vineyards, as well as an awful lot of hopeless cases. Inevitably, the demands of practising medicine and winemaking at the same time posed a considerable strain. In his book about doctors and wine, Max Lake listed the problems involved. These included "surveys, financial problems, pests or my initial lack of knowledge about sprays, pruning, cask technique, labour management, drought, hail, and intrusion on my ordinary family life and a busy practice". But he was kept going by his belief in himself. In the course of an interview, wrote Oz Clarke, "I lost count of how often he said 'I did that, I was the first one'."

The reinvigoration of the Australian wine business required not only prophets and missionaries spreading the gospel. There were also bloody-minded winemakers like Evans's old mate, the late Murray Tyrrell. Evans and Tyrrell shared what can best be described as linguistic fluency: not for nothing was Murray called "the mouth of the Hunter." The Tyrrell family had been established in the Hunter since the late 1850s, when the founder, Edward Tyrrell, planted a small vineyard with the "Aucerot" grapes (it is probably an Anglicized misspelling of Auxerrois) that Dr Lindeman, no less, described as the king of white grapes. According to Jancis Robinson, this term can be a synonym for Pinot Gris, or, to my mind more probably, Chardonnay, which Australians called Pinot Blanc until the 1970s. So it is quite possible that the Tyrrell family had Chardonnay in their vineyard throughout its history.

Edward Tyrrell's eldest son, Edward George (universally known as Dan) died in 1959 in his late eighties, true to his belief that "I want to wear out not rust out," although his health problems started when he slipped off a ladder at the 1956 vintage. He was succeeded by his nephew Murray, just as formidable a character, who had been a cattle dealer and a "Jackaroo" – the Australian name for an odd-job man – on an estate. Murray was helped by his father, a great vineyard expert who provided invaluable support. So Murray's son Bruce, who now runs Tyrrell's, is only the fourth generation of the family.

Evans and the gang took Murray Tyrrell under their wing. Rudy Komon gave him access to good foreign wines, and in 1962, Len Evans persuaded him to bottle his own wine. Unfortunately, Tyrrell's financial problems meant that he had to bottle his red wines rather earlier than he should have, taking them from the barrels on the dirt floor in the old tin shed the summer following fermentation. At that time, merely finding bottles was a problem, beer was much bigger a business, so Australian Glass Manufacturers, the monopoly bottlemakers, didn't care about wine bottles. Pioneers such as John Charles Brown had to scratch around for secondhand burgundy bottles.

Murray "not only made a lot of noise", observes Phil Laffer amiably, "he also made good wine". He also enjoyed acting as a mixture of monster and country yokel. In 1985, a party of Masters of Wine, the leading authorities on wine in Britain, reported that Murray, then sixty-three, was "humorous, tough, grainy, and very much an individual" – which, being translated, means a bloody-minded old B. They also found his winery "almost defiantly rustic". Tyrrell's was a contrast to the ultra-modern wineries they visited elsewhere and which were eventually the source of the complaint that Australian wines were technically perfect but lacked any form of individuality. At Tyrrell's "beaten-earth floor, open fermenting vats, the odd cobweb, all appeared to reflect the powerful character of Murray himself." "Leaning against one of the old vats, he told us about his family's business," Laffer continued. "His style was laconic, but he could not disguise his understandable pride in the Tyrrell method. . . and its results over the years."

Perhaps inevitably the Hunter was the magic region of the late 1960s and early 1970s. Inevitably, too, Len Evans, who loved the region and moved there in later life, wanted to invest in what he perceived as its winemaking potential. He and his close friend, the entrepreneurial financier Peter Fox, who shared his visions and was able to organize the finance for them, introduced the idea of raising funds through a syndicate of investors, an initiative that has been imitated by hundreds of similar groups in the past twenty years.

Rothbury Estate, the prototype for many others, was not itself profitable, for Evans wanted fun and new ventures rather than profit. The original syndicate behind his first and most ambitious venture, with 365 ha (902 acres) of vines and a fine winery, consisted of three businessmen, a surgeon, a radiologist, a dentist, and Rudy Komon, with Murray Tyrrell to make the wines. It was soon clear to insiders that Rothbury was started in too much of a hurry, not nearly as thoroughly prepared as Lake's Folly, and never made financial sense. Nor did Brokenwood, set up by Halliday and some friends almost as a "student prank". Two decades later, Halliday showed that he had learned from the Brokenwood experience when he established Coldstream Hills in the Yarra Valley, building himself a superbly sited house overlooking the whole valley. Unfortunately, he took his treasured estate public in October 1987, just before the crash. Although he subsequently sold out to Southcorp, he's still there, working like a maniac and acting as a consultant on some of the finest and most elegant Pinot Noir in Victoria.

Halliday and Evans were not alone. In the early 1970s, Penfolds sold the historic 520-ha (1,285-acre) Dalwood estate at Wybong in the Lower Hunter and moved further inland into the Upper Hunter, where they planted a dozen or more varieties, often from new and untried clones. The whole venture cost A$two million (£714,000), an immense sum at the time. The "old" Dalwood estate was bought by Perce McGuigan, who had made the wines there for Penfolds for twenty-eight years, and his son Brian. They renamed the property Wyndham Estate, after the original owner, the pioneer George Wyndham, and planted a dozen or more varieties.

Some total outsiders soon followed Evans into the region. WR Carpenter, then a Pacific trading company, had been taken over by a coalmining company, which established the Arrowfield winery in 1969 and almost collapsed six years later. One complete outsider who made the grade was Bob Oatley. Before he bought an estate in the Upper Hunter in 1968, he had been a trader in the world's finest coffee, from Papua New Guinea. He bought in the Hunter because it seemed fashionable, and he wanted to breed horses and possibly plant a few vines. Rosemount, the eighty-one-ha (200-acre) estate he purchased, had been settled in the mid-nineteenth century by Scottish immigrants who named it after a village outside Blairgowrie. But the vines, like so many others, had been pulled up after World War I because of the slump in demand for the type of wines produced in the Hunter.

In most cases, the boom in the Hunter largely ignored the suitability of the soil and the too-wet-in-summer climate for many varieties or, in some years, for vines of any description. The surge in plantings in the early years of the 1970s meant that a lot of unsuitable sites were planted with vines. They were unsuitable because the soils and sub-soils were hard, mean, and clayey. Moreover, many of the new vineyards lacked adequate or suitable supplies of water. Not surprisingly, around 1,700ha (4,201 acres) of these vines disappeared in the following two decades. Between 1969 and the peak of 1976, the land under vines had soared from 591ha (1,460 acres) to 4,137ha (10,223 acres) before subsiding to 1,600ha (3,954 acres) by the early 1990s. There's been little planting since. Today, less than one-fifth of the wine sold in the Hunter is made from grapes grown in the region. It has become almost a virtual region and has seen a considerable decline in the area under vines while most of the country's other well-established wine regions grew, in some cases enormously, in the last thirty years of the twentieth century.

But I mustn't exaggerate. There were many other pioneers where Evans's influence was not all that important. D'Arenberg is a classic example. In 1912, Joseph Osborn, a director of Hardy's, bought Milton, a well-known vineyard in McLaren Vale. Osborn's son Frank left medical school to take over and innovated. According to one account in 1920, his were the first vines in the district to be given "the dignity of posts and a training wire". In 1943, Frank's sixteen-year-old son, Francis d'Arenberg Osborn (always known as "d'Arry"), returned to the estate to take over the management from his sick father. By 1957, d'Arry was in charge, and the next year he sold his first wine in the bottle. In the 1960s, his wines, especially his Cabernet Sauvignon, were universally acknowledged as some of Australia's finest. D'Arry is a man of great gentleness and passion, and no mean winemaker. His burgundy (a blend of Grenache and Shiraz) has won no fewer than twenty-five gold medals – a tradition continued by his son Chester, who now runs the estate. The young d'Arry was greatly helped by Cuthbert Thornborough Kay (known as "Cud"), a much-loved winemaker in McLaren Vale. On one occasion, d'Arry took him two buckets of his unfermented juice and returned with two buckets of Cud's wine. He then kick-started the fermentation of his vats in a primitive but effective fashion.

But then, during the 1960s, there were signs of wine life all over Australia. Glen McWilliam planted some Cabernet Sauvignon at Hanwood near Griffith, making 500 cases in 1963, and many more varietal wines in the following years. Another venture on the Murray River came when Windy Hill-Smith planted Oxford Landing, a major vineyard on the Murray River near Waikerie. A third of the vineyard was planted with the then-neglected Cabernet Sauvignon. At the suggestion of his long-time winemaker Peter Wall, he bought forty ha (ninety-nine acres) of vineyard high above Pewsey Vale from Colin Heggie, a man whom Oz Clarke describes as "wild, argumentative, a be-whiskered bushwhacker born out of his time".

After immense effort choosing the correct varieties, the right clones, the right trellising, and the right density, Hill-Smith and Wall started producing the finest of Rieslings and Cabernets. Wall also set up a nursery that has proved crucial in providing new clones for the whole industry. One upmarket wine was The Menzies, a Coonawarra Cabernet named after the then prime minister, Robert Menzies, who had declared that the 1961 Yalumba Galway Vintage Special Reserve was the best red wine he had ever tasted – surely a joke from a prime minister who normally revered and copied the habits of the British establishment, which would never normally have touched a "colonial" beverage.

But what James Halliday described as "the most important event of the decade" came in 1963. Then Karl Seppelt bought 356ha (902 acres) of land eighty kilometres (fifty miles) northwest of Coonawarra in a region called Padthaway-Keppoch, which had the same sort of red soil as

Coonawarra itself. It was not a blind bet. In 1944, a CSIRO report had identified Padthaway, with its virtually unlimited underground water, as suitable for large-scale planting of early-ripening grape varieties. Seppelt was soon followed by Hardy's, which bought over 200ha (494 acres).

Luckily for both of them, the white-wine boom of the 1970s showed that Padthaway was better for white wine than for the reds for which Coonawarra was so justly famous. Both investments showed the increasing commitment of the major firms to new regions in their search for large areas to establish vineyards suitable for growing the newly prominent table-wine varieties, a search that was to intensify in the next decade.

8

Wake-up Time

In a single generation, Australia remade itself. It went from being a half-forgotten outpost of Britain, provincial, dull, and culturally dependent, to being a nation infinitely more sophisticated, confident, interesting, and outward-looking.

BILL BRYSON, *DOWN UNDER*

The series of innovations that enabled Australia to retake its rightful place as one of the world's great winemaking regions occurred during that underrated decade, the 1970s. The winemakers responded to the new demand for better wines with a quantum leap in winemaking techniques, and big business – much of it foreign – was at hand to transform the industry's previously rather lackadaisical business practices.

The change in drinking habits in Australia, as in Britain, was largely due to the baby-boomers, those born in the decade after World War II who drifted away not only from fortified wines but also from beer, the country's traditional alcoholic drink. Beer consumption reached a peak in the mid-1970s and has been in decline ever since. One key moment in the study of Australians' drinking habits had nothing to do with alcohol. In 1975, Kevin McLintock, then with a major distributor and later managing director of McWilliam's, noted for the first time that sales of that eminently "Continental" beverage, coffee, exceeded those of tea, the historic Australian "colonial" beverage, for the first time.

The new Australia had first shown its face in 1972 with the triumphant election of Gough Whitlam at the head of an unprecedentedly forward-looking labour government, an event that marked a true generational shift. Next year, the end of the White Australia policy, by which only white immigrants had been accepted into the country, introduced a new world of Asian food, which was far more suitable for the Australian climate. The change represented a substantial cultural shift from the British food that had been traditional in the old Australia.

Nevertheless, in the 1970s wine was still not a normal feature of Australian life. Bruce Tyrrell remembers wooing a girl at the time. He naturally brought a bottle or two of wine with him when he was invited to Sunday lunch with her family. Before, during, and after the meal the men drank beer, and the women, totally unused to wine, got so plastered after a few glasses of Tyrrell's wine that they could not wash up. That was the last time the young Tyrrell was invited to that particular house.

In the cities there were a growing number of restaurants, and in the majority of unlicensed ones, BYO (Bring Your Own) wine became very fashionable. Yet in many parts of the country, such restaurants as there were closed at weekends. In some states you could eat in a restaurant or drink in a pub, but you could not do both on the same premises without breaking the law.

In 1970, the Gorton government had introduced a fifty cents per gallon (£0.37 per litre) excise tax on wine. It was halved in 1972 and totally removed by Whitlam six months later. But the already declining brandy industry suffered badly. Between 1965 and 1978, the excise duty on brandy jumped tenfold – admittedly from a low base of little more than fifty cents a bottle. Not surprisingly, production halved between the peak year of 1955 and the mid-1990s.

For the wine industry, the most important single action of the Whitlam government came in 1974, when retail price-fixing was outlawed. This set off a long fight based on heavy discounting and the emergence of a handful of major players in wine retailing. The biggest was Liquorland, a subsidiary of the Coles Myer department-store group, which operated not only as Liquorland but also as Vintage Cellars. The heavy hitters moved in to exercise unprecedented pressure on winemakers used to customers far smaller and less formidable. Sales mounted as prices – and thus winemakers' profits – fell sharply.

At the same time, smaller wineries started to discover cellar-door sales, which were to prove an ever more important weapon in their fight against the increasing power of major buyers and the major wine-producing companies that alone could deal with them on a more or less equal basis. The 1972, the Trade Practices Act released the growers from previous restrictions that had allowed sales of only between two and five cases from the winery. This restriction had had one helpful result, in that it had forced growers such as the De Bortolis to open distribution companies in major cities such as Sydney, thus widening their market.

But the situation before the 1972 act had crippled cellar-door sales. In the late 1960s, Dr Max Lake was refused permission to sell individual bottles from his vineyard, Lake's Folly, because he was told he was an "unsuitable person". When he replied that perhaps he should stop prescribing morphine for post-operative pain, he was told his unsuitability, in legal terms, derived from the fact that he didn't live at the vineyard. Many visitors had to buy cases, rather than single bottles, if the cellar door was unlicensed.

Lake was only one of the many newcomers who depended on sales from the cellar door in the absence of proper distribution. It was in the 1970s that enthusiasts started to drive from Sydney to the Hunter Valley to buy the new releases. This practice became almost institutionalized. At the peak of one pass on the old pre-motorway road to the valley you can still see the cairn Champagne corks erected by visitors like James Halliday who had paused awhile to admire the stunning views of the valley and enjoy a little light refreshment (Krug was a favourite) on their way to what was always Sydney's home farm, for wine anyway.

In the 1960s, however, as few as thirty people a weekend would visit the valley in search of wine. Probably – one can't be sure because successes like that of Hunter's cellar-door operations have many progenitors – the breakthrough came from Len Evans, who included a major facility to attract visitors to Rothbury. He was followed five years later by Murray Robson, owner of the Squire wine shop in Sydney. As Robson put it, the Hunter was the "number-one wine retailing area in Sydney". Evans's real contribution to the Hunter was not Rothbury, but his confirmation of the valley's position as the greatest wine-related sales outlet, not only in Australia but in the world – with the Napa Valley as the only competitor.

The growth in the flow of visitors encouraged wineries to follow the Tullochs' 1950s decision to bottle under their own name instead of selling the wine in bulk. The trend was not confined to the Hunter. Brown Brothers, admirably sited on the road to the increasingly popular skiing resorts in the Victorian Alps and one of the first wineries not to charge for tasting, found that the tourists provided a good test market, and as recently as the late 1970s, accounted for most of the firm's sales. Even today the 100,000 visitors make up a fair chunk of business. In the early 1970s in the Hunter, one of the jobs for the young Bruce Tyrrell was to develop a primitive mail-order business, sometimes by simply thumbing through the (then much slimmer) telephone directories of likely cities such as Sydney and Newcastle. These efforts helped to educate the public. Bruce Tyrrell claims that visitors would come in asking for "reverse" port instead of reserve port, and "rugby" Cabernet for ruby Cabernet, but the prize went to the buyer who asked for "gee-wizz tram driver" rather than Gewürztraminer.

With increased and more general consumption of table wines came swings of fashion, like that from red to white and back again; the resurgence of Shiraz in the late 1980s and 1990s; and the extraordinary growth in sales of sparkling wines between 1975 and the late 1980s, when the growth suddenly stopped. At one point Yalumba was landed with immense, and almost unsaleable, stocks of their previously triumphant product, Brandivino: a sweet white-wine liqueur with, as the name implies, a distinctive taste of brandy, which once sold a million litres per year. But the most dramatic change in fashion came in the mid-1970s, when white wines started to outpace reds. Previously, in the trenchant words of Murray Tyrrell, "White wine was only for ladies and woofters" – though, as elsewhere in the world, women's preference for table wine rather than sweet sherry, their previous tipple, when outside the home had helped boost wine consumption.

The swing to white was due partly to a scare that the histamines in red wine could be harmful. White wine was taken up even at the business lunches that formed such an important element in the country's wine scene. The trend to white was also due to the difference in the relative quality of wines of the two different colours. Too many of the red wines – with the honourable exception of those made by Penfolds and a handful of other conscientious firms – were like those described by one senior winemaker as "tired, hard, and lacking fruit character". By contrast, the overall quality of white wines had greatly improved. Following Colin Gramp's lead, they were cold-fermented and stored in stainless-steel, temperature-controlled tanks to ensure that they were fresh and fruity – albeit rather sweet for the palate of many of today's drinkers.

Nevertheless, the "crisis" for the producers of red wines should not be exaggerated. Sales, which had risen nearly fivefold between 1960 and 1970 to over twenty-five million litres and reached a peak of thirty-six million in 1975, had declined only to twenty-seven million litres in 1980. Overall, domestic consumption of table wine doubled in the 1970s to reach over sixteen litres per head – well above the levels in Britain and the United States.

For the majority of wine-drinkers, probably the single most important innovation was wine in the box, also known as "Chateau Cardboard". The development of what was basically a "bladder in a box" started in 1965. After two years of development, Angove's introduced a 4.5-litre pack, which consisted of a plastic bag within a cardboard box that collapsed as the wine was withdrawn. Two years later, Penfolds launched its own bag. At first, it proved too clumsy, so the box was replaced by a sort of biscuit tin, but the plastic bag inside it leaked and Penfolds had to recall two million bags because the wine oxidized.

Then Charles Malpas, a genius from Geelong, invented a flexible container for use in a cigarette lighter and adapted it so that the bag would collapse as the wine was poured out, thus avoiding oxidation. To get the wine out without dripping and destroying the bag, he used two seals, one fixed on the bag, the other fixed on a tap. The final solution was provided by an American company, Scholle, with its pre-sealed and multilayered silver liner. This device, along with better plastic, resulted in unprecedentedly cheap packs of white wine to be kept in the country's fridges.

Unfortunately, at first, these packs, like fortified wines, proved only too convenient for getting rid of inferior fruit. But they did help mop up the "wine lake" created by the gross overproduction of dual-purpose grape varieties such as Sultana. Thus, they helped the major producers by concentrating the growth of consumption on cheap, and thus low-margin, wines. Brown Brothers, unwilling to discount, developed boxes of up to ten litres, which may have been too big for the average household fridge but were ideal for restaurants, thus giving the Browns a lock grip on "house" wines.

Wynns was in the forefront, prepared to cannibalize its own market in flagons of "Wynvale" by buying up some of the patents for different-sized "bladders in a box" and introducing a 4.5-litre pack with an energetic advertising campaign. Between 1970 and 1985, sales of flagons dropped from two-fifths of the market to less than one-tenth, while casks soared to over three-fifths.

In 1974, Lindemans created its cask, Cellarpack, and Orlando its Coolabah cask. These casks came to dominate the sale of wine (not just white) and greatly helped the swing from beer to wine. By the 1980s, seventy per cent of all table wine was being sold in casks of over four litres. Not surprisingly Gunther Prass, the managing director of Orlando, described the cask wine as the "saviour of the industry". He was exaggerating, but casks did transform wine from an occasional purchase into part of the normal contents of the household fridge. They also proved to be ideal entry-level wines for the mass of new wine-drinkers.

In Australia itself, the growth and increasing complexity of the wine business during the 1970s led to some dramatic changes. Previously it had been a fairly cosy affair, involving relatively small and almost exclusively family-controlled companies. In Adelaide, their management was dominated by former pupils of the city's three leading schools. But by the end of the decade, the family companies' idyll had been gravely disturbed – albeit often to the advantage of the shareholders – by major outsiders. These were not confined to local firms, but included foreign groups anxious to "diversify" (one of the buzz words of the decade) by investing heavily, if not always wisely, in the business.

In the fifteen years after 1970, there were thirty-two major takeovers in the industry as an endless stream of newcomers, Australian and foreign, bought – and then often resold – most of the country's most famous names. The poker game continues to this day. According to James Halliday, writing in 1994, the merry-go-round has never ceased to spin: "Not a single one of the wineries [involved in the takeovers] is still in the same ultimate ownership or control."

Unlike many of their successors, some of the original takeovers made some business sense. It was the reduced margins, combined with the need to invest in ever-increasing stocks, that forced cash-strapped family companies into the mergers and sell-offs of the 1970s. Once a company embarked on the slippery slope of discounting, it was lost. "If you're going to get in the discount mentality," said Wolf Blass in typically trenchant mode, "where will you be when they finish discounting?" In any case, wine had traditionally not been a profitable business sector. As Robert Hill-Smith of Yalumba put it recently, "More prosperity has been delivered to the industry in the last two decades than the industry had ever seen previously."

Some of the changes were the inevitable result of family firms going public to acquire increased capital. This was essential, thanks to the squeeze on margins, the rise of sales – which involved ever-increasing capital expenditure on equipment, vineyards, contracts with growers, maturing stocks, and bottling and "casking" equipment. Pre-flotation Seppelt was a typically inward-looking, family-dominated firm. In the early 1960s, Phil Laffer, then a newly graduated winemaker, was promised a job with Seppelt, but the place was taken by an unqualified sprig of the family. Then Seppelt went public and the bankers insisted on an injection of professional management, in this case ensuring that a new chairman was appointed. Although he was a Seppelt, he was Karl, who had been excluded from management because his father had married a Catholic. He recruited a young Scottish immigrant, Ian Mackley. Born in Glasgow, Mackley had married a girl from Sydney and had fallen out with his employers, Sainsbury, then a family-dominated firm. Upon emigrating, he was snapped up as a marketing expert by Woolworths, a more up-market chain in Australia than it is in Britain, as the company's second-ever graduate recruit. At Seppelt, Mackley found that many members of the family were still living in the past; one was simply too lordly to be an effective salesman, while another tried to persuade the firm spend a fortune on advertising the fortified wines that were going out of fashion.

The first years of the 1970s witnessed two tax changes that greatly increased the strain on the finances of family-owned companies. The Whitlam government forced companies to distribute some of their profits, even if these were purely on paper, and due to the increase in value of stocks. The same government also repealed the concession granted back in the 1950s that enabled wine companies to value their maturing stocks at a nominal amount until they were actually sold. Instead, wine companies had to pay a tax of A$1 a gallon (£0.35 per 4.5 litres) on their maturing stocks within a five-year period. The results were explained by Henry Martin of Stonyfell and Saltram when he sold his company to Dalgety, an enormous British-controlled pastoral company that had diversified into selling wine. "Operating as a family company," Martin said, "our resources were stretched too far; we could not expand and that is what a company has to do. At least now we have the capital backing to do anything we think feasible: Pressures were increased by the sheer number of family shareholders – twenty-two in the case of the relatively modest Tulloch company. The takeovers naturally cascaded, and as shareholders saw the (often excessive) values placed on rival companies, they grew greedy.

Takeovers were easier than they would have been in a country less used to foreign control of many of its industries, and where tax concessions made them relatively cheap for foreigners – and locals. The new capital helped to increase the proportion of wine companies' grapes coming from their own vineyards from a tenth to a quarter in the early 1970s (a rise that resulted in one of the regular, and often unjustified, warnings of a forthcoming surplus of grapes). The first foreign bid had been as far back as 1961, when the Distillers Company (DCL), which controlled most of the Scotch whisky industry, bought one of the best-known Australian distillers, Tolley Scott & Tolley. In 1966, British company Reed Paper acquired Tullochs in the Hunter Valley, to which, in 1970, it added McLaren Vale Wine Company as well as a number of others.

By 1972, international companies, always lemming-like in their investment behaviour, had taken over the majority of Australia's leading wine concerns. The rationale was relatively reasonable: they were looking to diversify into an industry that was clearly on the move and was able to absorb their surplus cash flow. Allied Vintners, a partnership of the local Tooheys brewery with Allied Breweries, took over Glenloth and Seaview and in 1972 added Wynns to its portfolio of brands. In 1970, Reckitt & Colman took over the Gramps' Orlando business as well as the much smaller Morris in Rutherglen. The next year, HJ Heinz – helped by Len Evans – bought Stanley-Leasingham, though the Knappstein family continued to manage the company. 1971 also saw the sale of Lindemans for a record amount of A$22.5 million (£8 million) to the biggest company to enter the fray, the American Philip Morris. Lindemans had been released from receivership in 1947, and the family grip had been loosened by share issues after listing as a public company in 1953, partly because of acquisitions. In 1965, for instance, Lindemans had acquired Rouge Homme in Coonawarra. Dalgety bought Loxton Estate, as well as Stonyfell and Saltram and sold Saltram to the Canadian giant Seagram, which in turn tried to buy Hardy's. Tom Hardy's attitude was brisk: "If they think it's worth that much, we ought to keep it ourselves." The tobacco firm of Rothmans bought Hungerford Hill and Chateau Reynella.

These changes contributed greatly to the professionalization of the industry. As Gunther Prass, the widely respected boss of Orlando, told James Halliday: "The 1970s demanded more: professional managers, financial controllers, and above all, professional marketeers." The new-comers "were prepared to invest substantial sums of funds to increase capacity and introduce new processing techniques which were the foundations of the future". Among the many innovations was the idea of brands of consistent quality promoted regularly, whereas previously branding had been a rather haphazard business. With brands came up-to-date (and to the industry rather novel) ideas of how to market and promote wines.

But sometimes the new managers – in particular, Prass – did not interfere. In Rutherglen two of the most respected producers of fortified dessert wines were taken over, but both were lucky. In 1970, Mick Morris had been forced to sell up to Orlando because he wasn't prepared to borrow the money required to buy out his brother and his nephew. He was left alone by Gunther Prass. So was Baileys when it was bought by an Australian-owned conglomerate called Davis Consolidated Industries in 1972. A corporate planner called Harry Tinson was sent in as manager; he "went native" and produced fine wines – but not much of a profit.

Only a major outside group could afford to develop Karadoc, 1.6 kilometres (one mile) from the Murray near Mildura. The first major greenfield winery in the twentieth century, and the most imposing physical memorial to the 1970s. It was built in the early 1970s with the support of Lindemans' then owner Philip Morris, to cope with the new demand for wine in a box. Ray Kidd, Lindemans' managing director, bought up a 200ha (494-acre) dairy farm and employed a young winemaker called Philip Shaw to set up one of the country's biggest wineries from scratch. "The first crush," says one veteran, "was pretty amazing. There were no walls to the buildings, no catwalks above the giant crushers or the vats, but in 1976, they still crushed 12,000 tonnes, mostly Sultana and Gordo for cask wine – oh, and Canada Muscat for sweetening." At first the wine was sent to Sydney 600 kilometres (373 miles) away in tankers for bottling.

Karadoc never ceased to expand. At the end of the 1970s, a production line for cask wines was introduced. By 1986, the bottling line (later to be duplicated) had been moved from Sydney to Karadoc to create a fully integrated winery. By then, Karadoc was a real wine factory. Its own fruit "was a spit in the ocean"; the company depended on the local growers, at first mostly Italians, then intermingled with Turks and others. Karadoc's mere existence greatly boosted the development of Sunraysia, as the irrigated region at Mildura and on the Murray River was called.

Despite the money they poured in and the modern management techniques they introduced, none of the foreigners lasted for more than a decade and none of the wineries brought them any great profit. The multinationals were probably too ambitious; Philip Morris in particular had hoped to create a global brand, but this ambition was twenty years too early. Moreover, they were not always logical. Typical were the problems encountered by the Cognac firm Rémy Martin in the Pyrenees region of Victoria. The money for the investment came from Rémy's Australian importer, who had established a fund during World War II to help the firm set itself up in Australia had Hitler won the war.

Unfortunately, Rémy chose to plant Ugni Blanc, the variety used for producing Cognac at a time when the Australian brandy market was starting its long-term decline. So it then tried planting varieties in a totally unsuitable region. By 1985, when a party of Masters of Wine reported on a visit to the winery, they were more than doubtful. Why use Ugni Blanc as the base for an upmarket wine when it is prized largely for its acidity? They added that: "It seems that they are spending an enormous amount of money for a very tiny output."

By the mid-1970s locals had started the process of buying back the farm, usually on highly advantageous terms. Even in the first half of the decade there had been a handful of takeovers by Australian firms. As early as 1970, brewers Castlemaine Tooheys had bought the Seaview winery from its owner, Ben Chaffey. Two years later, Castlemaine bought the Wynn family business, which had been listed only a couple of years earlier – listing was inevitably an open invitation to a bid. Hardy's acquired Stanley-Leasingham and bought Chateau Reynella from Rothmans and the Quelltaler winery in Watervale in the Clare Valley from Rémy. Then, in March 1976, Hardy's bought the Emu wine business from the English-based Chaplin family. In bidding for Emu, Hardy's was up against the West Australian entrepreneur, Robert Holmes à Court, but Sir

James Hardy heard that the much-feared predator was after the business, and in the end illness prevented him from taking any personal part in the bidding process. Despite a higher bid by Penfolds, the owners preferred Hardy's. Emu's assets included a winery in Morphett Vale and a more important one near Perth, which produced Houghton White Burgundy, one of the country's best-selling dry white wines. Although sales of Emu wines had virtually dried up in Britain, the Canadians were still good customers and the sales network was extremely useful.

The biggest single takeover of the decade also involved a local bidder. In 1976, with Len Evans's encouragement, Tooth's, one of the handful of brewers that still dominated the market in alcoholic drinks, bought Penfolds for A$7.9 million (£2.8 million). The takeover was one symptom of the itch for diversification that has afflicted brewers the world over since they perceived that the demand for beer was finite and the thirst for table wine – at least the branded variety – was ever-expanding. Penfolds was in poor shape; it had stuck too closely to the declining markets in fortified wines and was still fermenting the white wines it did make in oak, thus leaving them way behind the trend toward the crisp, fresh, fruity white wines made by many other companies.

Unfortunately, Tooth's employed McKinseys, the famed management consultantancy firm to guide its policy. In its wisdom McKinseys decided that the sales functions of all its diverse companies should be grouped together. The executive involved, used to the beer business, assumed that volume was the be-all and end-all and that stocks were undesirable. The result was an amazing clear-out in the late 1970s of precious cases of Grange at ridiculously low prices, a boon to alert wine-lovers and to Farmers, a mail-order wholesale specialist, which sold largely to the inhabitants of Queensland, a state where sales of all liquor were still in the restrictive and ignorant hands of the breweries. Farmers provided its customers with what must surely have been the biggest bargain in the history of Australian wine, offering Grange at prices as low as A$9.95 (£3.60).

Big companies were not the only investors interested in the wine industry. For the first time for a century, wealthy individuals became interested in the potential profitability of vineyards, an involvement that has continued for thirty years despite a growing number of often well-publicized, loss-making ventures. Many of these projects were "boutique wineries," small ventures usually formed by the combination of an enthusiastic winemaker and a group of investors – although in the 1980s some winemakers were well-enough established to go it alone, raising the money themselves. The outsiders, who were involved in other agricultural projects as well, were named after the equivalents of Wall Street in the country's financial centres; those from Sydney were known as Pitt Street farmers, those from Melbourne as Collins Street farmers, while much later came the St Georges Terrace farmers from Perth.

In some cases, this impetus came from a disenchantment with corporate or professional life and an often romanticized vision of life in the vineyard. For, as John Charles Brown put it: "A wine-grower is a very fortunate kind of farmer. Imagine being a wheat farmer. You wouldn't get much pleasure out of sampling wheat, would you?" But most of the investment was more hard-headed. It derived from a tax system that gave more favourable treatment to capital gains than to income and, above all, the tax advantages available to the wealthy and high earners.

When the Whitlam government introduced universal medical insurance in 1972, the impetus for doctors to invest in vineyards was even greater. But they were not alone. In John Beeston's words, "It was almost as if every prosperous person of whatever profession who had ever sipped a glass of wine wanted their own vineyard. . . medicine, dentistry, the law, banking, all were well-represented. . . there were nurserymen like Garry Crittenden. . . and even press photographer-turned-abalone-diver Geoff Bull, who founded Freycinet Vineyards on the east coast of Tasmania in 1980." Fortunately, Beeston adds, "There were very few accountants," who, he assumed, would be mainly, if not exclusively, concerned with immediate profits.

The newcomers should have been deterred by a 1980 report issued by the Department of Agriculture that spelled out the figures for a new vineyard of four ha (9.9 acres) complete with winery and a cellar-door operation. The report outlined a negative cash-flow for five years, during which time A$170,000 (£61,000) would be spent – not including the cost of the land, which the statisticians reckoned rather optimistically could be recouped if the project went belly-up. In a study nine years later, the figures were revised, and the risk element increased, with the peak outgoings reckoned at A$1.23 million (£427,000). The potential for loss was considerable. In one A$30 million (£10.7 million), hit Peter

Pargeter of Vinescape Management Services planted 320ha (791 acres) for the Guild of Pharmacists' superannuation fund on completely unproven, salty land.

Inevitably, the Hunter Valley was the first target for the outsiders, and equally inevitably, the leader of the pack was Len Evans, whose efforts as a promoter gave the valley a viticultural prominence not justified by its very special nature. Unfortunately, Rothbury, his major project, proved to be the wrong vineyard in the wrong place. It was too big to be a boutique winery like Lake's Folly and too small to be truly commercial. Nevertheless, Evans's example was enthusiastically followed. The area of vines in the valley, a mere 600ha (1,483 acres) as late as 1969, had risen dramatically to over 4,000ha (9,884 acres) in 1976, out of a total for the country of 70,000ha (172,970 acres). By the 1990s, the Hunter area under vines was down to only 2,500ha (6,178 acres), as most of the new vineyards proved unprofitable.

Rothbury was an example of a tendency common in the 1970s and 1980s to think that it didn't really matter where you grew any variety of grapes. It's a belief now overturned in the quest for cool-climate vineyards, together with suitable and distinguished sites for specific varieties. By 1978, the less favourable sections of the Rothbury vineyard had been put on a "care and maintenance" basis. Not surprisingly, the shares were diluted over the years. After the December 1981 death of Evans's friend and business partner, Peter Fox, in a road accident, the project wound down. Fox was in his early forties, and Evans was devastated. In 1996, after a bitter battle, Rothbury was sold to Mildara Blass, after which Evans washed his hands of the whole enterprise.

Fox's death spelled the end of Evans and Fox's boldest dream, which involved buying a number of vineyards in Bordeaux as well as the Alexis Lichine wine business. In his own inimitable way, Evans loved France: "Garlic, BO; I'm back in France." In principle, the timing was excellent, for the economic and financial crises of the 1970s had reduced prices. Evans and Fox did succeed in buying a relatively unimportant estate, Château Rahoul in the Graves region south of Bordeaux. At the time of Fox's death, they were negotiating to buy Château Lascombes, the classed-growth estate Lichine had built up, as well as Château Suduiraut, one of the finest estates in Sauternes. Brian Croser – who had worked for Evans at Rothbury – was to run the worldwide empire and both he and

James Halliday still believe that it could have come off. They are sure that it would have been immensely profitable, given the rise in the value of estates in Bordeaux during the 1980s.

But Evans was not cut out to be an international businessman. Moreover, Fox, at the time of his death – which some people claim was suicide – had appalling financial problems and would not have been able to provide the finance. The failures did not deter Len Evans. He continued to come up with ideas and projects, none of them especially profitable, despite continuing heart problems and a heart bypass in 1976. The parties he threw on his fiftieth, sixtieth, and in 2000, his seventieth birthday lasted for days, involved the consumption of huge quantities of superb wines, and were the envy of the whole world of wine for their gaiety and the imagination shown by the host.

Len Evans was not alone in failing to make a go of winemaking in the Hunter. This was not necessarily because of lack of quality; indeed, Tower Estates, his latest venture, is producing remarkable wines. The region seems to have more than its share of ill-luck – like that of Andrew McPherson, whose ambitious ventures went belly-up but who has proved successful in a more recent venture based in the Goulburn Valley, near Tahbilk.

Typical of the 1970 ventures was Saxonvale, which owned an excellent vineyard in deep red-basalt country. In 1970, it merged with the publicly listed Pokolbin Winemakers, but then fell into the clutches of a wholesaler, Gollin & Co, just before it collapsed.

Probably the biggest mistake in the Hunter was made by a group of investors who, between 1969 and 1974, planted 485ha (1,198 acres) of vines, virtually all Shiraz, complete with a massive, state-of-the-art winery at Arrowfield, a spot made famous as the breeding ground for the winner of the 1920 Melbourne Cup. The vines started to produce just as the move to white wine was in full swing. After a series of changes of ownership (it's now owned by the local Coca-Cola distributor), the estate has shrunk by nine-tenths but is now producing a wide variety of excellent wines, both red and white.

Ironically, the most successful start-up in the history of Australian wine was based, if accidentally, in the Hunter. Bob Oatley is an improbable figure to emerge as the chairman of the biggest wine group Australia has ever seen. His greatest asset was his knowledge of the market for a fine agricultural product. In the case of coffee, this meant that he had to satisfy the requirements of the Hamburg market, which played the same role in the world coffee market as London did for wine. Not surprisingly, Oatley's first wine exports were to Hamburg.

His earliest venture had been to buy 600ha (1,483 acres) in the then unfashionable Upper Hunter, where the climate is less wet than in the Lower Hunter, which is nearer the coast. Like so many estate owners through the ages, he planted vines. In the mid-1970s came the bust in sales of Shiraz. Oatley could not sell his grapes and had to make his own wine. In 1975, he hired the laconic, decisive figure of Chris Hancock, with whom he formed a long-lasting partnership.

Hancock was the son of a metallurgist whose interest in wine stretched only as far as the decanters of port and sherry on the sideboard. In the late 1950s, Hancock's father decided that agriculture was the way of the future as far as Australia was concerned, so young Chris was despatched to Roseworthy to do a purely agricultural course. There he drifted into oenology and won the biannual scholarship to do the wine course.

After graduating, Hancock was snapped up by Penfolds, where he worked for some years for Max Schubert before becoming a sort of "itinerant production manager, which gave me some wide experience". By the time he was thirty, he was Penfolds' production manager for the whole of South Australia. He was then summoned to Sydney for a series of management jobs. At the time, he says, "Winemakers were not really valued."

He had not realized that Penfolds was conspiracy-ridden and in the final throes of discord and mismanagement. In 1976, one of the resulting upheavals led to his departure. Hancock formed an ideal foil to Oatley, who retained control of Rosemount's finances while Hancock concerned himself with producing and selling the wine.

Hancock's first success came when he remembered Charlie Carter, a brilliant grafter of vines with unique techniques whom he had first met while working for Penfolds in the late 1960s. He promptly employed Carter in a speedy exercise to regraft the Shiraz and Traminer vines – the latter used for a Ben Ean type wine (see page 127) – into Chardonnay. But the price they put on even their original wine was A$2.50 (£0.90) a bottle as against the A$1.50 (£0.54) charged by the competition. "We were always going to be upmarket, as Bob had been for coffee," says Hancock.

In 1977, Oatley sold his coffee-trading business, though he retained a ten-year management contract. He was always ready to take advantage of other people's mistakes, and the sale provided him with the capital to invest in further vineyards, which were (and still are) run by his son Sandy, a viticultural specialist. They bought two key holdings: Wybong, which Penfolds had created in the 1960s, and the Mount Dangar vineyard owned by an Adelaide company, Adsteam. In 1980, Oatley bought Roxburgh from Denman Estate.

By the early 1980s, Rosemount's winemaking team was led by Philip Shaw, the first winemaker at Lindemans' vast Karadoc winery. Philip Shaw mutters, so he is difficult to understand, but once you've learned how to interpret his language you realize the forward-looking good sense of his thoughts and plans. These immediately concentrated on finding new vineyards to exploit, not only in Orange and Mudgee (a particular favourite) but also further afield, in McLaren Vale, for instance, to produce the cross-regional blends he favoured (though at the top end he was happy to produce wines from single vineyards such as Roxburgh).

In a decade that witnessed an outpouring of new vineyards, new wineries, new regions, and new grape varieties, the single greatest contribution to progress was made by a handful of individuals – and none was more individual, or improbable, than a German immigrant called Wolf Blass. "Wolfy" has always been a contentious and often under-recognized figure. And there remains a sniffiness in many people's attitudes to this brash immigrant. Oliver Mayo writes how Blass "has used his remarkable palate to make and blend prize-winning wines of whatever kind the judges currently seek", though even Mayo admits "that some of the credit for the undoubted improvement in Australian winemaking is his – his influence, on balance, has been benign".

No one who heard it will easily forget the speech Blass made when he was awarded the coveted Maurice O'Shea Award for distinguished service to the Australian wine industry in November 2000. He was genuinely bitter that his contribution had not been recognized earlier. "I am preparing this speech since three years," he said in his unmistakable accent, part-German, part-Australian, part-cockney. "When I came here I was tall poppy," – inches taller than his present short, stocky, bow-tied self. All his speech lacked was the steady flow of expletives for which he is famous. After nearly forty years in Australia, his grammar is still fractured, sometimes deliberately. "I'm a character who makes a joke of being German," he confessed to me. "All this type of nonsense I can talk."

Blass was born in 1934 and suffered the privations common to his generation of young Germans. He came from a professional wine background; his maternal grandfather had had a wine-and-spirits business. According to Blass, "I got into the industry because my father didn't know how to fund me." He started an apprenticeship in Rheinhessen. "My first employer," he says, "was a bad man. I still dream about this man." Following spells in Champagne and with Averys, the famous wine merchant in Bristol, he was hired by Ian Hickinbotham to help him make Pineapple Pearl at Kaiser Stuhl after an interview in which, he confessed, "I didn't understand any of the questions."

When Grange arrived on the market, Blass saw the potential for wines like it, so he embarked on a career as a consultant, a courageous step for a young, unknown, and foreign-born winemaker. He sallied forth to wineries complete with rubber boots, his trademark bow tie and an intense attitude, "I had to prove myself to my colleagues," he recalls, even though, "Doors were shut in my face." He was particularly successful in helping the brandy producer Tolley Scott and Tolley to make table wines under the Tollana label. At the same time he was making his own wine. In 1973, he was sacked after he had set up a proper winemaking operation in the Barossa which automatically involved competing with his clients. There he found John Glaetzer, a great winemaker who since then has provided the crucial technical backup while Blass was on the road promoting his wines throughout the world.

His motto for the last twenty-five years has been "quality, character, and consistency". Like Max Schubert, Blass' wines relied on the use of oak. "No wood, no good," he would say, in his efforts to lead the counterattack by red wine against the flood of white. Blass was careful to use modern techniques (stainless steel, temperature-control) while he and Glaetzer were fermenting the wine, but notably unlike Schubert, they designed their wines to be approachable when young.

Chris Hatcher, now chief winemaker with Beringer Blass and therefore still working with Blass, started his winemaking career with Wolf, who, he says, "introduced the idea of consumer-friendly wines – not the tough, enormous monsters previously made," he added, "Yet, they had good tannins and some of them last twenty years or more." Blass changed the atmosphere. "Until Wolf Blass came along," says Ray King, "people were trying to make French wine better than the French." Blass' wines' young friendliness was dramatically demonstrated when, in the early 1970s, they won the Jimmy Watson Trophy[1] three years running for one-year-old Shiraz, a unique achievement. After the Jimmy Watson success, sales soared as did Blass' reputation as a character. "I absolutely enjoyed knocking the industry around," he chuckled. He also enjoyed indulging his favourite hobby: horseracing.

The biggest-selling wine of the decade was markedly less ambitious. It was Lindemans Ben Ean, named after a historic winery in the Hunter Valley. The wine, however, was originally made from Barossa Riesling and Gordo with more than a touch of residual sugar. Technical advances had ensured that, since the mid-1960s, sweet white wines could be safely packaged while still containing residual sugar. Ben Ean was so successful that its makers had to bring in some Sultana. The wine started a tradition represented today by another market leader, Queen Adelaide Chardonnay – what the Americans would call a "fighting varietal," sold at the time at between A\$4 and A\$5 (£1.43 and £1.74) a bottle. Ben Ean did not lack competition. Seppelt successfully promoted Muroomba, its answer to Ben Ean and its like and one of Colin Preece's many legacies to the company, using the pop song "BYO Muroomba". Ian Mackley was particularly happy when he heard kids singing the song on their way home from school.

But the future was not with Ben Ean. In 1976, Orlando launched a new range of wines, the Vineyard Series, named after individual vineyards around the Barossa. To fit in with the fashion of the time, there were three white wines – Lyndale Riesling, Kluge's Moselle, and Moorooroo White Burgundy – and just one red: Jacob's Creek. From the beginning, Stephen Couche, the man behind the range, was clear that "The market was being badly served by tired, big, firm reds which lacked fruit." So the product's key characteristics had to be fruit character, softness, and drinking appeal. The wines – including Jacob's Creek – were always going to be relatively inexpensive to produce; most of the fruit came from the Riverland, but Jacob's Creek included cool-climate Malbec from the new region of Padthaway as one of 150 different batches used for the wine, a

---

[1] Recently this prestigious award has been criticized because the wine is, inevitably, unfinished and its future cannot be predicted. But the same could be said of the six-month-old clarets on which buyers and journalists pronounce so authoritatively every year.

selection which ensured that the quality and style could be maintained every year.

To ensure that Jacob's Creek was "fresh and fruity", it was sold when it was two years old, leading to lower stocks of maturing wine. Short fermentation times were employed to produce soft wine, which helped efficient winemaking. The use of old wood also helped. The wine was an immediate success: the 1973, the first vintage, was a mere 18,000 cases, which was up to nearly 150,000 by the early 1980s, when the introduction of a Jacob's Creek Riesling spelled the end of the other wines in the Vineyard Series. After a hiccup it resumed its upward path after 1984. Since its introduction, the formula has not changed substantially, it has simply been refined and applied to an ever-wider range of wines.

Throughout the 1970s, producers had enough on their plate trying to cope with the vagaries of the domestic market to pay much attention to exports. As a proportion of production, exports tumbled from up to twenty-five per cent of the total just before World War II to a mere six per cent at the start of the 1960s, and reached a low of below 1.5 per cent at the end of the 1970s. Australia's major markets were relatively limited ones, such as New Zealand and Canada where the wines were fortified. Elsewhere, exports, above all in Britain, suffered from a general swing to lighter, table wines. As late as 1979 Britain was only the seventh-largest outlet for Australian exports, which were almost invisible in Britain's trade statistics. The 1960s had seen the effective demise of the trade in the "cheap-and-cheerful" rich red wines that had served the Australians – and British drinkers – so well for a hundred years. The decline obviously caused problems. In 1961, Emu stopped buying wines in bulk and after the 1964 vintage shut down its Tatachilla winery. This in turn created major problems for the local growers, though these were solved by Hardy's, which got the South Australian government to form a cooperative for 185 growers in the vales south of Adelaide.

In Britain, the few tentative initiatives to increase sales met the patronizing and indifferent attitude of the traditional British trade, an idle and often alcoholic lot mostly recruited from the less intelligent ranks of the British upper and upper-middle classes. In addition, Australian efforts in Britain were naïve and hampered by the strength of the Australian dollar. Angove's introduced a wine called Australian Dry Red, described in one British newspaper as a "plain, cheap, honest red from the Murray River" but in 1968 it wound up its long-time importers, Dominion Wines. In the late 1970s, Ross Duke, who specialized in buying wine for the home-bottling trade, tried to export through a group of small, high-quality producers, and managed to sell some Muscat Blanc to the Wine Society, whose chairman, Edmund Penning-Rowsell, the wine correspondent of *The Financial Times*, was one of the most influential writers at the time. But Penning-Rowsell was virtually alone. According to Duke, "The English wine merchants were so condescending – that's what made me riled."

The condescension was not totally unjustified. As Raymond Postgate, the founder of *The Good Food Guide*, put it in his foreword to *The Wines of Australia* by Harry Cox, everyone of middle age or above "remembers well the advertisements of white-haired doctors recommending to frail old ladies 'ferruginous flagons' of 'Australian Burgundy' ". The makers had still not abandoned the pitch, pioneered by doctors like Penfold and Lindeman 130 years earlier, that wine was above all medicinal.

> *"The wines corresponded to the propaganda almost too well." "They often tasted of iron, which was not very agreeable, and were of medicinal value only to the anaemic. They were sold in flagons, because they were not worth keeping (you can't lay down a flagon to mature). They were cheap because of Empire Preference – which was abandoned with Britain's entry into the then European Common Market in 1973. They were also pretty strong, and the frail old ladies could get tiddly quickly and with complete respectability. 'Coarse, strong and good for you' – that was the picture the Australians drew for us of their wines."*

This passage echoes what could have been written about cream sherry, a favourite tipple of secret, middle-aged, female drinkers at the time. Unlike Australian wine, it has never regained its earlier favour and remains a down-market beverage.

In the 1970s, most Australian wines were represented only by the Australian Wine Centre in Soho. In an unhelpful spirit of cooperative endeavour, the centre had to accept wine from any and every source. Even its smart, modern design could not offset the unsuitability of its offerings for British drinkers. Most of the wines were sherry and other fortifieds, while none of the table wines – with the notable exception of Wynns Coonawarra Cabernet – had any indication of their region of origin. Their names ranged from Halls Tonic Wine to Kopala and Imperium down to Chateau Downunda, Kanga Rouge and Wallaby White, and showed that winemakers were still pandering to the down-market image of Australia personified by Barry Mackenzie, the perpetually pissed anti-hero of a popular comic strip. Even worse was "Chateau Chunda" featured in the Monty Python shows. Not surprisingly, despite the sterling efforts of its manager Stewart Foulds, the wine centre shut up shop in 1980.

But within the story of "Kanga Rouge" lay the seed of future triumph. The brand was accidental, based on the fact that a Sydney wholesaler, Swift & Moore, had a load of red wine stranded in Marseille because French customs would not allow the drink to besmirch French palates. In desperation a British merchant, Michael Peace, sold it in Britain, getting it into Waitrose and Oddbins – both always pioneering chains. He was helped by the late Michael Hogg, who ran the Peterborough column in *The Daily Telegraph*. Hogg went on to ask his readers to find a name for the white equivalent in a competition won by the Bondi Bleach, after that Wallaby White seemed respectable. It wasn't good, but Kanga Rouge – which was in fact Shiraz from Rothbury – was clearly superior to the truly terrible plonk that formed the normal tipple of impoverished British drinkers at the time. Confirmation of the quality of the country's better wines came in 1979, when Murray Tyrrell's Pinot Noir – a favourite of Malcolm Fraser, who had succeeded Gough Whitlam as prime minister in 1976 – triumphed at the 1979 Paris "Wine Olympiad". These efforts did have some success.

But unfortunately it was one of the many false starts which marked the progress, or rather lack of it, of Australian wines in Britain in the 1970s and early '80s. To make matters worse, virtually none of the Australian producers were remotely interested. "It was all too complicated" was the reaction when such pioneers as Don Hewitson, a New Zealand-born wine-bar owner, tried to buy their wines. And when one company, Reckitt & Colman, which owned Orlando, did make a pitch, it got the wines wrong. The actual promotion was imaginative – and expensive. Colman flew a group of journalists (including Oz Clarke and Jilly Goolden) to Australia, and then launched the wines at Pinewood Studios, converted for the occasion into an imitation of the Australian bush. Unfortunately, the wines were imitations of the current ones available in Britain, and did not assert the natural characteristics of Australian wines.

Until the mid-1980s, only a handful of daring individuals in Britain were prepared to chance their arm. John Avery, a leading merchant in Bristol, was one of the first enthusiasts (he also supported wines from New Zealand) and he had more influence than many more publicized advocates. The late and always far-sighted James Rogers bought several containers of Australian wines for his family's Cullen chain of grocers. A more subtle appreciation appeared in one of Dick Francis's detective novels, published in 1976, and set in a wine merchant. There was a robbery in the merchant's cellars, but "in their rush" the burglars had left behind some Australian wine that, the merchant said, "could be superb". The narrator found that "It was indeed a marvellous wine, even to my untrained palate. Wynns Coonawarra Cabernet Sauvignon. You could wrap the name round the tongue as lovingly as the product." At the same time visitors to Australia were sometimes struck by the quality of the country's ordinary wines. When Oz Clarke toured the country with the Royal Shakespeare Company in 1975, he and actors such as Timothy West regaled themselves with inexpensive wine chosen by Clarke, which they found as superior as Anthony Trollope had done a century earlier.

Yet the sales efforts were both small-scale and patchy. As late as the early 1980s, Negociants, the trading subsidiary of the Yalumba business, was a net importer of wine. It started selling in Britain through an introduction by Kit Stevens, a wine broker responsible for Deutz Champagne and Guigal, among other brands. Stevens introduced Robert Hill-Smith to Andrew Hamilton, a small importer based in Somerset, who bravely declared that he would "rather sell 500 cases of Aussie wine than 100,000 of Liebfraumilch".

To produce more and better wines suitable for the international market required a constant stream of technical innovation backed by an unprecedented degree of scientific sophistication. Roseworthy College helped by appointing Richard Smart, the pioneer of canopy management (the art of ensuring that the grapes receive the appropriate amount of sunlight) to a lectureship in 1975. Even more important was Ron Potter, an engineer from Griffith and creator of a series of technical innovations, especially the Potter fermenter: a stainless-steel fermenting vat with a conical base that formed a removable drainer for the juice. This type of vat was generally adopted by the industry as standard equipment in the following decades. Potter went on to produce a rotary fermenter to enable winemakers to control the extent to which the fermenting grapes were mixed with the "cap" of skins – though this was decidedly not to the taste of such old-fashioned winemakers as Mick Morris: "I won't have these concrete mixers," he declared firmly. "They extract too much from the grapes."

Potter provided the institutional framework within which two remarkable men, Brian Croser and Tony Jordan, transformed the scientific basis of Australian winemaking. They were not, however, operating in a vacuum; the first wine technical conference had been held in 1970, and there has been one every three years since then. As is the way with scientists, neither Croser nor Jordan suffer fools at all, let alone gladly. The result of their work has been to put winemaking on a much more sound (indeed, advanced) technical basis than ever before. Jordan is characteristically blunt, He says that there was "a technological revolution" during "a decade in which Australia was transformed from a backwater of technological expertise in winemaking into the world leader".

As James Halliday points out, their basic lesson was the same as that preached by predecessors such as Perkins and Fornachon: the overriding importance of cleanliness and avoidance of oxidation. In preaching such a message, Halliday adds "They were fighting inherited habits." Potter was also largely responsible for setting up a rival academic institution to Roseworthy, which was still a general agricultural college, its courses not really suited to budding winemakers. John Charles Brown's son, John Graham, who hated animals, was forced to study animal husbandry there. Not surprisingly, Roseworthy attracted few potential winemakers anxious to acquire a specialist oenological training. Even in the 1970s, many winemakers preferred to do an appropriate scientific degree at Adelaide University. In 1960, Phil Laffer was one of the first students in Roseworthy's specialized wine course, one of only five in his year (one of whom ended up working with disabled children).

Tony Jordan was the son of one of the country's leading bookmaker but seemed destined for a purely scientific career. He gained a doctorate in physical chemistry and went on to do research in the United States and at University College in London. Then the research funds dried up and he came home. After an unhappy few months in the office of a patent lawyer, he saw an advertisement for a lectureship in physical chemistry and oenology. He jumped at the chance, for he, like many university students of the 1960s, had been turned into a "wine fanatic", thanks to Len Evans's writing. Jordan was not deterred by the fact that he knew little or nothing about oenology. He suspected that no one else in Australia knew much, either, and in any case, he felt that "doing a doctorate in science is problem-solving, and so was oenology".

The advertisement had been placed by Ron Potter and Don Lester, an agronomist and a future vineyard director of Orlando Wyndham. They were planning to transform a general agricultural course at the Griffith College of Advanced Education at Wagga Wagga, which eventually became Charles Sturt University. They set up a three-year course, originally offered part-time by correspondence, but by the mid-1970s it could also be studied full-time. It involved more oenology than the more general two-year course at Roseworthy, though Roseworthy soon followed suit with a three-year course. In 1991, when Roseworthy was absorbed into the University of Adelaide at the instigation of Brian Croser, it was renamed as the Department of Horticulture, Viticulture and Oenology, and the course was extended to four years.

Obviously the pioneers at Wagga needed someone to teach oenology. One of the first applicants was Brian Croser, who already knew Ron Potter. Croser had been born of Methodist (that is, non-drinking) parents but they lived in the heart of the Clare Valley. Although the valley was then devoted largely to wheat and sheep, Croser's school friends tended to be the sons of wine-growers. His vinous education started at Scotch College in Adelaide where Charles Fisher, the headmaster and the surprisingly enlightened son of an archbishop of Canterbury, introduced him to red wine. After a degree at Adelaide University specializing in microbiology, chemistry and horticulture, Croser went to work for Hardy's, followed by a couple of years at University of California at Davis. He did not finish his master's thesis at Davis before returning to Hardy's. There, in 1975, at the age of twenty-seven, he was able to produce a truly modern-day white wine, Siegersdorf Riesling. It involved "the selection of the right fruit, our own yeast cultures for slow fermentation, an unoxidized wine for quick bottling – Orlando and John Vickery at Buring were already doing much the same thing". He soon found conditions at Hardy's too restrictive, so he hightailed it for Wagga when he saw Potter and Jordan's advertisement.

Croser and Jordan agreed on the necessity of a scientific education. "We said that if you don't understand the science, you're going into wine-making blindfolded," says Croser. He taught largely from the works –

which he himself translated – of Professor Emil Peynaud, the practical scientist who had transformed winemaking in Bordeaux in the 1950s and '60s. They naturally attracted a horde of talented students, including such future stars as Robin Day, Chris Hatcher, Rob Bowen (formerly of Capel Vale and now at Willow Bridge), Stephen Henschke, and Geoff Weaver, in what Jordan describes as a "new-technology environment". They all came under the spell of Croser's crisp, intellectual confidence even though he was only a few years older than many of them and, as one of them put it, he "didn't know much more than us". The course at Wagga did not neglect the practical side. Formal education in winemaking in Australia has always included a spell as a "cellar rat", an informal apprenticeship at the (sometimes exceedingly) sharp end of winemaking.

By 1978, Croser and Jordan had set up their own consultancy, Oenotec. They were deeply, and probably rightly, convinced that they had a better grasp of the science of winemaking than anyone else in Australia at the time. As Croser told Margaret Rand in an interview in *Harper's* magazine, "Oenotec was about transferring scientific principles into wineries that had none and were suffering because of it." Their arrogance naturally upset a lot of people, but the depth of their knowledge and their passion for quality proved extremely useful to many of their clients. Typically, in the late 1970s, the Ritchie family, long established at Delatite in the high hills to the east above the Goulburn Valley, were desperately worried about their inability to sell the high-quality grapes they had planted in the late 1960s at a profit. Ros Ritchie, who ran the estate, called in Croser and Jordan, who agreed that Delatite was an ideal locale and recommended that, instead of selling their grapes to the Browns, they should make their own wine. The result – except in years like 1984 and 1989, when the grapes simply didn't ripen – has been some superbly aromatic wines, especially their Rieslings and Gewürztraminers, varieties that tend to produce "cloying" wines when grown in warmer vineyards.

After founding Oenotec, Croser and Jordan went their separate ways. Jordan went on to guide Moët & Chandon when the French firm decided to produce high-grade sparkling wine in Australia. He landed this job thanks not only to his own abilities, but to the lawyer who was handling Moët's application: one James Halliday. In the late 1980s and 1990s, Jordan guided the French to the Yarra Valley to set up an impressive winery, producing increasingly sophisticated wines. A disagreement over the firm's strategy led to a temporary and unhappy experience running Wirra Wirra, the winery of Greg Trott, one of the consultancy's clients. Jordan is now the managing director of Domaine Chandon, acting as overseer of the winemaking at Moët's other non-French wineries – most obviously Domaine Chandon in the Napa Valley, where the winemaker, Wayne Donaldson, is one of Jordan's former colleagues.

Croser was more ambitious than Jordan, not only founding his own wine firm but also playing a key role in the politics of the industry. As Len Evans says, Croser "has been instrumental in the creation of entities like the Label Integrity Program, the Australian Regional Winemakers' Forum, and the Winemakers' Federation of Australia", all by no coincidence aimed at ensuring that the voice of the small winemaker was heard loud and clear in an industry increasingly dominated by major groups.

As far as winemaking is concerned, Croser put his principles into practice. Not surprisingly, he is a passionate believer in the capacity of science not to dictate to the winemaker but to help him. As Oz Clarke puts it: "He argues that if you are aware of every possible chemical, organic, and mechanical tool, and are aware of the various applications for which these things may be suitable, it gives you enormous freedom as a winemaker. But not a freedom for you simply to interpret your own flight of fancy; rather a freedom to allow the vineyard every opportunity to express the ultimate quality of which its fruit is capable."

Unfortunately, people confused Croser's scientific approach with a desire to rely overmuch on technology. In fact, he fully grasped the need for the matching of sites and varieties. In the past, he complained, "Everyone planted fruit-salad vineyards. . . Good wine starts in the vineyard, so the rule is: choose your vineyard. The rest is incidental." In 1976, to prove his point, he set up his own vineyard, Petaluma, at Piccadilly in the Adelaide Hills, the only high-rainfall, cool-climate region in South Australia. He was backed by Len Evans, who became chairman and a large shareholder, unselfishly helping Croser make what can only be called "benchmark wines".

The Adelaide Hills was merely one, albeit one of the most high-profile, of the many ventures in which courageous, bloody-minded pioneers attempted to establish new vineyards in climates that had been considered too cool and therefore relatively unproductive during the previous half century or more – although Adelaide Hills, like many of the "new" regions, had housed many vineyards during the nineteenth century. Cool-climate vineyards could be profitable if there was a demand for the superior wines they could produce at far greater expense than their warm-climate rivals, if only because yields were so much lower than in hotter vineyards.

The classic case is that of another scientist-turned-viticulturalist, botanist Dr Andrew Pirie. In the early 1970s, he had decided to do his doctoral thesis on cool-climate viticulture in Australia, even though, or perhaps because, there was so little of it about. He was also obviously influenced by his studies and travels throughout France. He settled on northern Tasmania, which had been virtually vine-free for the previous 130 years. In 1974, he established Piper's Brook, now the producers of some of the finest Pinot Noir and, after five years of effort and A$5 million (£1.8 million), some of the best sparkling wines in Australia.

The basic story, especially in Victoria, is, as Max Allen puts it: "Region finds wine, region loses wine, region finds wine again." Many of these born-again vineyards were in Victoria. Yet, despite the state's viticultural importance in the nineteenth century, its revival was very slow. As late as 1960, nearly a century after phylloxera had first struck, there were only twenty-four vineyards in the whole of the state, of which eleven were in the northeast, together with Tahbilk in the Goulburn Valley and Seppelt and Best in the Great Western region.

Inevitably it was difficult to resurrect the old vineyards, and not only because modern winemaking demanded a new type of viticulture, one based on quality rather than yield. The balance is a tricky one. The vineyard John Charles Brown had bought in the 1950s at Everton Hills, northeast of his base at Milawa, proved too cold for the regular production of wine that could be sold at an acceptable price. Had he tried twenty years later the result might have been very different. Yet the experience did not prevent him from investing in one of the highest vineyards in Victoria at Whitlands, 800 metres (2,624 feet) above the King Valley. Once the pioneers – who were few and scattered during the 1970s – had come into prominence, they were perceived as a dangerous challenge to the advocates of warm-climate viticulture.

The most obvious region for exploration was the beautiful, wooded Yarra Valley, even though the last vines in the valley had been pulled up in 1921. Not only was it close to Melbourne, but it had also been the site of some historic vineyards in the nineteenth century – a point made when Chateau Yarrinya won the Jimmy Watson Trophy in 1978. Nevertheless, it was an act of arrogant confidence, which still marks the man, that led Dr Bailey Carrodus (the doctorate is in plant physiology) to invest in a vineyard there in 1969. The location of the vineyard, like that of Lake's Folly a few years earlier, was the result of painstaking research.

To the untrained eye, the only clue to its potential for making world-class wine comes in the grey colour of the thin layer of soil overlaying the hidden limestone – and what Carrodus calls "a warm spot in a cool climate", a mile south of the Yarra River. He and his partner Reg Egan, a barrister who had already planted a small vineyard near Melbourne, found institutional funds to buy twelve ha (thirty acres). Since then, he has been producing some excellent wines, inevitably from a wide range of varieties. After tasting some superb Pinot Noirs, Merlots, and Cabernets on a visit in late 1998, I spotted a cask of port in the corner. Asked why he bothered, Carrodus replied, "You have to have a go!" It didn't taste much at the time, but apparently it has emerged a few years later as a great (though probably unsaleable) drink.

In 1969, Guill de Pury planted a few ha of vines, and two years later Dr John Middleton, a doctor from Melbourne, established Mount Mary nearby. His wines, made from Cabernet Sauvignon, Merlot, Cabernet Franc, Malbec, and Petit Verdot, now have a cult status enhanced by the owner's scorn of journalists and critics. Not without reason was he described by Len Evans as "a cantankerous old bugger". His scorn is especially strong for critics who, like me, find some of his wines rather thin and weedy. In 1972, Middleton's medical partner, Dr Peter McMahon, and his wife Margaret established the Seville Estate. In 1975, SEK Hulme, a distinguished lawyer, established Arthur's Creek, though he did not actually release any of his precious Cabernet Sauvignon until 1992.

Probably the most "pioneering" region in Victoria was the Mornington Peninsula, Melbourne's favourite seaside holiday destination, a region as cool as any other on the mainland and one that had had virtually no vines even in the great days of the nineteenth century. In the 1960, wine merchant Douglas Seabrook had experimented with some Rhine Riesling vines at a friend's holiday home, but they were burned in a bush fire and were never replanted. It was not until the mid-1970s that a few brave souls – like the publisher Brian Stonier, maker of some of the country's best Pinot Noirs – established more long-lasting ventures. But, as in the Adelaide Hills and most of the other "new" regions, none of the estates were big. The same applied to such new-old regions as Sunbury, Ballarat, where Ian Home established Yellowglen, soon famous for its high-grade, good-value sparkling wines, and Geelong, where one of the earliest ventures, Prince Albert, had first been planted by none other than Monsieur Pettavel, one of the original settlers from Neuchâtel.

Some of the most fascinating ventures were in the Macedon Ranges west of Melbourne. For instance, Alec Epis, a former Australian Rules footballer of Italian origin, invested the money he had earned as a sportsman to buy a vineyard and employed a great jobbing winemaker called Stuart Anderson, who had already established himself in Bendigo to make fine, French-style Pinot Noir and Chardonnay. It is the story of another vineyard in the region, the Virgin Hills estate, that provides all the elements in the roller-coaster ride that is almost inevitable with new vineyards in cool-climate regions combining the pioneering enthusiasm of outsiders in a new region, the role of postwar immigrants, the travails of newcomers, and the tangles that are inevitable when small wineries are involved with the stock market.

Virgin Hills was the creation of Tom Lazar, a Hungarian refugee who had studied in Paris, but who, in the words of John Lewis, had decided that "He didn't want to join the 2,000 starving sculptors in Paris."[1] He failed to emigrate to Canada, his first choice, and he arrived penniless in Melbourne in 1951. By the end of the 1960s, his restaurants – Little Reata and Lazar's – were successful enough for him to realize his great ambition: to make wines like the clarets he had drunk in Paris. Studying the maps and a favourable report from the Victorian Department of Agriculture, he decided on the virgin region of Kyneton, where, starting in 1968, he planted the Bordeaux varieties, plus of course, some Shiraz. By the mid-1970s his wines, made in a truly marginal region, subject to frosts well into the spring, had been recognized by James Halliday as "some of Australia's great wines".

Yet Lazar grew too ambitious. He closed his restaurants and opened one at Virgin Hills, just as the imposition of drink-driving laws hit the tourist business. To make matters worse, the new restaurant burned

[1] John Lewis, *Australian Wine Selector: Budburst*, 2000.

down. He was rescued by Marcel Gilbert, a Melbourne businessman, who maintained the estate's high standards until he sold to Vincorp (one of whose directors was Virgin Hills winemaker Mark Shepherd).

Within two years of going public, Vincorp was on its knees, offending lovers of Virgin Hills by trying to add Coonawarra and Margaret River wines to the range and using synthetic bottle closures that proved impossible to open. In 1998, Virgin Hills was rescued when it was bought for A\$7.19 million (£2.57 million) by another relative newcomer, Michael Hope, a former pharmacist, who, in 1994, had bought six ha (14.8 acres) in the Hunter Valley and at the time of writing owns forty ha (ninety-nine acres), including the Saxonvale winery, abandoned for years. Hope's wines, made unusually with wild yeasts and a wide variety of oak, now have an excellent reputation. Indeed, his Verdelho has featured on Qantas's first-class wine list. Not surprisingly, Hope has firmly rejected all the invitations to launch his company on the stock market. Nevertheless, Victoria remained a minority taste. At the end of the 1950s, its share of the country's wine production was a mere seven per cent. In the 1970s and 1980s, it rose sharply to nineteen per cent, but outside the Murray region, because of the relative smallness of its vineyards, it could not keep pace with the growth in production in the rest of Australia.

The miracle region of the 1970s, first identified in the 1960s, was not in Victoria at all. It was the small and, its rivals would say, rather over-publicized Margaret River, a Mecca for surfers and other holiday-makers in Western Australia, a hundred miles south of Perth between Cape Naturaliste and Cape Leeuwin. Both Naturaliste and nearby Geographe Bay are named after the two ships of Commandant Baudin, who charted the coast in 1801. The French names are entirely appropriate because the wines are reminiscent of those of Bordeaux. Indeed, on my first visit I became positively homesick for the French city after I had tasted Cabernets as elegant as fine clarets. In the words of David Hohnen, one of the region's most distinguished winemakers: "The weather is Mediterranean, [there is] virtually no summer rain. . . we sometimes don't have a real winter so the vines are never properly dormant, which results in irregular budding and fungal diseases." Like so many other regions, Margaret River has its own particular problems, including the ravages of birds from the neighbouring forests.

The heart of the Margaret River region, a maximum of seven kilometres (4.3 miles) from the coast and between 150 and 200 metres (492 and 656 feet) above sea level, is a long strip – or rather two strips – of decomposed granite. The best vineyards are on a ridge, once an island, on one of the oldest land masses in the world. To the east are the "sunlands", some of the richest mineral sands in the world. The soils of this extraordinary region are ideal; its iron-rich clay is low in organic matter and so provides the stress so useful for making great wines.

It is the only great wine region first defined by a geologist, or rather two: Harold Olmo, when working for the West Australian government in the 1950s, and Dr John Gladstones, whose work inspired the first winemakers. The surveys also showed the potential of regions well to the south of Margaret River. In 1965, the West Australian Department of Agriculture planted two experimental vineyards at Frankland River and Forest Hill, near Mount Barker.

But it was Margaret River, a mere three-hour drive south of Perth, that was naturally the first stop for winemakers. The region has continued to dominate the wine scene for the whole state, its estates taking a great deal of fruit from further south. Because of its relative proximity to Perth, it is also becoming a sort of "Hunter Valley" of Western Australia, with the advantage, which it shares with the Mornington Peninsula south of Melbourne, of having been a well-known holiday resort before any vineyards had been planted.

The pioneers in Margaret River were almost all doctors. The first was Tom Cullity, a cardiologist, who established Vasse Felix in 1967. He was soon followed by Bill Pannell (father of Steve Pannell of BRL Hardy) at Moss Wood. On the southern part of the ridge, Xanadu was founded by the Langans, husband-and-wife doctors who had fled the troubles in Northern Ireland in the late 1960s. The pioneers – who retain a considerable pride in the date their estate was founded – also included Tom Cullen, a well-known doctor who founded Cullen, and whose daughter Vanya now makes some landmark wines mainly from Cabernet Sauvignon. Another doctor, Peter Pratten, was largely responsible for the development of Capel Vale, to the north of Margaret River. Pratten had returned to Perth n 1974 after working in the United States, and bought a fruit farm that he transformed into the Stirling Estate vineyard.

After the doctors came the financiers. Some, like the late Robert

Holmes à Court, bought existing wineries, in his case Vasse Felix: an estate that was kept by his widow, Janet, despite the appalling financial problems she faced after her husband's early death.

Denis Horgan is one of the financiers who made Perth the centre of a financial boom in the 1980s. He faced similar battles when he developed his own property, the 650ha (1,606-acre) Leeuwin Estate. Its potential had been spotted by leading American wine producer Robert Mondavi in the mid-1970s, but he was unable to develop the site when his backers withdrew their support. In the late 1980s, Horgan had to sell most of his shares in the estate when Perth suffered through the collapse of many "entrepreneurial" (and often dubious) financiers, one of whom, Alan Bond, even went to jail. Horgan's friends rallied round and he has now bought back many of the shares. His wife Patricia still runs the estate, and for the past fifteen years has produced the Art Series, one of Australia's finest Chardonnays.

For both the Horgans and the Holmes à Courts, vineyards were a matter of passion, not high finance. More orthodox financial motives have ensured the expansion of the ambitious firm of Evans & Tate. In 1909, Lionel Teitelbaum arrived in Australia from the Ukraine as a young boy. In 1971, his son John Tate bought a small vineyard in the Swan Valley in partnership with John Evans. After their Gnangara Shiraz won the Jimmy Watson Trophy, they expanded, and by 2000, under John's son Franklin (who took over in the course of the 1990s) and his wife Heather, Evans & Tate had emerged as the region's most dynamic and commercial firm, pushing further east to the slopes round Jindong. This has a more Continental climate because it is further away from the sea breezes, so it is warmer by day but colder at night.

David Hohnen was one of the few winemakers among the West Australian pioneers. He studied at Fresno State University in California and worked at Taltarni, a cool-climate vineyard in western Victoria. In 1972, his brother planted vines at Cape Mentelle, which was named after two brothers who had accompanied Baudin: Edmond, a geographer, and François-Simon, a cartographer. The Hohnens, says David, "had yet to write the textbook on how to grow grapes". "There was no infrastructure to support what was happening," he added, "and getting about was very difficult." Undeterred, in 1985 Hohnen and his brother founded the glamorous Cloudy Bay estate in New Zealand, where he made a legendary

Sauvignon Blanc. Nevertheless, four years later, a family disagreement led to a sale of both estates to Veuve Clicquot.

Hohnen, like the other pioneers, took fifteen years to go further than the local, limited West Australian market. Even cellar-door sales were confined to visitors from Perth, a far smaller city than Melbourne or Sydney. Nevertheless, the early winemakers at Margaret River continued to dominate wine in the state, buying fruit from the whole of the Great Southern region – Pemberton, Frankland River, and Mount Barker, which can produce wines as good as most of those from Margaret River – on the very south-west tip of the continent. But Margaret River got there first and is closer to a major city.

Western Australia was not alone in possessing "colonial" regions that had difficulty in establishing their separate identity. At the end of the 1960s, Colin Gramp had set the example by buying a ninety-five-ha (235-acre) estate in the Eden Valley, seventy of which were suitable for vines. That particular region has managed to establish its own identity. Less independent has been Langhorne Creek, near the mouth of the Murray in South Australia, whose grapes formed the basis of many of Wolf Blass' wines. Like a number of successors, Blass especially appreciated the cool nights, called by one winemaker the "air-conditioning provided by the ocean breezes sweeping in from the nearby coast across Lake Alexandrina".

A number of other largely "colonial" regions are situated to the west of the Great Dividing Range in New South Wales, where the climate is drier and the vineyards can be planted on hills of up to 1,000 metres (3,280 feet) to provide the necessary cool climate. These regions extend right down from west of the granite belt in Queensland south to Mudgee, Orange, and Cowra, ending up in Tumbarumba. There's even Great Southern, a highly promising region virtually on the peak of the range, halfway between Sydney and Canberra, one of the highest wine regions in Australia, with an average altitude of 600–750 metres (1,968–2,460 feet).

With the development of new regions came new varieties. At the end of the 1960s, vineyards had been dominated by non-premium varieties such as Doradillo, Gordo Blanco, Palomino, and above all Sultana, which alone accounted for at least one-third of the total. The only premium variety suitable for producing fine wine to be properly established was

Shiraz; there were only 1,700ha (4,200 acres) of Cabernet Sauvignon, of which a quarter was too young to provide fruit. The lack of new varieties (or different clones, for that matter) was not only due to the historic lack of demand for table wines but also to the near-impossibility of importing new rootstocks.

In the 1960s the Department of Agriculture introduced more varieties, such as Gewürztraminer and Colombard, to suitable growers such as the Browns. Unfortunately, the department measured the suitability of the clones and rootstocks it imported by their productivity, as though wine were merely just another agricultural product. When the scientists, above all Alan Antcliffe, responsible for producing new varieties at the CSIRO wanted new stocks, they would not go to Montpellier because of a rather ridiculous fear that the rootstocks could be infected.

Instead, they went to the Davis campus of the University of California, the Mecca of American viticulture, because the scientists there, like scientists throughout the world at the time, were promoting the most productive rootstocks. This policy did enormous damage to vineyards in France, and above all in Germany, where new overly productive hybrids ruined the country's reputation to this day by making thin, rotten wines. Fortunately, Antcliffe's successor, George Kerridge preferred to go to France, above all to Montpellier, to get clones to start a much more sensible rootstock breeding program.

The most notable introduction in the 1970s was Chardonnay. At the beginning of the decade, the area planted was too small to be recorded separately. The variety had been around for 150 years; a pre-phylloxera clone discovered at Mudgee was described by Professor Paul Truel, the great French expert on wine varieties, as one of the best he had ever seen. It had almost certainly been introduced by James Busby, but was dismissed as a minor variety called Pinot Blanc or Pinot Riesling and was planted as such by Penfolds in its vineyards in the Hunter Valley in the 1960s. Penfolds used the wine in a blend called "white Pinot", made from Chardonnay and Hunter Valley Riesling, a name often used for Sémillon.

Enter Murray Tyrrell, the self-proclaimed "inventor" of Chardonnay. To listen to him in full lyrical mode, you would have been led to believe that even the Burgundians learned about the variety from him. To be fair, he was always an enthusiast for "new" varieties, above all Burgundian ones such as Pinot Noir and Chardonnay, but also for Cabernet Sauvignon.

The normally critical Max Lake remarked that he was "one of the few who is able to make a really delicate wine and yet retain the exotic character of this variety". Today, Murray's son Bruce makes one of the country's finest old Semillons (written in Autralia without the é) and only the lucky few are allowed to buy a case of Vat 9 Shiraz, a wine that is the epitome of the qualities to be found in a relatively cool climate.

The story of the "discovery" of Chardonnay – which may even be true – is that Murray was a friend of the foreman in charge of pruning the vines of the Penfolds vineyard planted with the variety next to his own land. Tyrrell apparently did a deal with the foreman, who announced one day, "We've finished pruning. I'm off for a beer for a few hours." To the day of his death, Tyrrell would show visitors the barbed-wire fence he claimed to have climbed in order to get at the precious prunings. These became the foundation of his first Chardonnay, the fabled Vat 47, probably the first ever sold in Australia under the varietal label which he introduced in 1973.

According to James Halliday, Tyrrell

"Added a stiffening jab of Semillon, and then, after scrupulously cleaning the wine up – lees are dirty after fermentation – transferred the wine to a mix of new and used French oak of indiscriminate parentage for a couple of months' barrel ageing. The grapes were grown in a climate similar to that of Montpellier, the yeast was an industrial one; there was no specification of oak forest or degree of toast; there was no barrel fermentation; no lees contact; no skin contact; no whole-bunch pressing; no oxidative juice handling; no malolactic fermentation; and, yes, there was acidification."

Nevertheless the wine was more distinguished than virtually any of the other dry white wines available in Australia at the time.

By the end of the 1970s, Chardonnay had spread, but was still not a major element in the vineyards of Australia. Typically, when those serial pioneers, the Wynns, had sold out their original business, they invested in Mountadam, high above the Barossa, devoting the bulk of the 1,000ha (2,471 acres) they bought not to vines but to water to ensure a regular supply. David Wynn finally managed to get the first Chardonnay vines allowed into South Australia and to produce wines that remain some of the most rounded and elegant in the state.

It took twenty years of soaring production to discover that "the fair ship Chardonnay" as produced in its original form (though not by the Wynns) as "pure, unalloyed fruit in a bottle" had its limitations. For it could be coarse or too full-bodied, leaving drinkers unwilling to ask for a second glass – unlike more elegant, less in-your-face wines, from France in particular. But for a long time, the Chardonnays were welcomed because they were fruity, so clean, and so well-made.

9

A Decade of Two Halves

It took us fifteen years to become an "overnight" success in Britain.

ROBERT HILL-SMITH

British football managers and commentators often talk of a match as being a "game of two halves", a description that perfectly fits the story of wine in Australia in the 1980s. As domestic consumption rose in the 1960s and 1970s, the area under vines increased by a third to over 70,000ha (173,000 acres). In the early years of the 1980s, it fell to a low of below 57,000ha (141,000 acres). Yet the second half of the decade saw the first stirrings of the renaissance that was to mark the 1990s.

The story of the 1980s can be encapsulated by the drama surrounding Peter Lehmann, the uncrowned king of the Barossa, immortally described by Len Evans as "a cheerful, light-heavy-weight with a face lined like a dried mudflat". Lehmann's story is also, not coincidentally, a perfect illustration of the guts, winemaking know-how, and sense of showmanship required for survival as an independent force.

The rush to white wines had hit the Barossa particularly hard. In 1983, Dr Richard Smart, even at that stage a respected viticultural authority, predicted that, by the end of the millennium, the Barossa would no longer be a major winemaking region, estimating that only 3,700ha (9,143 acres) would be covered with vines, less than one-fifth of the 1981 figure. Until near the end of the 1980s, it seemed only too likely that his dire prediction could have been near the truth.

Peter Lehmann was the fifth child of a Lutheran minister descended from one of the early settlers. He was a restless lad, happy in the Barossa but "made to feel like Herman the German" at school in Adelaide at the end of World War II – even though his mother had only ever spoken to him in English. By the age of sixteen, he was working at Yalumba under the great Rudi Kronberger, who Lehmann described as "a meticulous record-keeper" and who taught him all about work in the laboratory, the cellar, the distillery, and the cooperage. The apprenticeship lasted a full decade – he had intended to go to Roseworthy, but had married when he was only twenty.

Then followed a twenty-year spell at Saltram, only a couple of kilometres away from Yalumba and then owned by the Martin family. He was lucky that his employers there were one of the few in the country to be making dry table wine. In 1972, the Martins sold out to Dalgety, which luckily, put a visionary, Frank Dunstan, in charge. "He was too early," says Lehmann. "He didn't have enough of an export market." Moreover, his attempts to buy up other companies were blocked by the Foreign Review Investment Board, which was trying to limit foreign penetration of the industry.

In the late 1970s, because of what Lehmann describes as "an horrendous surplus of red grapes", he received a letter from the Dalgety company secretary telling him not to buy any grapes. "I was frantic," he recalled, "I'd given the growers my word at the behest of the company." Miraculously, the chairman allowed him to form an independent company to buy the surplus grapes and make wine from them. With a mere A\$120,000 (£42,900), raised mostly from his second wife Margaret's relations, Lehmann bought A\$2 million (£714,000) worth of grapes on credit. He covered his costs by selling the white wine at a handsome price, so the red was pure profit. Dalgety was delighted and was prepared to allow Lehmann to do the same deal for the next vintage. On a visit to London, Margaret nearly managed to raise the money to buy Saltram, which Dalgety had put on the market, but the Lehmanns were pipped at the post by the Canadian giant, Seagram.

At that point Lehmann took a decisive step: he gathered his grower friends and told them he was going to declare his independence from Seagram. He had plenty of willing supporters; during his two decades at Saltram, the weight of grapes crushed had increased fifteen-fold to 6,000 tonnes. He could also rely on the clannishness of the Barossa Deutsch community. Journalist Philip White, who first visited the Barossa in 1959 and lived there for the latter half of the eighties, "soon discovered that a newcomer was anybody who did not arrive on the first ship, or their descendants". "A stranger," he reckoned, "was somebody who'd lived there for twenty years or less. Everyone else is a tourist."

Yet the Barossa community *was* businesslike. Even the Barossa Club was not just for drinkers; it was the forum where Wolf Blass first met winemakers. The close-knit nature of the community could be seen in the organization of the first Vintage Festival in 1947, the first in Australia. This was instigated by Bill Seppelt, who had seen the Colmar festival in Alsace just before the war. Other examples of Barossa local initiatives were the 1975 creation of a group called the Barons of the Barossa, and later campaigns to publicize the region.

On October 13, 1979 – a date that is indelibly etched in Lehmann's memory – he and his loyal band of supporters turned the first sod for a new winery. On February 10, 1980, it was ready for its first crush, which amounted to 10,000 tonnes. The wine was made by a new recruit, the now long-serving Andrew Wigan. Just over half the shares in the company were bought by Cerebos, a subsidiary of British flour and bread group RHM, which had hired Dunstan after he had left Dalgety. The Lehmanns took a fifth, with the rest in the hands of the Anders family, local farm machinery merchants and blacksmiths who had become fascinated by the wine business.

To show what a gamble everyone knew it to be, the company was named after Sky Masterson, the gambling antihero made famous by Marlon Brando in the film of Damon Runyon's short story, *Guys and Dolls*. A photograph of Damon Runyon still hangs on the wall of the weighbridge, where Peter Lehmann sits throughout every vintage. During the first vintage, the finances were so tight that Lehmann survived only thanks to a payment of A$50,000 (£17,800) in advance by Joe Fassina, owner of two local wineries, for whom he was doing some contract crushing.

The choice of his post was not accidental. "In his days at Saltram," says Margaret Lehmann, "he did all his winemaking from the weighbridge, because it's the first point of contact when the grower brings in his fruit." From there the fruit can be directed to the appropriate crusher and vat. Today, the little hut by the weighbridge is practically a national monument – but then, so is Peter Lehmann himself. The supervision he exercises is pretty nominal, since the fruit weighed at the bridge has been inspected just before it was harvested, and will be examined even more critically before it goes into the crusher. But hospitality remains the same, complete with offers of a *Schlug* (a generous glass) of wine and a slice of *Metwurst* (an appetizing German sausage made from a fermented blend of pork and veal) for the growers who bring in their fruit, many of whom are the sons and grandsons of his early suppliers. One year Lehmann handed out a tonne-and-a-half of *Metwurst*. "But then," he says laconically, "it *was* a large vintage."

The new company survived – just. In 1987, ructions within RHM resulted in Cerebos selling out to an investment company, MS McLeod Holdings, which already owned the Basedow and Hoffmanns wine businesses. By then the Barossa wine lake was in the process of drying up, thanks to the sudden thirst of the Swedes for wines not contaminated by fallout from Chernobyl, and by the steadily increasing demand from Britain for wines that Lehmann had been selling under his own name since 1982. "I was never going to supply premium bulk wine," he says "and play golf the other eight months." Lehmann's luck ran out in 1990 when he contracted bowel cancer – cured, according to Margaret, by the award of the Jimmy Watson Trophy for the best one-year-old red wine at the Royal Melbourne Show.

In November 1992, McLeod was in dire financial straits because of an unwise investment by a new managing director in a chain of loss-making, duty-free stores. "We were going to be sold off in bits," says Margaret Lehmann, "in effect, asset-stripped. It proposed selling off the winery, plant, buildings, and equipment as one lot, and the stock and the brand as another. It would have completely destroyed what we'd worked so hard to build up."

Facing the third big challenge of his career, Lehmann decided to buy the winery with the help of his friends and his son Douglas, who became general manager. When McLeod put on the pressure, demanding up to A$11 million (£4 million) within a few days, Fassina again came nobly to the rescue, giving a guarantee that he would provide A$4 million (£1.4 million), a gesture that allowed the Lehmanns some breathing space.

Independence was not total, however, and the Lehmanns had to go public the next year with the help of some small stockbroking firms to raise enough capital. As Peter puts it, "I really felt comfortable when I had to send letters refusing money because the offer was oversubscribed" – a clear demonstration of the general confidence in him. With the money, he was able to buy a number of vineyards, including Stonewell, source of most of the fruit for the wine of the same name which became a Barossa icon after the third vintage had won the Jimmy Watson Trophy in 1989.

The low point of the decade came in the mid-1980s, with the vine-pull scheme designed by the South Australian government to get rid of unfashionable varieties, particularly dual-purpose ones. Unfortunately, it was not totally successful because the price of Sultana was supported by a sudden increase in the demand for grapes for drying. The scheme did, however, result in the destruction of a great many old Grenache and Shiraz vines – pulled up because they were lower-yielding than the younger vines. They would have been invaluable when old-vine Grenache and Shiraz came to be appreciated at their proper value in the 1990s. Nevertheless, the scheme did result in the destruction of far more second-rate vines – Doradillo, Palomino, and their like – than it did of nobler varieties. I've never been able to find any figures on exactly how many vines were pulled, but I know that many old vines, particularly in the Barossa, were protected by informal arrangements within the community.

It is difficult to exaggerate the depth of the crisis so far as Shiraz was concerned at a time when white wine was triumphant. For a time some of the mass of surplus Shiraz juice was even transformed into Shiraz muffins. "It was a real underdog," says Stephen Henschke of Hill of Grace, "so people put the name of the estate on the label, not the variety." But in the late 1980s, Shiraz began its dramatic return. Production of the variety had jumped from 15,000 tonnes in 1966 to an unbelievable 73,500 tonnes in 1976 and fell to 47,000 tonnes in 1984. But by 1996, production was up to 81,500 tonnes.

The real loser in the vine-pull was Grenache, which fell from a peak of 53,000 tonnes in 1979 to 34,500 tonnes in 1989, because of the decline in production of the fortified wines which formed its major outlet. As Robert Hill-Smith put it: "In the past three decades I've seen the region go from pre-eminent to apologetic to pre-eminent again." The Barossa has retained its particular Deutsch style, with bakers selling *Vollkornbrot* and *Bienenstich*. Still, there are a few makers of non-German background, like Grant Burge, whose top Rhône blend is called the Holy Trinity. And today, Lehmann and the other Barossa Deutsch old-timers face fierce competition from the likes of Charlie Melton, whose 1998 Shiraz beat Grange and Hill of Grace in a tasting conducted by *Wine Magazine* in early 2002.

The federal government did not help the winemakers. The worst step was the doubling of the tax on brandy in 1983, which contributed to the decline of consumption noticeable since the mid-1970s, but ensured that revenue from the excise tax remained stable as consumption fell. The biggest effect on company finances was the excise tax on the spirit used for fortifying wines. This was introduced in 1983, originally at A$2.61 (£0.92) a litre, but was altered after only a month; subsequently, the rates were juggled around. It was difficult to avoid, as unlike its predecessors, it was levied on the spirit itself and not, as before, on the final wine, in which the exact proportion of spirit was difficult to measure.

In 1984, a sales tax of ten per cent was introduced on table wine, a rate doubled two years later despite the firm recommendation to the contrary by a committee of enquiry set up by the federal government itself. Unfortunately, because of the Byzantine rules of the General Agreement on Trade and Tariffs (GATT), which then regulated international trade, when a wholesale tax was imposed on wine in 1983, taxes on the then booming sales of imported wines had to be halved to a mere ten per cent, thus giving them an unfair advantage.

By and large, the tax increases were absorbed by the industry, and served merely to put further pressure on winemakers' profit margins. In the early 1980s, the country's department stores suddenly became interested in wine retailing. Coles Myer bought up three chains in Sydney alone, and after buying two fine-wine stores in Melbourne, owned ninety outlets, while Woolworths expanded throughout New South Wales. The results of the competition can be seen in the statistics. Increases in the price of wine lagged badly behind that of the general retail price index while the industry absorbed the tax increases. Not surprisingly, a government enquiry found that, by the mid-1980s, nearly half the country's wineries were operating at a loss.

Faced by the double threat from the government and the retailers, the winemakers had to found their own pressure group. At the time the only representative body was the Australian Wine and Brandy Producers Association, where the voting was, quite literally, weighed, since votes were allocated according to the tonnes crushed by each member. The response of the smaller winemakers was the Australian Regional Winemakers' Forum, set up by Croser, Tony Smith of Plantagenet, and Tony Jordan. It led the fight against the increasing tax burden, but its underlying aim was to counter the trend toward what Croser calls "bland wines made in huge factories in hot, irrigated areas." The founders of the forum felt that unless they did something, "the lowest-cost producer making commodity wine will win", a trend symbolized by Ray "Cap'n" Kidd of Lindemans, the godfather of Karadoc. (Lindemans has since changed and is no longer known, as it was then, for providing bulk wine at the lowest cost).

Kidd and Jim Williams of Penfolds, the heads of two of the biggest companies, both fought for the break up of the Australian Wine and Brandy Corporation, founded in 1981 as an umbrella body designed to improve the wines, to encourage research, and to support the industry at home and abroad through the formation of the Australian Wine Export Council. Croser recognized the need for the support of the bigger companies and managed to persuade Penfolds and Lindemans to rejoin.

By the early 1980s, these large companies included an unlikely new-comer, Adelaide Steamship, usually called Adsteam, run by John Spalvins, an immigrant from the Baltic and one of the many corporate "larrikins" (dubious but charismatic fellows) who graced the Australian business scene in the 1980s. Spalvins was described by David Combe, the export director of Southcorp in the 1990s, as "a darling of the limitless debt-driven, high-flying eighties". He exploited the cash flow from the business of providing the tugs in Adelaide harbour by developing a 200ha (494-acre) vineyard called Mount Dangar, which used under-ground piping for irrigation. After the pipes blocked and had to be replaced, Mount Dangar was sold to the ever-hungry Rosemount. He did even worse with a venture into producing salt at Shark Bay.

But Spalvins was clever and lucky in buying Tooth's. He made a for-tune by stripping its assets in what he called Operation Plunder, a term that so delighted him he gave his yacht the same name. However, he retained Penfolds, by then being run by Ian Mackley, who had moved to Sydney, his wife's home town. Mackley remembers Spalvins as an ideal boss: "He would look at the figures and your plans and immediately say yes or no." South Australian insularity prevented him from also acquiring Seppelt, which ended up in the hands of a slightly reluctant South Australian Brewing, with a thirty-per-cent stake in the hands of the state government.

Hardy's also took advantage of the low prices being asked for wineries in the 1980s, acquiring Chateau Reynella, which had retained its old-fashioned air but also, surprisingly, had some useful clones of Cabernet Sauvignon. Hardy's also beat out Rothmans, buying the Stanley family's Leasingham business just after the stock-market crash of October 1987, as well as Balgownie near Bendigo, Krondorf in the Barossa, and Rhinecastle, a major distributor of wines in Sydney.

Even more acquisitive was Ray King, an underestimated figure who was responsible for salvaging the historic Mildara business and subsequently for merging with Wolf Blass, forming one of the big four that dominate the wine scene. Always a loner – he is a cycling fanatic who still rides in veterans' races – he had been a schoolteacher before becoming marketing director and general manager at Wynns, where he helped pioneer the bag-in-box idea. In 1982, he was called in to salvage Mildara, which, as he says, was "losing money. . . it was in a bad shape". A few years earlier Mildara had nearly gone under when Gollin & Co, its Australian distributor, went bankrupt. It was saved only when William Grant, the Scotch whisky company, provided new capital. But Mildara still relied largely on selling bulk wine to other companies – "Not a licence to print money," as King puts it.

It did not take King long – a mere three or four months by his own account – to understand what was wrong: a lack of new products and an over-reliance on fortified wines. As a result, he introduced three products within a mere three months and continued to innovate for the next eighteen years until he retired. His principles were simple; he claims that he has "never done anything original in my life". His first success was Benjamin Port, sold in a newly designed bottle, and a Chardonnay-based sparkler. But he knew he was living on the edge. "There's a very fine line between excitement and terror," he says.

Through the acquisition of brands such as Yellowglen (the country's best-value sparkling wine), Krondorf, and Yarra Ridge, King built up his stable of brands. He also copied labels and names quite freely his office was usually stacked with other firms' offerings. Typically, the labels of one range of wines in flower-patterned bottles were copied, as he was the first to admit, from leading Beaujolais producer Georges Duboeuf. He stuck to middle-priced wines where there was "a bloody great market gap" in accordance with his principles, which were unusual in the industry at the time. "I was a return-on-investment freak, so naturally I focused on the top end," he admits – by his definition, anyway. This was unusual at a time when most attention was being paid to the volume of sales and not their profitability. By the time he retired in 2000 King's firm was, by his reckoning, one of the most profitable wine companies in the world.

The key to King's success, as a close associate put it, was that he "understood brands and the need for simplification." In this he was unusual – at the time, anyway. According to Wolf Blass, "Brands did not matter. When Fosters bought Elders it had to write off A$100 million [£35.7 million]" – because the brand itself was not considered to have any value. When Ian Mackley, as head of Penfolds, bought Kaiser Stuhl and Tollana, it was not because of the value of the brands but because their wineries hemmed in Penfolds' key winery at Nuriootpa in the Barossa, which was badly in need of room to expand.

It was only in the mid-1990s that brands acquired a value in wine groups' balance sheets. In buying brands and in running his group so well, King "made a lot of people rich", according to Blass. Still, the ever-cautious King hedged his bets by buying the business of Douglas Lamb, a leading Melbourne merchant, which had some then-valuable import agencies, including that for Pommery and some German wine brands.

Perhaps inevitably, given the dramatic times through which he had led Mildara Blass, King's policies had limitations. He believed, "There are limits beyond which you cannot build a brand, so we have a portfolio of products from which we choose if you think you're anywhere near the limit." He could never have envisaged the existence of brands like Jacob's Creek selling millions of cases the world over. Not surprisingly, he was not a great believer in exports, stating firmly that they would only work if they made a decent profit from day one, and refusing to indulge in the patient brand-building required for success in foreign markets. Yet overseas markets were badly needed. "We need strong export markets," said d'Arry Osborn, "because of the fickleness" – and he could have added the limitations – "of the home market." Making it even more difficult was a factor never really grasped by outsiders: the parochialism of Australian drinkers, especially in New South Wales. "It was," said John Charles Brown "easier to sell in London" – where Brown Brothers was a pioneer – "than in Sydney."

The major wine producers' belief in long-term investment was only one of the factors behind the astonishing success of Australian wine exports since the mid-1980s, above all in Britain. At the end of the 1970s, Australia was a lowly nineteenth in the league table of the international trade in wine, and Britain barely showed up in the figures.

Today it is difficult to understand the patronizing attitude and lack of interest within the English wine trade at the arrival of the Australians in the early 1980s. When Wolf Blass tried to sell his wines, "Doors were shut in my face," he says. "Each time I was trying to get to the finishing post I fell over." It seemed that, in a period of greater ethnic tolerance, the Australians (and the Irish) remained legitimate objects of satire and condescension. Perhaps the older British generation's experience of cheap-and-cheerful brands such as Emu contributed to the attitude. Though the idea of "Brand Australia" had been applied to beer before it became so firmly attached to wine, none of the brands – Fosters and Castlemaine XXXX in particular – were exactly upmarket. The beers were renowned for their strength and the atmosphere of mateship they conveyed, not their quality.

Because of the low esteem in which Australian wines were held, drinkers demanded proof of their quality, which required a major effort by the Australians and enthusiasm for the wines by at least one major chain of liquor outlets in Britain itself. By a happy coincidence, all these factors came into play in the mid-1980s.

The starting gun for the great surge in exports was fired in 1983 by Paul Keating, who was then the federal treasurer (Chancellor of the Exchequer) when he floated the Australian dollar, which had been more or less overvalued since the great boom in Australian mining in the late 1960s. For the next twenty years, the Aussie dollar's weakness provided exporters with a currency that allowed them to export at a profit for the first time. It also helped that competition and the increasing development of container ships led to a collapse in the price of shipping, so that by the mid-1990s, it cost little more to send wine from Australia to Europe than from Adelaide to Perth.

Although they did not realize it at the time, the newcomers were knocking on an open door. "People were fed up with cheap, not well-made European wines," says the Australian Wine Bureau's Hazel Murphy. The quality of the branded wines most popular in Britain at the time – Hirondelle, Piat d'Or, and Liebfraumilch such as Black Tower and Blue Nun – was far inferior to the Ben Eans the Australians had been making in the 1970s. During the mid-1980s, the pace was being set by the Bulgarians with their rough red Cabernet Sauvignon and Merlot. These wines, the "vulgar Bulgar" as they were called, sold up to a million-and-a-half cases, higher sales than the Australians achieved until toward the end of the 1980s. But, like these wines, succeeded by selling on price rather than quality.

Australian winemakers provided the new generation of British drinkers with clear labels, giving varietal and regional names with which they could be comfortable. Wine-buyers did not feel confused or patronized as they so often did when confronted by the labels from the Old World. These consumers were ready for reliable, properly marketed brands because they realized that they knew little or nothing about wine, had no preconceptions and were unaware of the unfavourable image of Australian wines imprinted on the palates of their elders. But the future showed that many Australian brands could provide a guarantee of quality. "It was a marriage made in heaven," says Oz Clarke. "It created the modern British wine trade."

The timing of the Australian winemakers was superb, if accidental, for they caught the fancy of a whole new generation of wine-drinkers who were moving into wine from beer – or from a whole slew of mixed drinks. Such drinkers were bewildered and put off by the typically French language of vintages, estates, and *terroir*, not to mention the complex labelling characteristic of most French and, above all, German wines. They were looking for wines that were fruitier and more approachable than their European rivals, and were not surrounded by the ineffably patronizing odour that accompanied the sale of French wines in particular.

To cater for the new drinkers there was a new generation of outlets. The 1980s saw the transformation of the wine trade in Britain from a gentlemanly, socially exclusive trade into a professional business. At first, it was dominated by quirky individualists who were succeeded by chains of off-licences and then by major supermarkets anxious to talk in terms of brands and the "price points" at which they could sell wines – in other words, by business habits and language.

That crucial year, 1985, saw the arrival of the person who was to provide Australia with one of the most effective promoters ever employed by any group of winemakers. Hazel Murphy is a rare case: a square peg who found a square hole during the eighteen years she worked for the Australians before she left in early 2003. Not surprisingly, her employers have appreciated her: she was awarded the much-prized Order of Australia, and in 1996 received the Maurice O'Shea Award, the industry's ultimate accolade.

Murphy is small, feisty, and no respecter of rank or tradition (yes, she did once pass the port the wrong way at a formal London wine-trade lunch). Born in Manchester, she has the strength and independence typical of the women who traditionally went out to work in her native Lancashire. Left on her own at the age of fifteen when her father died, she learned French shorthand at a commercial college – though, not surprisingly given her determined character, her first job as a secretary didn't last long. She first showed her potential as one of the few women to sell textiles in Europe for what was then a major Lancashire textile company, Tootal. But she was sacked for telling the company's unbelieving directors the obvious fact that they needed different sizes of coverings for different markets. A short-lived marriage and weariness at too much travelling led to a job as a researcher looking at possible outlets for Australian consumer goods with the Australian Trade Commission in Manchester.

"Luckily," she says, "I've often found chaps who pushed me." One of these was her boss in Manchester, who suddenly announced, "I'm going and you have the ability to take over." Even when the Australian Wine Centre in Soho closed in 1980, Murphy "thought wine had a future". The next year at a tasting of Australian wines at the London Wine Trade Fair – then a tiny event – she got together with fourteen enthusiasts led by Don Hewitson to find ways of promoting Australian wine. Her triumph in putting Australian wines on the map in Britain was largely a matter of common sense, vision, and strength of character. In the words of one sympathetic observer: "Hazel had to drag people together. She was the archetypal sergeant-major, especially when she tackled the CEOs of the major companies."

It was an Australian-born journalist, the late Tony Lord – whose efforts to promote his country's wines in *Decanter* had been derided as mere patrotism – who organized a group of importers at the fair to set up a generic office to promote Australian wine. Walking back from the fair with Chris Hancock of Rosemount and his London agent Mike Rayment,

Hazel said, "I could do it for less." With the support of eight other companies and A$100,000 (£35,700) from the Australian Trade Commission she managed to scrape together the minimal sum required to start work. Until 1986, promoting Australian wines was only part of Murphy's job, but by then she had managed to establish them on the British market by ensuring that the country's opinion-formers understood their qualities.

Hancock's backing was crucial in launching one of Murphy's first triumphs. In 1985, thirty-four Masters of Wine – respected because of the severe examinations, both practical and theoretical, they have to pass to gain the coveted distinction – spent a fortnight touring the vineyards of some of the country's most enterprising companies. Unfortunately, the Australian Wine Board (AWB) had been unable to find the necessary sponsorship, and financing the trip was left to individual companies. Chris Hancock passed the hat around firms such as Tyrrell's, McWilliams, and Browns. The MWs were treated like royalty and conveyed mostly by private aeroplanes. They had a whale of a time and returned full of enthusiasm for the country's wines.

Even before Hazel Murphy arrived on the scene, Rosemount had started selling wine in Britain. Its efforts had been kick-started by the award of a trophy to Rosemount's 1980 Chardonnay at the 1982 International Wine and Spirit Competition, an event then taken far more seriously than it is today. Oatley and Hancock naturally came to Britain to receive the trophy. After the dinner, they were strolling past Big Ben when Oatley said, "We must do something about this." So Hancock stayed behind and hired an agent, Mike Rayment, who by the following April had an office devoted to selling Rosemount's wines. This ended the era known to insiders as "BC" – Before Chardonnay.

At that year's London International Wine Fair, Rayment and Hancock managed to sell their Chardonnay to Peter Dominic, then the trendiest chain of off-licences. To this day, seeing Rosemount Chardonnay promoted in the window of the Peter Dominic branch in Orange Street in the heart of London's West End remains a memorable moment for Hancock. Shrewdly, Rosemount had priced the wine at £4.99 – high for the time, and thus avoiding the usual scrum at the lower end of the market. Hancock's decision on market position staked a claim to the ever-increasing market for mid-priced wines which Australia was set to dominate before the end of the twentieth century. Yet at that stage they were not ambitious, hoping to sell 3,000 cases the first year, up to 7,000 in the next few years, with a long-term goal of 10,000 cases.

Their entry into New York later that year was equally happy. Rupert Murdoch had installed an Australian as editor of the newly purchased *New York Post,* and he gave the arrival of Rosemount front-page treatment. It helped that their Show Reserve Chardonnay had beaten fifty others in a competition organized by Terry Robards, by no coincidence the *Post's* wine-writer. By then, Rosemount had decided to go it alone instead of appointing an agent: a brave step for what was still a tiny operation. Oatley and Hancock hired John W Gay, as head of their office, who has now become the head of all the Southcorp-Rosemount operations in the United States. Although in 1983 Alan Bond put Australia on the map in the United States by winning the America's Cup, it was not until the success of *Crocodile Dundee* in 1988 that Americans took note of Australian wines.

The Masters of Wine had thought in terms of "Brand Australia" rather than individual wines. Their official report stated that "generic advertising needs to be spent to inform the consumer that Australia produces quality wine". But Hazel had different ideas. She always scorned generic advertising which left the individual companies to blow their own trumpets. Rather, she promoted "Brand Australia" through events. "We went all over the country," she says, "where there were already customers": at sporting events such as golf tournaments with their "natural" links to Australia. She then invented the now-legendary tastings held in late January on the country's national day, Australia Day, the first ever launched by a winemaking country, with the initial one held, naturally enough, at Lords Cricket Ground in London.

Until 1986, all the efforts had been on a relatively small scale. The step-change came from Oddbins, a chain founded by a Persian marketing genius called Ahmed Pochee, and it was not surprising that his equally enterprising successors should have provided the Australians with their opportunity to break into the mass market. Even then it required the courage of a single buyer, John Ratcliffe, to achieve the breakthrough. "We didn't really get going," says one veteran, "until John Ratcliffe risked his career."

Ratcliffe's father was librarian of Cambridge University; he had gone to Oxford and achieved a third-class degree in classics – not surprisingly, he was prouder of the fact that he had taken over management of the college bar and made a profit. On leaving university, he gravitated to the wine trade and finally secured a job with Oddbins as a buyer. Recalling that his father had brought back some splendid wines after a trip to Australia, he organized a tasting with his two far more senior and respected colleagues.

Ratcliffe loved the wines, but the prevailing attitude was best summed up by one of his colleagues, who objected to them because they were "too fruity" – the exact quality sought by the new generation of drinkers. Ratcliffe then asked his bosses if he could start importing the wines on a large scale, but they set him an apparently impossible task. They agreed only if he could raise the then-enormous sum of £50,000 from the suppliers to support Oddbins' sales effort. He was saved by Ian Huntley, the sales director from Penfolds, who pledged half the sum: enough to persuade his bosses to go ahead.

In the event, Ratcliffe made his – and Oddbins' – name as the Australian specialists with the backing of a handful of suppliers, most importantly Ian Mackley of Penfolds. The first batch of wines naturally included a number from Penfolds: two vintages of Grange were modestly priced at £17.99 and at £19.99, respectively. Ratcliffe also took advantage of the surplus of Shiraz in the Barossa with wines from a local cooperative, Barossa Valley, although none of them was a pure Shiraz. These wines were advertised in Oddbins' newsletter – another innovation – the *Australasian News*.

Jane MacQuitty, one of the youngest of the new generation of wine-writers, wrote a glowing article in *The Times* in 1986, praising the wines being sold for £2.69. "How can they ship these wines from Australia and still make a profit?" she wrote. The article had an immediate effect on sales; in those days, British wine-writers had more influence than they do now. But there was still a doubt, even in her mind: "Whether they will take off in the same way as California wines will be interesting to watch." The reaction to her article was unprecedented. Previous recommendations – like those by Oz Clarke in *The Sunday Express* and Tony Lord in *Decanter* – had been unavailing.

Within a year Oddbins' sales of Australian wines were up in the hundreds of thousands of cases, but it took time for other major chains to follow. "We stocked 200 wines," says Ratcliffe. "We had the field clear for two whole years before the supermarkets caught on to the opportunity." And by then Oddbins' lists had blossomed, complete with the unforgettable, cheeky cartoons by Ralph Steadman, a world apart from any other wine publicity and showing that wine was fun. In December 1988, I could legitimately hail Oddbins in *The Financial Times*, in a parody of Douglas Adams' words, as "wine merchant to the world, the universe, and everything".

Hazel Murphy took full advantage of the breakthrough by homing in on Jane MacQuitty's contemporaries, who had already started to rave about the new wines. The older generation had been rather sniffy – the only real supporter was the late Edmund Penning-Rowsell, who had loved Penfolds Bin 60A in particular because it reminded him of a classic Pauillac. The new writers, such as Robert Joseph, Charles Metcalfe, Anthony Rose, and Oz Clarke, were attracted not only by the wines but also by the relaxed, open, and honest attitude of the Australian winemakers – such a contrast to the stuffiness, secretiveness, and arrogance of so many of their French equivalents. Hazel Murphy provided these writers and their colleagues with a tour that amounted to an "immersion course" at a raft of vineyards – later echoed in mass visits by Dutch and Belgian wine-writers.

It is important not to exaggerate the progress of Australian exports even in the latter half of the 1980s. Historically, the latter half of the 1970s and the first half of the 1980s were an exceptional period, the only one in which wine imports exceeded exports. So the last few years of the 1980s merely represented a return to historic normality. It really wasn't until the 1990s that the growth in exports grew sufficiently to form a larger proportion of Australian production than in the previous peak period before 1939.

Even then, albeit outside Britain, there were several false starts. The most obvious was the *rosé nouveau* sent to Japan, but the most serious came when the Australians took advantage of Swedish worries about radiation in European wines after the Chernobyl nuclear disaster. The Swedish state monopoly turned to Australia. Unfortunately, while the prices of the wines may have been low, the quality was not great, to put it mildly, and it took a decade or more to improve the image and start to regain the market.

By the end of the 1980s, foreign companies were again taking an interest in Australia, despite the losses made by the multinationals in the 1970s. The first to arrive in 1986 was Moët & Chandon, shrewdest of groups. Three years later it launched a range of sparkling wines made *à la champenoise* in the Yarra Valley. Although they have suffered from changes of name involving the unwillingness of the mother company to put the precious name of Chandon on non-French wines, today they are among the best and best-selling premium sparkling wines in the country. The same year, the Veuve Clicquot division of the group made Moët's first-ever investment in table wines. The move, initiated by the far-seeing Joseph Henriot, resulted in the purchase of two premium, high-profile vineyards: Cloudy Bay in New Zealand and Cape Mentelle in Margaret River, both run by David Hohnen. Because of family quarrels – as David Hohnen wrote, "Who was it that said 'Thank God for family; otherwise we'd have to fight with strangers'?" – the Hohnens sold up, but David remained to run the vineyards on the light rein characteristic of the group.

The most unlikely and, in the event, by far the most important new-comer was French company Pernod-Ricard, then known almost entirely for its pastis. For a long time, Reckitt & Colman had wanted to sell Orlando, and eventually did so to a management buy-out, encouraged and backed by the South Australian government, which took a stake in the business. The buy-out was led by Christopher Roberts, an entrepreneur whose previous experience had largely been in the aerosol business. Roberts promptly got rid of the much-respected Gunther Prass and soon bought Wyndham Estate.

Originally, Wyndham Estate was George Wyndham's pioneering estate in the Hunter Valley. It later became Penfolds Dalwood and was sold when the firm made its unhappy move to the Upper Hunter. Wyndham relied on the winemaking skills of Brian McGuigan (son of Perce), who specialized in slightly sweet wines, particularly but not exclusively white, which contained some residual sugar. With backing from a couple of banks, Wyndham Estate had been a leader in the renaissance of the Hunter in the 1980s. But then it virtually collapsed through a mix of overexpansion, an unwise choice of financial associates, and McGuigan's family problems. Roberts' purchase proved a dud and he was lucky to get Pernod-Ricard to buy the newly formed Orlando Wyndham at a considerable profit. Yet Pernod purchased Orlando Wyndham purely as a distributor for its pastis in Australia. The French never guessed that within little more than a decade, one of the firm's wines would be rightly labelled "Australia's top drop" and would be selling over five million cases worldwide.

10

New Horizons

Producers in the Old World lacked economies of scale, developed few real brands, and were shackled by rigid traditions (not always observed). Even today, while many great wines come from three countries [France, Spain, and Italy], most are very ordinary, poorly made, and aimed at the low-price end of domestic and export markets.

DAVID COMBE

Orlando Wyndham was not the only victim of the depression that marked the end of the 1980s and the first years of the 1990s. It was a disaster which, in particular, afflicted the entrepreneurs of the 1980s, and none more so than John Spalvins of Adsteam. He had finally overstretched himself by buying Woolworths – ironically, it was possibly the best of his many acquisitions – and had refused to give up control by issuing additional shares, which would have given him a sounder financial base. His downfall had disastrous side-effects, since shares in Adsteam had formed part of the core portfolio of all respectable members of Adelaide society.

The first vulture to swoop was Ray King, who brought together the bosses of the major companies to form a syndicate to buy the wine interests from the beleaguered group. Yet he was outwitted by Ross Wilson of South Australian Brewing (SAB). Wilson followed John Spalvins into the toilet at a Grand Prix Ball and offered him a price so high he couldn't refuse. Wilson's bid, which resulted in the merger of Penfolds and Lindemans to form by far the biggest force in the industry, cost SAB a mere A$423 million (£151 million), and was rightly hailed as the deal of the decade. The new group also included Seppelt, earlier the object of a two-yearbattle triggered by a bid from Adsteam. This had been defeated by a bid from SAB supported by the state government, an offer that was politely described at the time as "fully-priced".

By 1993, the remaining brewing interests had been sold to the Lion Nathan Group from New Zealand, and the name of the group has been changed to Southcorp, with the wine division being called Southcorp Wines. Wilson and Ric Allert added major firms in packaging, storage water heaters, and other non-wine businesses. Unfortunately Wilson, who was something of a visionary, soon went off and eventually found a well-paid job running the Victoria Gaming Board.

The final result of the upheavals was the formation of four groups, Southcorp, BRL Hardy, Orlando Wyndham, and Mildara Blass, which together accounted for four-fifths of Australian wine production. In this atmosphere of financial stringency and forced sales it was not surprising that Wolf Blass took fright. "I was burned out," he told wine-writer Margaret Rand. "The industry was changing; there was a surplus of products; there was discounting; my marriage was breaking up. I needed more capital." (His critics say he had overinvested in vineyards and wineries and had rather lost touch with market realities.) He continued:

> "So, I decided we had to get bigger, by either a takeover or a merger, and it all happened in a very rapid period. . . When SAB took over Penfolds and had thirty-six per cent of the total industry, it was the most frightful moment of my professional career. . . we went to the chief executive of SAB and tried to buy bits and pieces they might not want but they were not forthcoming. That caused a change in my attitude. In order to succeed as a public company we had no choice. We weren't taken over; we were a willing partner. But the merger word didn't exist. The media took it as a takeover."[1]

Moreover, it was publicized as a takeover by a firm headed by Ray King, never a man with whom the flamboyant Blass was going to work happily, for King never grasped the fact that Wolfy himself was by far the most cost-effective advertisement for his wines.

The most dramatic story was that of Hardy's, the only remaining major firm still owned by the founder's family. Tom Hardy, the presiding genius of the firm in the 1970s, had died young, and his successors, including a

---

[1] Interview with Margaret Rand, *Harper's,* June 1, 2001.

relative, Alex Fletcher, had big ideas – including the disastrous purchase of the famous Chianti business, Ricasoli. By the early 1990s, Hardy's losses were heavy enough to end the firm's long independence in a crisis triggered by the problems of the State Bank of South Australia, a government business that had grossly overexpanded. Hardy's was forced to merge with BRL, the giant Berri-Renmano Cooperative, which was producing twelve per cent of all the country's wines.

By the time of the merger the cooperative had greatly sharpened up its act. Until 1977, says one old-timer, it had been managed by accountants; then came a new chairman, Jack Hill, from the dairy industry, bringing with him a rather broader outlook. In the early 1980s his successor John Pendrigh, a key figure, started to abandon dual-purpose varieties and bring in premiums, notably Chardonnay, which became something of a BRL specialty. They even started a proper brand, Berri Estate, replacing the earlier wince-making name, Mine Host. In 1979, BRL invested A$3 million (£1.1 million) in new winemaking facilities and hired a well-known winemaker, Ian Mackenzie. In 1989, in a major breakthrough for a cooperative, BRL won the trophy of trophies, the Australian Show Wine of the Year, for its Chairman's Selection Chardonnay.

Wolf Blass' worries were as nothing compared to those felt by many family firms such as Yalumba, which like Brown Brothers, was among the most innovative of all the firms in the country. On their 1985 trip, the British Masters of Wine had been greatly impressed by Yalumba's technical sophistication and the scale of its laboratory. Yalumba also had a nursery set up by Peter Wall, the chief winemaker, which has proved crucial in providing new clones for the whole industry. Its business base was stronger than that of other family firms because Yalumba owned an important distribution company: Negociants.

The brunt of the financial shocks was borne – largely because of his own actions – by Robert Hill-Smith. He is a deceptive figure. With his big, innocent blue eyes and floppy blond hair, at first Robert looks like a figure out of PG Wodehouse. In fact, he's both tough and ambitious. Even at school, noted a contemporary, he "had the air of someone born to rule". He had a hard act to follow. Hill-Smith had grown up in the Yalumba "compound", a warm, Victorian-era workplace-cum-home, by all appearances a casual and good fellow with a love of horses inherited from his father, Wyndham (Windy). In his first job as sales director, his greatest success came from the introduction of a cask with a difference – it was two litres, not three, and it was premium and, above all, varietal wine. As managing director in the late 1980s he had continuing battles with some of his relations. They, he once said, "had to be overhauled and dragged kicking and screaming into the modern age". So in 1989, he and his brother Sam, an art dealer, bought out the rest of his family. As his cousin Michael put it: "Rob and his family had decided that their sense of immediacy was more immediate."

Like his father fifty years earlier, Robert Hill-Smith had taken over at a time of crisis. In the days of sky-high interest rates, the "key banker," in Hill-Smith's words, "took a rather dim view of our inability to meet some repayment schedules and control growth". But what he really missed "was the comradeship that family brought" – though it was the takeover he initiated that had done the damage. Even his aged father, who died in 1990, was worried, pointing out that it had taken five generations for the family to achieve financial stability. "I know you're a bit of a gambler," he said (but then, so was he), "but don't bloody lose it all in one generation." Helped by a salary freeze immediately accepted by the whole staff, in the end, peace broke out in the family. Two of Robert Hill-Smith's cousins, Martin Shaw and Michael Hill-Smith (the first Master of Wine from out-side the United Kingdom), immediately got together to found Shaw & Smith, now one of the most prestigious names in the Adelaide Hills.

Robert's boldest step came in 1992, when he sold all the family's inter-ests in fortified wines and spirits, complete with stocks and trademarks, to Ray King of Mildara Blass. The reasoning was simple, if courageous: "If products do not have an international future," he told *The Wine Industry Yearbook*, "their value has to be questioned within the portfolio." With the money, he updated the winery and bought the Menzies Vineyard, an important estate in Coonawarra. It was a major step in Hill-Smith's declared policy of channelling "our energies into sustainable success in the fine-wine market" and focusing "on value growth rather [than] vol-ume growth". He decided to play down the cask market because "there is plenty of room just in the premium sector".

In the early 1960s, Windy had bought Oxford Landing, a major vine-yard on the Murray River near Waikerie. Although most of it was planted with Doradillo to make fortified wines, a third of the vineyard was planted with the then-neglected Cabernet Sauvignon. In 1990, Robert took advantage of his father's initiative by launching Oxford Landing, a brand which now forms the basis of the family's cash flow. Hill-Smith's flair for publicity showed in the splendid slogan: "This is a hell of a fuss to make over a six-dollar wine." It was in line with his motto: "We're here to deliver value to our loyal drinkers." He could rely on the vines his father had bought from Colin Heggie and brands such as The Signature, a Cabernet/Shiraz, and he added other upmarket wines like The Octavius, an old-vine Barossa Shiraz.

Another historic family firm, McWilliams, which had been the king of fortified wines in the 1960s, faced the same sort of problems. It was not that the family lacked talent. Doug McWilliam was a machinery freak. The academic Bryce Rankine recalls asking for the managing director and finding "an elderly man in overalls running the still". On another occasion Rankine found the remarkable Glen McWilliam, then production director, "building new 500,000 gallon [22,800 hectolitre] stainless-steel storage tanks on site, using the new argon-welding technique". But the firm seemed to have lost the plot by not emphasizing table wines strongly enough – this despite the proud memory of Maurice O'Shea.

Fortunately, in 1992 the four branches of the McWilliam family took the drastic step of hiring the first outsider to head the firm. Keith McLintock was an obvious choice. He was a South African with a distinguished record in his home country. An aborted joint venture with McWilliams led to an invitation for McLintock to head the whole firm, though he only agreed after the family had accepted his plans to change its emphasis. The shareholdings were complicated since there were four groups of family shareholders, three with a twenty-eight per cent share each, the other with fourteen per cent. The arguments were between the shareholders within the groups, one of which had a mere fourteen shareholders, another no fewer than 150.

McLintock brought a combination of shrewd marketing and the ability to communicate his own enthusiasm to the team he inherited, which led to success for ranges such as Hanwood, which was making more profit than the whole of the fortified wine division by the turn of the century. His greatest coup came in 1997 with the formation of a joint venture with American giant Jim Beam Brands. McLintock's idea was simple: create a whole range of wines under the umbrella name of Barwang (an Aboriginal word for "swiftly moving bird"). In 1988, the McWilliams family had bought the Barwang Vineyard at Hilltops, south of Orange and Mudgee, from the late Peter Robertson, who had established it in 1975. But even in 1989, the 400ha (988-acre) property had only thirteen ha (thirty-two acres) of vines. Nevertheless – as with Jacob's Creek and many other brands – the name could be used on wines from a number of regions, which could be sold by Jim Beam's sales force worldwide.

The idea received a major boost with the formation of the Maxxium joint-distribution venture which brought together Jim Beam, Rémy-Cointreau, and Highland Distillers. The objective was to sell up to 250,000 cases of upmarket wines, with the enormous advantage that Barwang, as a joint venture owning the brand name, did not demand any upfront marketing investment by McWilliams. The brand was profitable from day one, and seemingly successful shortly thereafter. Two years later, McWilliams followed up with a joint venture with Gallo, the world's largest wine company, which had already tried to sell Australian wine under its own label. These deals ensured that McWilliams retained its fifth position in the sales and export rankings, albeit well behind the big four.

Alister Purbrick took another path, one that also involved a joint venture with an American giant, though it is still not clear whether his firm, Tahbilk, and McWilliams can remain independent given the vast disproportion in the size of the Australian firms to their American part-ners. Purbrick was the third generation of his family to run Chateau Tahbilk, and the first qualified winemaker to be involved with the estate. He had had a hard apprenticeship. In 1978, when he returned to Tahbilk after completing his education, his father John, who had never shown much interest in the family property, announced that he was going to live in Sydney and that the twenty-three year old Alister was on his own, helped only by his ageing grandfather. In a gesture of cultural indepen-dence, Tahbilk has dropped the term "Chateau" and reverted to its original name of Tahbilk Wines and is controlled by a trust with voting control in the hands of a single person.

Alister Purbrick made a great start by being awarded a gold medal for his Semillon at the first show he ever entered – a feat compared by Australian winemakers with getting a century in your first test match. As far as the red wines were concerned, he was guided by his grandfather, who would bring out a cherished vintage to persuade his grandson not to change the winemaking methods. As James Halliday says, Tahbilk retains the traditional approach to winemaking precisely as it was fifty years ago, which results in "unbridled extraction of colour, flavour, alcohol, and tannin during fermentation", maturation in large oak casks and then in the bottle to soften the astringent tannins. The vineyards have expanded from a few ha inherited by his grandfather, Eric, to 220ha (544 acres) today. And apart from the Tahbilk 1860, made from the original vines, Purbrick still makes some excellent Cabernet Franc and the traditional Marsanne. He doesn't want to make more than 100,000 cases of wine under the Tahbilk label, half of it sold through the cellar door or by the highly successful mail-order operation run by his father.

Once Purbrick had got over the difficulties caused by the depression of the early 1990s, he embarked on an investment policy through joint ventures with well-known winemakers. These included Trevor Mast at Mount Langi Ghiran; the more populist Geoff Merrill; and, most ambitiously, he helped the veteran Andrew McPherson build a winery next door to Tahbilk, designed to produce reliable, low-cost wines for supermarket sales throughout the world. Their venture was successful enough to attract the interest of Brown-Forman, owner of Jack Daniels. Purbrick admitted that he was so naïve and parochial that he'd never heard of the American giant, but this did not prevent the formation of a joint venture, which sold 750,000 cases in the United States in 2002.

As successor to Brian Croser as chairman of the Winemakers' Federation of Australia, Purbrick was deeply involved in the tangled arguments over tax levels. The tax arrangements showed clearly the fundamental hostility of the federal government to wine. It seemed to be an attitude that combined the greed automatically and permanently associated with any finance minister with the lingering relics of an outdated puritanical attitude toward alcohol. This was summed up in the remark made by an Anglican archbishop and primate of Australia, who likened the industry's stance on wine taxation to "a study that set out to prove that the Golden Triangle poppy-growing region was beneficial to the Thai and Burmese economies" (even teetotallers might find that the equation of opium and wine was going a bit far).

By the early 1990s, the wine industry had sprouted an increasingly complex net of official bodies, including the Australian Society of Wine Education and the Australian Society of Viticulture and Oenology, both signs of the increasing power and sophistication of the industry and of a new-found willingness to work together. The tax fight started when the federal government appointed a commission in an attempt to prove that wine should be treated like beer or spirits. Brian Croser, one of the commission members, managed to prove to the economist, who was the independent member, that the wine industry would be disadvantaged by a tax based on quantity, that the industry had a good future, that, incidentally, it was not really responsible for alcoholism, and that a value-based tax would not hurt fine wines.

Nevertheless, in August 1993, the Keating Labor government proposed to raise the tax, first levied by Keating's predecessor, Bob Hawke, nine years earlier, by eleven per cent to thirty-one per cent. The wine industry reacted more strongly than ever before; two months later, the government climbed down (a little) reducing the immediate increase to twenty-two per cent (up two per cent on the existing level), though it would rise to twenty-six per cent by 1995. In 1997, as a result of a general rearrangement of excise taxes, the federal tax rate was increased to forty-one per cent, though this included taxes previously levied by individual states, which were compensated for the income they would lose.

Then in 2000 came the infamous Goods and Services Tax (GST), which covered an even wider spectrum of products than its British equivalent, Value Added Tax. The government swore that, as far as the wine industry was concerned, it would be tax-neutral; that is to say, other imposts would be reduced to allow for the new tax. They weren't, for a simple political reason: the government had imposed the tax on soft drinks and didn't want to be perceived as apparently favouring wine. In the event, drinkers defied a level of tax higher than that in any other wine-producing country and the gentle upward sales trend continued undisturbed. In 2000, domestic sales were a third higher than they had been in 1990; sales in flagons and in bulk were virtually non-existent, and sales of fortified wines had fallen even further.

During the 1990s, exports rocketed above all to Britain, where Hazel Murphy continued her progress, by now supported by all the major companies. Occasionally, however, her ambitious schemes didn't come off. She tried to hire a Boeing 747 for £250,000 to hold an Australia Day tasting in Australia, but in the end had to make do with a less ambitious event, the 1992 "Wine Flight" that took 110 movers and shakers from the

British wine industry around Australia in three buses guided by three British journalists: Oz Clarke, Tim Atkin, and Robert Joseph. "It was a nightmare," she says, "but it had an amazing knock-on effect. It created a band of influential missionaries, and made a lot of friends because we had the product." She thus achieved her objective of translating the goodwill created by all the tastings she organized over the previous seven years into national distribution.

Thanks to the continuing weakness of the Australian dollar, the wine companies could meet the price points required by the increasingly powerful UK supermarkets – for example, the £3.99 and £4.99 at which Rosemount was selling its Chardonnay. Although the average price the producers received for a bottle of wine sold in Britain decreased slightly in 2001–2, Australian winemakers are still not competing to any great extent – in Britain anyway – in the bottom sector of the market, which accounts for half the sales of wine. The growing importance of Australian wines reflects improvement in taste. As Tim Atkin, editor of *Harper's*, the industry's weekly magazine, wrote: "For Don Cortez and Black Tower, read Koonunga Hill Shiraz and Jacob's Creek Chardonnay." Indeed, by 2001, Australian wines such as these occupied the majority of places in the top-ten UK brands.

The leader in the pack was that former laggard, Southcorp, whose British subsidiary was run by Mike Paul, a wine marketer who for love of wine, had turned his back on a promising career selling spirits. As late as 1991, he had been told by John Roberts of Penfolds to forget about exports, they didn't have enough spare wine – though fortunately Roberts soon left.

Ian Mackley soon found enough stock to provide 30,000 cases of Penfolds Bin 28 after the wine had won the Wine of the Year award at the International Wine Challenge in London, which, as David Combe put it, had become "in commercial terms the most important wine show in the world". Nevertheless, as one of Mike Paul's colleagues said, "He had no real help from head office; he was operating on his own instincts, which were usually sound." Not surprisingly, Paul left Southcorp in 2000. Penfolds – and Rosemount – were not the only firms to cash in. Most of the others did, too, including Yalumba, which established a branch of Negociants in Britain representing not only Yalumba and other brands from Australia, but brands from New Zealand and the Napa Valley as well.

Mike Paul had enjoyed the support of Ross Wilson and Ian Mackley. Indeed, three key brands – Lindemans Bin 65, Koonunga Hill Chardonnay, and Rawson's Retreat from Penfolds – were developed for export only. By 1998, David Combe, then Southcorp's export director and formerly Australian Trade Commissioner in Hong Kong, could claim that Southcorp had developed "the best global distribution capacity of any wine company in the world". Previously, Penfolds had been decidedly un-export-conscious. By contrast, Mackley and his successors aimed to sell as much bottled wine abroad within five years as at home, and even bought vineyards and wineries outside Australia – learning lessons the hard way by investing, albeit for a short time, in Moldova, one of the most backward winemaking republic split off from the former Soviet Union. Management also learned about some of the problems of working with the French, when Southcorp became involved with a massive coop-erative, Val d'Orbieu, which did not, in the view of the Australians, fulfil its basic role of supplying wines of a consistent quality.

Yet while Southcorp was by far the biggest group in the industry, throughout the 1990s, it was facing an increasingly effective challenge from Mildara Blass, BRL Hardy, and Orlando Wyndham, as well as the smaller family-owned companies. Even in the late 1990s, however, the Australians still could not believe in the long-term nature of their success even though it was none too surprising in the world context. (The 1990s were a decade of ever-increasing international sales of wine, as consumers in many countries without a wine-drinking tradition – not only Britain, but, for instance, Scandinavia as well – took to wine in a big way. In 1994, James Halliday had written of sales to Britain: "With around six per cent of the total wine market and twenty per cent of the bottled wine market above £5 a bottle retail, growth could not be expected to continue indefinitely, and certainly not at the rates achieved between 1989 and 1994." Even he could not believe that the momentum would be main-tained, that exports, which had trebled in the six years up to 1994, would nearly treble again by 2001, although largely concentrated in the off-trade. (The off-trade is made up of retail outlets such as off-licences, supermarkets, and so on. "On-trade" refers to wine consumed in bars, pubs, cafés: that is, away from home).

It was against this background that Brian Croser induced the Winemakers' Federation of Australia to produce what appeared to be an absurdly over-optimistic document, *Strategy 2025*, launched in June 1996. It talked boldly of the "Australian Wine Revolution 1966–1996" and of the way "the industry's successful development should not be seen as a recent, unrepeatable phenomenon". *Strategy 2025* described Australian winemakers' "total commitment to innovation and style from vine to palate" and also forecast that, by 2025, the industry would "achieve A$4.5 billion [£1.6 billion] in annual sales by being the world's most influential and profitable supplier of branded wines". The document provided a whole host of "competitiveness factors" to back up this apparently wildly optimistic view reaching 6.5 per cent of the value of world wine production storage facilities. But this would require massive new plantings and investments in wineries and Australian producers would achieve a suspiciously precise 8.3 per cent share of the wine market in Britain by 2001.

All the *Strategy 2025* forecasts, for sales as well as rates of planting, were soon exceeded – largely because the original figures had been much higher but had been reduced by exporters who wanted to be seen to be exceeding expectations. The most important landmark was reached in August 1999, when the industry announced that it had already achieved the target of an annual export rate of A$1 billion (£357 million) a year early. By 2001, production was already around 1.4 million tonnes, against an estimate of 1.65 million for 2025, and in the three years to 2002, exports had doubled to A$2 billion (£714 million) – the estimate for 2025 had been a mere A$2.5 billion (£893 million), albeit at 1996 prices.

Despite Southcorp's export successes, all was not well within the group. After its creation there had naturally been a great deal of reorganization, much of it seemingly sensible. All the sparkling-wine production was moved to Great Western in Victoria, the "premium" wines to Nuriootpa in the Barossa, and what were called the "semi-premium" or "commercial" wines to Karadoc. As a result, Karadoc could soon boast of being "the biggest modern winery in the southern hemisphere", producing ninety million litres of wine a year, including such export-oriented products as Bin 65 Chardonnay. Even Lindemans, a well-run firm, was subject to what one insider calls a "great deal of angst" as the Penfolds management took over the entire group. All the many brands were subordinated to what James Halliday calls "the Penfold superculture". Apart from Bin 65, the emphasis was "Penfolds, Penfolds *über alles*", in the bitter words of one refugee.

This virtual dictatorship combined with an increasing weight of bureaucracy to stifle initiatives and the development of most of the group's brands, dozens of which had been accumulated over the decades. Throughout the 1990s, Southcorp suffered from a double bind. The management, headed by Bruce Kemp, a former engineer, appeared not to have a coherent plan for its many brands. Worse, management was unable to decide whether Southcorp would become purely a wine company; attempts to offload other divisions, especially the troubled water-heater business, appeared half-hearted. As a result, Kemp's more positive steps, notably his unprecedented and enlightened attitude to women in management and winemaking, went largely unappreciated. For Southcorp, the 1990s were, to a great extent, a period of missed opportunities.

On the other hand, for BRL Hardy's the decade was little short of miraculous. In the decade after the 1992 merger of Hardy's with the BRL cooperative, the group more than held its own as one of the big four. Its market value soared from a mere A\$100 million (£35.7 million) to over A\$1.3 billion (£464 million). The success of a group which combined a virtually bankrupt family firm and a cooperative with few serious brands was itself improbable, but not nearly so unlikely as the man who made BRL Hardy work and flourish: Stephen Millar. An accountant by training, Millar won a scholarship to attend General Motors' corporate "university" in Michigan but grew restless with what he saw as "formula management". He subsequently worked with Australia's leading manufacturers of brooms and brushes for twenty years, ending up as managing director. Looking back on his old job, all he can say is, "It was much harder to make money [in brooms and brushes] than it is here [in wine]." A row with the chairman (who saw the brooms and brushes company fall to its knees after Millar's departure) led him to take the reins of BRL in August 1991.

Then followed by far the most exciting year of Millar's working life. A world tour convinced him that even a cooperative as big as BRL – which in 1982 had merged with Consolidated Cooperative Wines – needed a merger with a company that had brands to offer. The first step was to allocate shares to the members of the cooperative. These amounted to over an eighth of the total capital before the takeover and are now held by an

International wine investment fund, presided over by John Pendrigh, former chairman of BRL, and since 1992, chairman of the combined group. The "merger" (effectively a takeover) of Hardy's, crippled as it was by its Italian losses. BRL was not the only suitor, but the worst problem was Hardy's enormous debt to the Bank of South Australia. With the help of a creative investment banker and a "comfort letter" – in effect a guarantee – from a major British trading group, Millar won the day. The combined group was listed on the Australian Stock Exchange at a low point "black Wednesday" in early 1992 at a ridiculously low valuation in stockmarket terms, reflecting the general feeling that the combination didn't have much hope of survival.

Millar, however, was always confident. "There were more synergies than people thought", he said. The key to success was the development of individual brands, control of distribution, and using individual markets as springboards. His inheritance included the superb, and then underexploited, name of Hardy and the "quality of the people, a strength which had not been properly harnessed".

He immediately discontinued BRL's own brands, and his first breakthrough came with Leasingham, which was designed as a premium regional brand and the first proof that Millar's formula of "giving them the tools" – that is, enough investment – would work. He repeated this success with Nottage Hill and Banrock Station as well as Houghton, maker of Australia's leading white wine; the quality of Houghton White Burgundy had slipped before the merger.

BRL also played its part. By the time of the merger it had a first-class facility for making bag-in-box wines from premium varieties planted by the cooperative's 550 members, many of them immigrants from Turkey, Greece, and India, as well as Italy. This equipment enabled BRL Hardy to dominate the market while reaping better profits than its rivals, who were making cask wines from less-valued varieties. Millar took full advantage of the Berri facility, Renmano, a few kilometres up the road, remained a relatively modest operation but Berri expanded enormously, taking on over 200,000 tonnes of fruit and growing every year. The expansion is based on the grapes planted by the members of the cooperative before the merger – though even the gigantic winery's facilities can become stretched. There are stories of growers waiting half a day for their trucks to be unloaded (normally, arrivals of white grapes at least are timed to start around 10pm and continue till dawn, the only relatively cool hours of a Riverland summer).

Hardy's shrewdest stroke was to buy Banrock Station, an overgrazed property on the banks of the Murray River, near Berri. The sheep were removed to make way for irrigated vineyards, and consequently, the reeds and native vegetation along the property's significant river frontage returned. The project has been championed internationally as an environmental triumph. Boxes for the first Banrock bag-in-box wines were made with wild seeds impregnated in the cardboard, which would grow if they were soaked in water. Advertisements for the "clean, green" Banrock hit even the pages of *National Geographic* magazine.

In Australia, BRL Hardy "followed the market upmarket", not neglecting cask wines but improving them. Profits from Australia provided the funds for the attack on Britain, where BRL Hardy has concentrated on its own brands, above all the super-successful Nottage Hill. Britain provided the impetus for an attack on the US market, where as late as 1998, Millar had only one person selling under 30,000 cases. Then came a partnership with Villa Banfi, a major importer of Italian wines in the US, a market where, says Millar, "such a partnership is the only way to succeed", sales reached over 400,000 cases. BRL Hardy then formed a joint venture with its future owner Constellation, the second largest wine concern in the United States, proof of the way Americans were prepared to treat Australians on equal terms, with initial sales of 700,000 cases. In 2002, the joint venture bought a major vineyard, the St Francis winery in Sonoma, and BRL itself formed another joint venture, with Stellenbosch Vineyards, to sell the South African producer's wines in Europe.

The next target is Germany, which Millar reckons is like the UK market in the late 1980s, albeit one "not so concerned with quality". After that, Canada, and then that unpromising market, Japan, where the only possible wine is French. But there's no forgetting New Zealand, where BRL Hardy has recently acquired Nobilo, and France. There, BRL Hardy has used its Australian winemaking expertise to transform the excellent local grapes into an increasingly successful brand, La Baume, which by 2002 was selling well over 200,000 cases. Yet says Millar, the experience has shown that "It's easier to build an Australian brand than a French one, for French-branded wines have a – generally justified – poor reputation."

Possibly the most orthodox success story of the 1990s is that of

Mildara Blass. In the middle of the decade, Fosters, the biggest name in beer in Australia, had a dilemma. Like many breweries before it – including Tooth's in the 1970s – it had an ever-increasing pile of cash and didn't know what to do with it. Fosters chairman Ted Kunkel had been trained as a winemaker, and he saw the future for premium wines. In 1996, Ray King at Mildara Blass accepted a friendly bid by Fosters. King now had the backing to buy more brands: Maglieri and Len Evans's cherished Rothbury, which by then included Saltram, Baileys, and St Hubert. Not surprisingly, King's Rothbury bid resulted in bad blood between the two incompatible principals: King himself and Len Evans.

Fosters brought in Cellarmasters, the world's largest mail-order wine business, which later provided the basis of a worldwide, direct-mail empire by buying similar businesses in Holland and Germany. As Ray King pointed out, "Wine clubs can rely on the fact that everyone has a surplus of something which wine clubs are ideally placed to buy." He also expressed the rather cynical view that clubs can target "a group of customers who don't want to buy through a retailer because they don't want to show their ignorance, so clubs can get a premium for spoon-feeding them".

Cellarmasters had been built up by Terry Davis, who was persuaded to stay on when it was sold to Fosters. As he said, "It's an excellent outlet [in which] to position new wines. Today people will have a go if they're described accurately. We've got two million active club customers, three-quarters in Australia, [as well as] in Holland and Germany, and a few thousand in Britain, shifting three million cases a year." Davis did not believe that Cellarmasters was competing with retailers. It might have been selling the same wines but "as a service to its customers – not at a beat-any price. So it's high service, higher price". This attitude accorded with King's passion for profitability. The company still stays faithful to Ray King's object: to concentrate on the most expensive twenty-five per cent of the country's wines. But King had eschewed exports (he thought they were unprofitable) and when he left they accounted for a mere fifth of profits, a far lower proportion than any other major Australian wine company.

When Davis succeeded Ray King in 2000, his first job was naturally to increase exports to catch up with his Australian competitors. Within a couple of years they had risen from a third to a half of sales, helped greatly by the strength of the Wolf Blass brand in the United States. Davis appreciated Blass' qualities and employed him systematically as a global ambassador for his brand. Mildara Blass also provided Blass with a spanking new winery in the Barossa, capable of treating up to 75,000 tonnes of fruit a year. But real expansion would involve a major takeover. Davis decided to concentrate not on Europe but on the United States, "where profitability was far higher". Even there only three firms were big enough to be worth bidding for: Kendall-Jackson, Beringer, and Mondavi. Pat Jackson was a buyer rather than a seller, and the Mondavi business was too personal for comfort. When Davis asked himself the question, "Would brand enthusiasm survive if the Mondavis left?", the answer was clearly no. That left Beringer. Even at A\$2.56 billion (US\$548 million £914 million), it was a relative bargain since sales had been growing at sixteen per cent annually for some years and the share price was depressed because three-quarters of the voting shares were owned by the Texas Pacific Company, a group of ultra-rich individuals. This domination naturally led investors to fear that the majority shareholder would neglect the interests of the minority.

According to Davis, it took "a long courtship" for Mildara Blass to acquire Beringer, combined with a straight cash offer to ward off other bidders as well as a promise to keep the existing management in place. The Texas Pacific top brass had told Davis: "We've got thirteen other CEOs in the group and they'll be watching to see how you treat them." In reality Davis was happy to keep the whole top team. Beringer owned some very fine vineyards and had a profitable lock-grip on the market for white Zinfandel, thanks to what Davis calls the "Australian philosophy" of paying top dollar for the best grapes. Moreover, says Chris Hatcher, "They showed the way to charging more for our top commercial wines." But, like so many American businesses, exports were a sideline, a means of disposing of surplus stock, and accounted for a mere four per cent of sales. Hence the double task: of exploiting Beringer's brands, such as Chateau St Jean, in Europe, and using Beringer's sales force to increase the already healthy sales of the Wolf Blass brand in the United States. The name of the group was changed to Beringer Blass, which greatly pleased Wolfy because of the emphasis on his name. The combined group's first acquisition came a few months later with the purchase in 2000 of Castello di Gabbiano, makers of the second highest selling Chianti in the

United States, reinforcing Beringer Blass' claims that it was "the world's leading premium table wine group".

Davis was lucky in benefitting from the Greg Norman phenomenon, a lesson in how a wildly successful new brand can be based on methods precisely opposite to those taught in any marketing school. It so happened that Ted Kunkel was a friend of the golfer Greg Norman, himself a wine-lover. They agreed that a premium wine named after Norman might be a success. Ray King's reaction was predictable: "You must be f. . . g joking." Nevertheless they went ahead, forecasting sales of 35,000 cases. This was natural: before the Greg Norman brand was launched, only 5,000 cases of Australian wine were being sold in the United States at above $15 a bottle and four-fifths of the total of four million cases were priced below $8. Within a year, the three Greg Norman wines, offered at well above $15, were selling at a rate of over 100,000 cases annually and within a couple of years at double that figure, making them the biggest-selling wines selling at $15 and above in the United States.

The success is unlikely to be transitory. The wines themselves are a nice blend of a famous name and respected regions. The Chardonnay (lean and limey) is from the Yarra Valley, the Cabernet/Merlot blend is a typical wine from (where else?) Coonawarra, and the Shiraz, from the Limestone Coast, is elegant and spicy. None of the wines is too obviously overfruity. As Bruce Tyrrell points out, "Mrs Norman in particular has a good palate and is learning all the time." Moreover, "for Americans the name of Greg Norman is better known than Coonawarra" – and a single visit by the Great White Shark to any American restaurant guarantees an honoured place on the wine list.

Sales of Australian wines in the United States did not, of course, start with Greg Norman. In the late 1980s, a tourist publicity campaign based on Paul Hogan's success in the film *Crocodile Dundee* ("Throw a shrimp on the barbie") made Australia the flavour of the month in the USA. Although sales in the United States had boomed during the 1990s, reaching A$280 million (£100 million) in 2000 (second only to those in Britain), this represented less than one-fortieth of wine consumption in the country. The independent ventures (as opposed to the many partnerships between Australian and US companies) were still largely dependent on two brands, Rosemount and Lindemans Bin 65, which had been crafted by Philip John at Karadoc, complete with some residual sugar, to please the relatively unsophisticated palates of most American drinkers.

By 1997, Lindemans Bin 65 was selling over a million cases a year thanks to José Fernandez, Penfolds' man in the United States. Fernandez is a Spanish-Irish-Brooklyn sales genius who trained as an orchestral conductor at the Julliard School of Music. He left Southcorp to embark on an (inevitably unsuccessful) dot-com venture before returning to his old trade at BRL Hardy. But the rest of Southcorp's wines lagged behind badly. Even Penfolds did not take full advantage when the 1990 Grange was named wine of the year in 1996 by the powerful American magazine, *Wine Spectator*. The magazine's canny, commercially minded owner, Marvin Shanken, recognized not only the quality of the wine but also the importance – and therefore the ever-increasing advertising budget – of the firm making the wine.

The Australian wine industry's problems in the United States are caused by the sheer size of the market and the very different legal situation in different states, most of which require an elaborate and expensive three-tiered system of agents, wholesalers, and retailers. For those companies without a US partner, the possibilities are niche imports through specialist merchants or sheer volume. Power in each state is concentrated in the hands of a handful of wholesalers whose sales reps have enormous portfolios. Effectively, only the big four can afford their own networks. Such problems ensured that Brown Brothers, for one, simply gave up exporting to the United States in the mid-1990s. Bruce Tyrrell goes for downmarket "box movers", while in Britain he has been able to move up-market by working with Paragon Vintners, the agent for Veuve Clicquot Champagne and other prestigious brands.

In late 2001, Davis, frustrated at not getting the top job at Fosters, unexpectedly left Beringer Blass to join Coca-Cola as senior man Down Under. He was succeeded by Walter T Klenz, a long-serving executive at Beringer. But he had been forced to admit the failure of Wineplanet, the website established to sell wines to ordinary drinkers over the internet. Despite an expensive and glitzy international launch and the backing of Cellarmasters, the venture soon followed the majority of similar e-initiatives into the ether. It was a salutary warning, for as Davis pointed out, "If we can't make a go of it with Wineplanet, then nobody can." Similarly, by 2002, Winepros, launched by a galaxy of wine stars headed by Len Evans and James Halliday, had also been wound up.

The biggest success story of the 1990s is obviously Jacob's Creek, promoted as "Australia's Top Drop." Although sales in the late 1980s were a mere 500,000 cases, they grew rapidly. In 1994 the Jacob's Creek range received the Maurice O'Shea Award, the first wine to be so honoured. By 2001 it was selling 5.4 million cases, 4.5 million outside Australia, making it the world's biggest internationally traded brand. The widespread idea that the brand's success depends on a magic secret amuses those responsible for it. "If they do find it, I wish that they'd tell us," was one reaction. Like everyone else in the firm, Orlando Wyndham's managing director, Christian Porta, attributes the brand's success to "over-delivery of quality for the price".

The all-important reliability of the brand is based on a blend of hot- and cool-climate grapes, mostly from outside sources, because Orlando Wyndham has never owned as many vineyards as the other members of the big four. Indeed, the range has gained an increasing number of awards over the years – over 230 in 2001, two-fifths of them gold or silver. This consistent quality is due to the stern discipline imposed by the man responsible Phil Laffer, the former winemaker at Karadoc, and one of the most distinguished of refugees from the Penfoldization of Southcorp, although Laffer himself gives more credit to Stephen Couche, who has been in charge of marketing the brand for over two decades. Laffer's only failure is the rather jammy blend of Grenache and Shiraz (which, he says grimly, "will be dealt with"), but this is excusable given the number of wines in the range.

Thanks to Laffer, Porta can claim, justifiably, that the wine "is getting better vintage after vintage. . . We've managed to increase quality and quantity at the same time". This is remarkable, because the single most astonishing feature of the great export boom of the late 1990s was that it was achieved at a time when a shortage of grapes had forced winemakers to accept any grapes they were offered and make wines that inevitably grew more and more bland over the years because of the need to mask the poor quality of the raw material.

Not surprisingly, the first thing Pernod-Ricard did when it took over Orlando Wyndham, then not in good shape because of the loss-making Wyndham Estate, was to install a hatchet man. Throughout the early

1990s, Pernod-Ricard kept Orlando Wyndham on a tight rein, unwilling to invest enough to expand sales, even of Jacob's Creek. It is only recently, after Orlando Wyndham had helped the group introduce its pastis into the Swedish market, that Pernod-Ricard started to appreciate the previously hidden value of its Australian subsidiary.

Things started to change with the arrival of more positive bosses, but they really moved when Christian Porta hit the Australian scene in early 2000. Porta is a relaxed, elegant high-flyer, with an appropriately international background. Alsatian by birth. After an education in a high-grade French business school, he worked for four years with the giant accountancy firm Arthur Andersen before moving into Pernod-Ricard's finance department. He spent two years with Campbell Distillers, Pernod-Ricard's Scottish subsidiary, before coming to Australia. As a result, Porta's English is perfect. He's greatly helped by the relaxed attitude of the parent toward its subsidiaries – or at least to those as successful as Orlando Wyndham now is. "It's real decentralization," Porta says enthusiastically. "We agree an annual budget and a three-year plan and once that is agreed we have three formal meetings a year."

Porta's most important contribution has been to nag Laffer into introducing new varieties and to back the brand extension designed to recapture buyers who had moved upmarket. The Jacob's Creek Reserve range sells in Britain at nearly double the price of the basic range. At the top comes the Limited Release: "A quality statement attached to a few thousand cases of wine and designed for drinking on special occasions by existing buyers." Above Jacob's Creek comes Wyndham Estate, wines of real quality that can be sold in quantity, thanks to the impetus provided by Jacob's Creek.

Today, Pernod is an enthusiastic supporter of its Australian wines, distributing them throughout the world. Orlando Wyndham is one of Pernod-Ricard's top-five priority brands and Patrick Ricard, the chairman, now refers to the company as being in "wine and spirits". Progress has been made even in Japan, where Pernod is well-established with Wild Turkey Bourbon. Nevertheless, Porta admits that, though the brand is familiar to thousands of Japanese in Australia, in Japan they "need educating". Jacob's Creek is even on the shelves of Carrefour, one of France's largest chains of supermarkets – surely the ultimate accolade for an Australian wine.

11

The Vines, The Wines – and Where They Come From

I'd like to work toward the hierarchy of single-vineyard wines – grand crus if you like – at the top of our portfolio, followed by distinctly regional wines, followed by the cheap blended wines at the bottom end of the pyramid.

STEVE PANNELL

Historically, the vast majority of Australian wines have been made from a relative handful of varieties, without too much regard to the specific region or site where the grapes were grown. For Australians, what the French call *typicité* is not linked, as it is so indelibly in most of Europe, to the qualities of the vineyard in which the grapes are grown. In Australia the spotlight is on a winemaker or a brand, one sometimes vaguely related to a geographical location – like Jacob's Creek – which has long outgrown the vineyard of that name. As a result, there was far less of a link in drinkers' minds between the wine and its birthplace.

The assertion by an English journalist that Australian winemaking "throttles regionality in the cradle" is still largely true because of the gulf between the grape-grower, the winemaker some hundreds of kilometres away and the blender possibly in a third place. There is still a very varied balance between marketable names for wines and the fact that the grapes were grown in specific regions. Does the drinking public know or care that the fruit for McWilliams Barwang originally came from Hilltops in Victoria? Or the variety and regional origin of the three Greg Norman wines, even though they are given on the label?

From the start, transport was the key to the relationship between growers and winemakers. Reliance on horse-drawn transport (and paddle-steamers along the Murray) severely limited the distance grapes or juice could be carried. But all this changed in the 1920s with the arrival of the first trucks. Ever since, one of the phenomena of Australian winemaking that most sharply strikes the European visitor is the casual way in which grapes, juice, and wine are transported breathtaking distances as a matter of course, while Europeans are reluctant to cart their produce more than a few kilometres. Today, trucks routinely make even the two-day journey across the Nullabor Plain from the vineyards in the extreme southwest of the continent to South Australia, often without refrigeration.

Not surprisingly, before the imposition of regulations over the labelling of wine in the 1990s, a great deal of "imported" wine was sold as genuine local produce, especially in the Hunter Valley. It was known as coming from "Shepherd's Creek," after the transport firm that carried the grapes, the juice, and the wines to the Hunter. (If these wines were posh enough, they were known as coming from Chateau Shepherd.) One day, so it is said, the irrepressible Murray Tyrrell was caught by some visitors transferring wine from a tanker to one of his vats. "There," he said, "you can see that other regions are buying our wines."

"It sometimes pays," wrote Australia wine journalist Max Allen, "to follow the winemakers rather than the vineyards." This adds another influence to those of regions and varieties, as the winemaker's own style can be imposed on both. Today, the "multiregional" blending tradition epitomized by Grange has some firm adherents, notably Chris Hatcher of Beringer Blass, who, indeed, takes it much further: "I select from up to 150 wines," he says, "and I don't even know what variety they are. I'm simply selecting on their style and finding the quality suitable for particular blends" – a blending technique he learned from John Glaetzer.

Nevertheless, the top-of-the-range Black Label Wolf Blass wines, for which Hatcher is responsible and which are now labelled simply "Barossa Shiraz," will soon carry the names of specific sites. The names of individual regions are becoming increasingly important as are what Australians, naturally reluctant to employ French terms, refer to as "distinguished sites" rather than the French term *terroir*. For example, when Milawa became the production centre for Beringer Blass in the King Valley, the name of the vineyard would go on the bottle only of the best wines.

Australians have never been fond of authority, hence their opposition to French ideas of "regional distinctions" now referred to as "geographical indicators" of origin. The long process began in 1963, when all the states passed Pure Food Acts. So far as wine labelling was concerned, Bob Roberts, an early arrival in Mudgee, started the ball rolling with a voluntary self-funding appellation scheme administered by the Society for the Appellation of the Wines of Mudgee. In 1989, when the Australian government started negotiations over wines with the then European Economic Community, a crucial step was taken with the introduction of the Label Integrity Programme, which aimed to ensure that labels meant what they said. A year later the law was tightened, allowing the authorities to audit claims made by wineries over the vintages, varieties or regional origins of wines. These claims could be checked at the weighbridge when the grapes arrived to be crushed, at the cellar sales desk, and wholesale desk. They were defined, among other criteria, by the region's reputation and the length of time the mark had been used.

These developments were merely preliminaries to the 1993 agreement with the European Union which allowed the importation of virtually all Australian wines to the EU. It was the first such agreement the EU had made with a significant non-member wine-producing country. It was a triumph for the Australians; it took the Canadians nearly fifteen years before they were allowed to export their *eiswein* (ice wine) to the EU. The agreement was useful for Australian winemakers, even though they don't like to admit it. It stopped the use of names such as claret and burgundy, which had been misappropriated for the previous 150 years. This single crucial step ensured that the previous automatic comparisons with "the real thing" would no longer be made and that Australian wines would be judged on their own merits.

It is difficult to exaggerate the confusion that had reigned until then. In the words of John Charles Brown, eldest son John Graham, in the early 1960s: "There was a white which we called hock, but actually it was a Riesling. We had a light port, a dark port, a claret and a range of 'sherries'. Claret, was usually a Shiraz, or a Shiraz and Cabernet plus Mondeuse. We were the first to call wines by their correct names, but that came a few years later."

Len Evans put the idea brutally. "When the hell is Australia going to grow up?" he ranted. "How can you expect to develop any form of reputation anywhere in the world when you produce 'Australian Beaujolais'?" When Evans confronted Brian McGuigan of Wyndham Estate about his "Australian Chablis", McGuigan simply said, "It sold more wine." By contrast the producer of Australian Asti Spumante changed the name of his (increasingly successful) wine to Gaia Spumante.

Also useful, albeit also much contested at the time, was the requirement in the agreement to define Australia's wine-growing regions. Yet the definitions provided some guidance to consumers and forced the winemakers to declare the origin of the grapes used in their wines. Of course, it was only too easy to label most of them as coming from that super-region "Southeastern Australia," which covered three states adding up to the size of most of Western Europe.

To an outsider, the definitions of wine-growing regions seem eminently sensible, since they do not come with all the tiresome restrictions – on varieties and yields, for instance – imposed by the French in their system of *Appellations d'Origine Controlée*. The Australian system leaves a lot of liberty to the producers. Not surprisingly, to the French the definitions are simply laughable. As Madame Bienaymé of the *Office Internationale du Vin* (International Officer of Wine) pointed out to Australians: "You do not have a system of geographical indications for wine. You have a system of indications of source for your grapes."

Nevertheless, the winemakers had legal tradition on their side. As leading Melbourne lawyer Stephen Stern pointed out: "If particular conduct is not specifically prohibited, then our legal system provides that it is permitted. Thus our system is far more flexible than that of other countries or jurisdictions." But, as he also points out, there is legislation, the Food Standards Act, that "deals with those winemaking techniques and practices that are permitted or prohibited and those additives that are also prohibited or permitted".[1] Even so, wines could acquire regional labels even if they contained up to fifteen per cent of grapes from outside the region; this practice is also allowed in California.

In accordance with the agreement with the EU, regionality started to come into force in 1994, when a federal act started the process of division into zones, regions, and sub-regions, each of which had to have at least five independent vineyards with at least five ha (12.4 acres) of vines and

[1] Stephen Stern, *Analysis of Australia's System of Vitiviniculture*, private paper, 1998.

a total minimum crush of 500 tonnes of grapes. Inevitably, most of the divisions, even those far smaller than the southeastern Australia zone, were not homogenous. As Stephen Stern notes, "When you consider the diversity of grape varieties, viticultural practices, and vinification methods used in any particular region, as well as the youth in wine terms and the sheer size of many of the regions, how can they be defined in wine terms?" Perhaps, he suggests, "Reputations should come first and then lines on maps second."

An obvious case is McLaren Vale, which journalist Philip White describes as a "mad hotchpotch of soil types, like the deep Blewett Springs sands that give red wines a delicious peaty aspect." "There is that huge sink and temperature stabilizer called the Gulf," he states, "constant humidity which produces wines softer than the tough hardliners of Clare." For Steve Pannell, McLaren Vale is "fantastically well-suited to Grenache". "You get weight and texture and elegance, which is comparatively rare." Chester Osborn of d'Arenberg describes it as "a warm region with mitigating circumstances". We can leave the fruit on the vine in April and it stays at 14 degrees Baumé because of the sea breezes and the cool nights," he explains. "But all the time we're developing big, ripe tannins."

The winemakers were quick off the mark. In the first year, 1994, 650 possible names were submitted to the EU before being winnowed down to 128. Since then, there's been a steady flow every year, and by 2002 there were sixty-five regions, all approved by the Geographical Indications Committee (GIC). They include lots of new regions and sub-regions, like Henty in the remote southwest of Victoria, which even in the mid-1990s had only a handful of wineries.

This process was useful for ambitious regions, such as Heathcote in the middle of central Victoria, which was historically part of Bendigo but which now has two regional groups both aiming for individual recognition. Then there were sub-regional appellations such as the Goulburn Valley's Nagambie Lakes, which already housed wineries as well-established as Tahbilk and Mitchelton. The winemakers' preferred name for the whole region was High Country, but Miranda had a brand of that name so it had to be called Central Victorian High Country. Sam Plunkett, whose family had been there since the 1960s, objected, but as he told Tony Keys, although the name didn't roll off the tongue as smoothly as Napa Valley or Bordeaux, "I just ran out of steam at the end.

I didn't find the committee easy to deal with. About half the people in the region are now looking to found a separate region called Strathbogie Ranges."[2]

In Western Australia, it was not clear if Pemberton, a well-known name, should be renamed Warren Valley or Manjimup. The region Capel Vale was delineated by Robert Bowen, then winemaker of the estate of the same name, by the simple method of defining the vineyards drained by the local river system.

As the GIC's Ernie Sullivan maintained "We don't have boundary disputes in Australia; what we're doing is resolving boundaries. It's just that some boundaries take longer to resolve than others." This overly optimistic pronouncement was designed to deal with the only big problem: Coonawarra. In the event, the argument over a naturally much-coveted name justified Dr Richard Smart's quip: "Appellations are things created by the French to make New World producers fall out with one another."

The first problem was that Coonawarra, strictly defined, is only one example of a specific type of soil: terra rossa ridges above a subsoil of limestone left as the seas receded millions of years ago. Other ridges crop up all the way through Coonawarra, Wrattonbully, and Padthaway, an area summed up in the name of the whole zone: the Limestone Coast. Coonawarra's terra rossa soil was discovered early, and the region has been associated with only a couple of varieties – a rare phenomenon in Australia – for nearly a century. Its hallmark is the elegant, leafy Cabernet Sauvignon (though its Shiraz is just as distinguished). Nevertheless, Robin Don, a visiting Master of Wine, is not alone in feeling that, as in most fine vineyards, it is the nature of the subsoil and the drainage it provides that are crucial. So, in his view, it is the underlying limestone that matters and fine wines can also be produced on the "black stuff," the richer soils either side of the central ridge. Don also noted another key element, the supply of pure water, although yet another factor, the (modest) height of the ridges, goes largely unmentioned, even though such minimal slopes have proved equally important in the Médoc north of Bordeaux, which itself is based on a series of ridges, albeit of gravel rather than the limestone found in the coast of that name.

Most of the major groups were naturally keen to acquire land there.

[2] Tony Keys, *Harper's Australian Supplement*, January 2001.

For Penfolds, Max Schubert bought choice terra rossa land at the north end of Coonawarra from the Redmans, and in the 1970s Penfolds, Lindemans, Mildara, and Wynns expanded their holdings. If Coonawarra had been delineated earlier there would probably have been only a few objections. But then came Brian Croser, who bought Sharefarmers, an excellent outcrop of terra rossa, which was unfortunately ruled to be outside the strip. Croser has never been the most clubbable of men and the "mates" who defined the region at the time didn't include his property, despite the geological evidence. By the time the geographical indicators were being defined, other major companies had bought property, some on the "black stuff" on which they grew grapes they marketed in bottles bearing the sacred name of Coonawarra. They objected to the original definition, which in truth was pretty weird, in agricultural terms, for it included ponds and other unlikely slices of *terroir*.

Eventually – someone will write a book on the subject sooner rather than later – the whole dispute was exposed to the full rigours (and expense) of the law. In October 2001, the Federal Administrative Appeals Tribunal handed down a seemingly common-sense ruling after appeals from forty-four grape producers, mostly the big groups, who had been excluded from Coonawarra two years earlier. The tribunal rejected nineteen and admitted twenty-five, with Justice Deirdre O'Connor, the president of the tribunal, admitting, "There is no absolutely correct boundary for the region." Even then the appeal process continued, with more parcels being added in 2002 after a number of major groups had appealed. This should close the affair. As Eric Sullivan, the secretary of the GIC cynically put it, "Hopeful people will now look at the money spent on legal fees by those Coonawarra vineyards over the last few years and think twice before entering into legal action." In other words, now that the big boys are satisfied, no one can afford to enter the battle.

Yet even the new, broad definition of Coonawarra ensures that its *terroir* is far more homogenous than, say, that archetypal French appellation, the 800ha (1,976 acres) of vines whose owners can make a fortune from using the name of Pomerol. Coonawarra, though not confined to the terra rossa, is based on a very particular type of subsoil, while Pomerol is a mix of several types of clay, gravel, sand, and even some rich loam. Now that Coonawarra has been defined broadly enough to include vineyards not situated on terra rossa, the name of the brand under which the wine is sold has become of even greater importance than it was earlier, when a buyer could generally rely on the fact that the grapes in a wine labelled "Coonawarra" really had been grown on the red stuff.

Such was the attraction of Coonawarra that the major groups hunted around to see if the low limestone ridge on which the vines are grown was peculiar to that region. In the 1960s, Karl Seppelt had discovered that somewhat similar, though not identical, conditions prevailed a hundred kilometres (sixty-two miles) to the north in what became Padthaway, and he was followed by other major players. Between Coonawarra and Padthaway lies Wrattonbully, originally known as Koppamurra, but a company of that name objected. Today, the whole stretch from the sea up to Coonawarra is known, and increasingly appreciated, as the Limestone Coast.

The name is now used not only in the Greg Norman range but also by Hardy's in its Regional series, itself an indication of the increasing importance attached to "newer" regions. The major companies were not active only in Coonawarra; they can sometimes transform a region from being merely a supplier of grapes or the home of a few (small-scale) enthusiasts into one with its own identity. In the "new" region of Canberra, which previously had only a few small wineries, BRL Hardy's has established a 2,000-tonne winery fed by 250ha (618 acres) of vineyards. In the Pyrenees region of central Victoria, Seppelt has planted an unprecedentedly large vineyard covering 146ha (361 acres).

There is an ever-changing balance between regions that have their own strong identity, generally acquired long ago, and the newer regions, many of which were also first planted long ago and are largely, if not entirely, exploited as anonymous sources for blends. The obvious cases are the Riverland, Langhorne Creek, Padthaway, and Wrattonbully. Yet many of these, even Riverland, are now establishing some form of individual identity.

The struggle can be tough. An obvious case is the cry of "fruit from Pemberton", heard as proof of quality throughout Western Australia. Typically, Evans & Tate says that the Pemberton fruit in its Cabernet/ Merlot blend "gives us the chance to produce a wine style with the trademark elegance and mouth-feel of our Margaret River reds, but with more subtlety and softer tannins". The old Houghton winery north of Perth now has substantial holdings not only in Pemberton but also in

Frankland River, Mount Barker, and Moondah Brook, north of the Swan Valley near Perth. In the 1990s, Houghton increased its fruit intake from the south from a third to two-thirds of the total, using the grapes for its finest wines such as the Jack Mann range. Newer arrivals built in the availability of southern fruit from the start. At Capel Vale, Peter Pratten has always looked for fruit from different regions, while Vasse Felix uses Riesling from Mount Barker for its premium wines. Such is the struggle that Howard Park, one of the biggest and best-respected southern wine-makers, has shifted its winemaking and cellar door to Margaret River, even though an increasing proportion of the fruit is coming from its original home.

Some regions can rely on their own identity, even if the vines disap-peared for fifty years. The most obvious case is the Yarra Valley. This has been planted not only by prestigious newcomers such as James Halliday and Moët & Chandon, but also by wineries from outside the region. An obvious case is De Bortoli. In 1987, it bought a winery in the Yarra, build-ing what is acclaimed as the finest Italian restaurant in the region. The upmarket move was signalled by the fact that it was the first time the De Bortolis had ever planted varieties of vines to suit the specific type of soil. The Yarra, of course, is a naturally cool region, and support for the idea that, as it were, cool was "cool" has naturally grown over the years. Yet the hotter regions are fighting back. In 2002, a year of positively European weather, the Riverland produced some Cabernets that were fully the equal of many of those from more distinguished regions, while I heard warm-climate enthusiasts gloating at the failure of the ultra-cool Mornington Peninsula to produce many ripe grapes that year.

The model cool-climate region is probably the Adelaide Hills, on the slopes of the 727-metre (2,384-foot) high Mount Lofty a few kilometres east of Adelaide. The region was given Brian Croser's blessing when he established his Petaluma estate in its northernmost sub-region, Piccadilly Hills, in 1979. But, like so many other regions, the Adelaide Hills had flourished in the mid-nineteenth century. Indeed the tiny two-ha (4.9-acre) Grove Hill boutique winery was established as early as 1846 – the stone buildings are still there to prove it. Today, the region's average quality is high with names such as Chain of Ponds; Nepenthe the Lenswood Estate vineyard, once owned by the Henschkes and the vineyard established in the same sub-region by Tim Knappstein after the family company,

Stanley, had been sold; and Shaw & Smith. The estates are all small, ranging from the absurd 0.33ha (0.8 acres) of Samphire Wines to Croser's seventy-ha (173-acre) estate.

Adelaide Hills is never going to be a major region; there's too little water, and much of what little there is is required by the city. Moreover, environmentalists keep an exceptionally beady eye on such a beautiful, wooded region so close to Adelaide. Back in 1909, there had been 1,000ha (2,471 acres) of vineyards around Adelaide but virtually all, including most of the historic Magill estate, disappeared under brick and concrete over the next sixty years, leaving merely the names of roads to remind inhabitants and visitors of the grapes once grown there.

Unfortunately, the current situation is not as rosy as it appears at first sight, since the regional identity of these idyllic slopes is now gravely compromised because so many of the "wineries" lack any form of physical reality. They are "virtual", owned by hobbyists attracted by the region's deserved place in the fashionable sun. According to Philip White:

> *"The Adelaide Hills wine region booklet touts thirty-eight 'wine producers', and there are more. But apart from a few tiny new ones taking shape, there are really only four wineries: Paracombe, Petaluma, Nepenthe, and Shaw & Smith, at which formidable qualified rivals. . . also make, or have made, their delicious wines. . . If our Hills are to retain their premium image, the hobbyists will have to sell better fruit, while the 'wine producers' will have to be more honest about who makes their wine, or learn to make it properly themselves."*

As so often, White is exaggerating, forgetting such names as Chain of Ponds and Hillstowe, but he has a point.

By far the best example of the growing importance of micro-regions and their micro-wineries lies in Tasmania, where, a number of wineries produce wines with the real, slightly sour-cherry, Burgundian feel. In fact the island includes several distinct regions, with the south representing a mere 3,000 tonnes, a quarter of Tasmania's production, but involving no fewer than sixty-three wineries. The regions remain very individual and the climate fickle – the distinguished Champagne firm of Louis Roederer was not alone in abandoning a venture there – but today both Southcorp and BRL Hardy are trying to establish vineyards to supply the precious high-quality, cool-climate Pinot Noir and Chardonnay they urgently require for their best sparkling wines. It is a classic example of the big companies acknowledging the importance of regionality.

An alternative way of finding the much sought-after coolth is to move up the hill, possibly the single biggest element affecting regional shifts over the years. An obvious case is the Central Victorian High Country. As that veteran, John Charles Brown, points out, "The northeast of Victoria enjoys a climate very suitable for viticulture, in that there is a wide range of micro-climates and soils to choose from. In a distance of one hundred kilometres [62 miles] from the Murray River at Wahgunyah to the hill-tops of Whitlands [where Browns has a vineyard at 800 metres (2,624 feet)], just about any climate from the Mediterranean to northern Europe can be matched" – with a corresponding multitude of types of soil. Not surprisingly, central Victoria is full of abandoned regions rediscovered by pioneers making icon wines. By 1891, Beechworth had 71ha (175 acres) of vines, a figure that fell to 41ha (101 acres) by 1901. By 1916, the area under vines consisted of a mere 1.2ha (three acres). It was revived only in 1981, when Rick Kinzbrunner established the Giaconda vineyard growing icon Pinot Noir, Chardonnay, and Cabernet Sauvignon. Within twenty years there were forty ha (ninety-nine acres) of vines in the region – enough for it to ask for its own name.

Nevertheless, the Central High Victorians face competition, height-wise anyway, from Orange and Mudgee. Orange lies on the slopes of a volcano, Mount Canobolas, on the drier western side of the Great Dividing Range. Typically of the new regions, it lies at an altitude of between 600 and 1,050 metres (1,968 and 3,444 feet). Much of the wine is used in multiregional blends, but a number of companies, including Rosemount, use the name. The recent history of the Orange region is typical, as are its winemakers. Two of the first were Stephen and Rosemary Doyle who, in 1983, bought a smallholding called Bloodwood. They commuted the 250 kilometres (155 miles) from Sydney and stayed in the back of their Land Cruiser while making some superior Cabernet Sauvignon. Contrast that with Cabonne, a very ambitious scheme started in 1995 through a quoted company, which invested A$45 million (£16.1 million) in Little Boomey with 900ha (2,224 acres) of vines and a winery capable of processing 20,000 tonnes of grapes. The whole venture is now supervised by a well-known winemaker, Jon Reynolds.

To the north lies Mudgee, another high-altitude region, its suitability for grapes shown by the presence of stone fruit such as peaches. Its history, again, is standard stuff. Three German families – the Roths, the Kurtzs, and the Buchholtzs – arrived in 1858. The region was helped by a minor gold-rush in 1872 and flourished until a bank crash in 1893. One pioneer, Dr Thomas Fiaschi, continued making wine until he died in 1927, but the other fifty-five wineries disappeared.

Mudgee was rediscovered in the 1960s and found a prophet in Bob Roberts of Huntington Hill. Peter Edwards developed Hill of Gold, which he sold to David Davenport of Mountain Blue. This in turn was absorbed by Rosemount, which sells a deep, fruity Shiraz and a Cabernet Sauvignon under the Mountain Blue label and expanded the vineyard to 140ha (346 acres). It was much the same story further south in Tumbarumba, where Southcorp bought a vineyard first established in 1982 in a typically high, dry, and remote region in the Snowy Mountains.

All these regions are still largely colonial: that is, dependent on sales of grapes to winemakers in the Hunter Valley. The region defies all the rules, if only because the climatic conditions, above all at harvest time, are so different from those prevailing elsewhere in Australia, except to a certain degree in Coonawarra. The Hunter's difficult and distinctive climatic conditions during the harvest period involve what Bruce Tyrrell, one of the few real experts on the subject, calls the "Hunter mentality".

"Our viticulture is very different," he says. "We have to spray every fourteen days because of the rain." Moreover, because of the likelihood of rain during harvest, "We have to get the grapes in early at 11.5–12.5 degrees Baumé, so it's always possible that the reds won't have reached proper phenolic maturity. At the worst, as in 1958, 1960, and 1962, we can be nearly wiped out with hail, and we can have one-and-a-half inches [3.8 cm] of rain in a day. . . but it's regular rain that does the damage – our best insurance is to have vineyards scattered all over the valley."

Tyrrell is naturally a staunch defender of the Hunter. "It's only twenty kilometres [12.4 miles] from the coast so the nights are cool, and there's enough cloud cover to ensure that there's no burn." As a result, "The wines have good acids and a large natural tannin." The proof lies with his wines – and not just the Chardonnays for which his father was so famous. His aged Semillon, Vat 1, is one of the two greats. When I tasted the 1996 vintage in early 2002, it was still young and vibrant. The few hundred cases he makes of Vat 9 is a perfect example of rich but not heavy Shiraz.

To demonstrate the versatility of the region, he even produces small quantities of a Pinot Noir, which is the real thing.

It was Len Evans who stated that "The best winemaking region in Australia remains to be discovered," which begs the question: best for what? Until very recently, Australian winemakers had assumed that every region could produce fine wine from a relatively wide spectrum of varieties. Evans himself made the point when he stated that "Most Australian wine regions have still to find their own niche" – citing some of the few exceptions such as Rutherglen and its fortified dessert wines, and the Shiraz and Semillon from his beloved Hunter Valley.

The underlying problem was that, for too long, most of the varieties were mislabelled – the descriptions of the grapes as fanciful as those of the wines themselves. There were a handful of exceptions. In 1941–2, François de Castella did a thorough report for the Phylloxera Board of South Australia and identified the "Rhine Riesling" in McLaren Vale as Albillo (Chenin Blanc). It was known locally as "the sherry vine". Only in 1976 did Paul Truel, the great French expert on grape varieties, visit Australia's vineyards and provide the right names. This had never been easy. As Max Lake noted in 1966, "The firm identification of a variety can be extremely difficult," and Lake's list of variations is long.

> "Aucerot could be either Chardonnay or Pinot Gris, both Palomino and Chasselas were called Sweetwater and so on. Crouchen was called Clare Riesling, Semillon Hunter River Riesling. Typically, it was assumed for a long time that Houghton White Burgundy was made from Semillon with a touch of Tokay. Later the 'Semillon' was found to be Chenin Blanc. The most complicated case I came across was at All Saints vineyard. It's called 'Rutherglen Pedro Ximenes' – now known to be Dorado – and a wine called Chablis was made from it."

On their 1985 trip, the Masters of Wine were told that there were no fewer than fifty-seven varieties being grown in the Barossa Valley – though I'm not sure whether this wasn't a Barossa Deutsch joke, with the number plucked from a Heinz label. Nevertheless, if there are, if anything, too many regions for effective promotion, precisely the opposite applies to the varieties – for the moment, anyway. By 2000, the area planted of the big three, Chardonnay, Cabernet Sauvignon, and Shiraz, accounted for over half the total. Their rise had been sudden and unprecedented. In the

1990s, the land under these three varieties increased five times or more. Yet as recently as 1990 that multipurpose old warhorse, Sultana, had accounted for a tenth of the total: more than the big three combined. Not surprisingly, in the 1990s the area planted with it dropped by a third during a decade in which the total surface of vines doubled.

In a sense, and only partly because of Grange, Shiraz is Australia's icon variety. Australia's only competitor in terms of Shiraz is the northern Rhône Valley, whose winemakers are friendlier with their Australian counterparts than those of any other French region. Australian winemakers even provide them with cuttings from their vines, more ancient than any found in France, and Chapoutier, one of the Rhône's leading firms, has recently established a vineyard at Mount Benson in southeastern South Australia.

The concentration is not surprising. "The Shiraz is our greatest asset," says Matt Harrop, a leading young winemaker. Typically, Shiraz provides what Steve Pannell describes as a "viticultural orgasm when all the tannins are ripe". Even more importantly, as Dr Bailey Carrodus points out, "Shiraz does very well wherever you plant it in Australia." "But," says Bruce Tyrrell, "we're often short of flavours. Sometimes [Shiraz] has all the subtlety of an oversexed bus." Nevertheless, winemakers realize that they've a long way to go with the variety. Hot-climate Shiraz, like the splendidly rich and sturdy wines made in the Barossa, is not the only type in Australia. Those from the Hunter are more peppery, spicy, and Rhône-like. For me, the single most satisfying wine in the 1998 London Yalumba museum tasting was the 1978 vintage from the fabled Hill of Grace vineyard: long, rich, and peppery.

The best wines have one major factor in common: they are made from grapes grown on "old vines." Although the term is as vague as the equivalent French expression *vieilles vignes,* it is generally taken to mean the centenarians scattered all over the Barossa and a few other long-established regions. There are some, for instance, at Chateau Tahbilk that date back over 140 years, for vines on their own roots last far longer than grafted vines. As John Duval, until recently the guardian of the Grange heritage, says: "When we've chopped off sick branches from hundred-year-old vines to train them on trellises they got a new lease of life." D'Arry Osborn found that they could get six tonnes per ha (2.4 tonnes per acre) from some of his old vines in McLaren Vale. Such vines provide an unparalleled depth of concentration in the wine they produce.

The rise of Cabernet Sauvignon is far more recent and, notably unlike Shiraz, the variety had never previously been an important element in Australia's vineyards. Because of its low yields and unsuitability for transformation into fortified wine, it had virtually disappeared in the first sixty years of the twentieth century. In 1967, when a mere 630 tonnes were harvested, Max Lake noted, "Wines made from straight Cabernet can be counted on the fingers of one hand and are mainly either collectors' curios, out of balance or have some other fault." Growth was merely steady until the mid-1990s. It had been hampered by attempts to imitate the style of claret, resulting in green, leafy wines. But now Australian Cabernets are very varied, the cool-climate wines from Coonawarra and Margaret River contrasting with the splendidly rich, hot-climate wines from much of South Australia.

People talk as if Australian Chardonnay is going to take over the world, yet even now the area under this magic variety is little more than it is in Burgundy or Champagne, and certainly not as much as in California. For all the talk of surplus in 2002, that year winemakers were still desperately looking for grapes of the variety of decent quality. Nevertheless, its progress has been remarkable. It was unmentioned as a separate variety until 1980–1, when 337ha (833 acres) had been planted, and thus played virtually no part in the great white-wine boom of the 1970s.

Contrary to popular opinion, Australian Chardonnays vary enormously. As Max Allen puts it:

> "Even though they've had only a quarter century to play with the Chardonnay, Australian winemakers have tried almost every conceivable trick in the book with the variety. They have fermented it in barrels to produce a savoury, toasty, complex style of wine. They have put it through malolactic fermentation. . . to augment the variety's naturally round, rich texture and flavour. They have kept the wine in contact with the lees. . . to increase complexity. And they have cold-fermented it in stainless-steel tanks to produce a light, fruity, crisp wine."

And, he could have added, they've been making an increasing number of excellent sparkling wines from it.

John Beeston goes further. Since the 1970s, he wrote in 2000, Australian winemakers "have left few Chardonnay stones unturned". "There have been flirtations with many types of French oak. . . not to mention American and German, as well as more exotic kinds such as Yugoslav, Hungarian, Portuguese, and even (in the late 1990s) Russian. Then there came into vogue various degrees of wood-charring: light, medium, and heavy toast." And while they were juggling with their casks, they were also looking at "skin contact, malolactic fermentation, low sulfurs, no sulphurs, oxidative handling, non-oxidative handling, maturation on still and stirred lees, whole-bunch pressing, early bottling, late bottling, and, in the last few years, unwooded Chardonnay with or without malolactic fermentation."

What is most encouraging is the general mood of dissatisfaction among winemakers which, combined with the gradual reduction in the use of wood, is reducing the monopoly of buttery richness that made the country's Chardonnays – most obviously those from Rosemount – so famous in the 1980s. "The high end of Chardonnay," declares Michael Hill-Smith flatly, "is improving more rapidly than any other variety." The new Reserve Chardonnay from Shaw & Smith now comes from a single vineyard; its name, M3, comes from the Christian names of the firm's partners, Martin Shaw and the brothers Michael and Matthew Hill-Smith. M3's grapes are grown in a cool-climate vineyard in the Adelaide Hills, only a few kilometres from trendsetter Brian Croser's Tiers Vineyard.

The superiority of its wines emerged from the tastings to select his Petaluma Piccadilly Chardonnay. Len Evans regularly chose them from wines from the vineyard's five other "distinguished sites" (Croser's words). A (belated) geological survey conducted in 1997 showed that all six sites had apparently similar soils: free-draining, red-brown soil facing northeast and thus protected from the prevailing winds. But the Tiers subsoil was a rare rock type found only in Tiers, which was also the lowest, warmest, and best protected of the six. For some years, Croser insisted on keeping it in the Petaluma Piccadilly blend to maintain its quality, but in 1996 he accepted that he had enough great fruit to make 150 cases of Tiers wine that was instantly recognized as outstanding. Despite its strength – 13.8 degrees Baumé – it's not a heavy wine and there's so much fruit that the fourteen months in new oak is easily absorbed. Its intensity, length, and absence of exotic fruit or grapefruit makes it the most Burgundian of all Australian Chardonnays. Its only real rival is the Art Series Chardonnay from Leeuwin Estate, or rather from a particular parcel of vines, Block 20 or the front gate, which shares its elegance. When the first (1995) vintage of Yattarna, a top-end Chardonnay, was launched by Southcorp, it was too rich to match the competition. Now, thanks to fruit from the Adelaide Hills, it is closer to the elegance of its competitors, with lovely overtones of pink grapefruit.

All three dominant varieties – Shiraz, Cabernet Sauvignon, and Chardonnay – are pretty tolerant of growing conditions, but some of their leading rivals have suffered from the (now receding) Australian hubris that they could be grown anywhere: that they were not, as they say, "site-specific." Unhappily, as Oz Clarke and Margaret Rand put it:

> "Until Chardonnay overtook it in the early 1990s, Riesling was the most planted white grape in Australia, reflecting the belief current among many growers at the time that if you took a noble grape variety you could plant it anywhere and get great wine. It was (and still is) grown in many regions far too hot for such an early ripener. The resulting wines gave the variety a bad name."

As a result, Riesling became increasingly unfashionable; indeed, the hectarage dropped by a third in the last fifteen years of the twentieth century. But by the end of the 1990s, because more care was being taken over siting the vines, it had re-emerged as a variety capable of great aromatic freshness, mainly in wines from the Clare and Eden valleys. Today, even Clare Rieslings are subdivided into those from the warmer area round Clare itself, those from the cooler terra rossa of Watervale, and the even more intense, (one might almost say "European") styles associated with the wines from the stonier soil of Polish Hill River. Wolf Blass, whose Rieslings have been favourites even with judges who find his red wines too oaky, organized a National Riesling Challenge that attracted 130 wines from eighty companies in its first year. It seems the query "Do they make Riesling in Germany, too?" is not entirely ridiculous.

The biggest sufferer from the "grow anywhere" syndrome was that pickiest of varieties, Pinot Noir. The result was summarized by Remington Norman on behalf of the Masters of Wine after their 1985 trip. "Achieving an acceptable alcohol level was not difficult" he said, "but the essential fruit characteristics tended to be masked by the overall weight of the wines. Two Padthaway and one Coonawarra wine were shown. On each wine the heat was destructively evident. The wines were not internally cohesive or, in cooperative terms, appealing."

As Peter Gago of Penfolds, who is now in charge of making Grange but is nonetheless a Pinot fanatic, puts it: "Most Australian Pinot Noirs are okay for young, primary, fruit flavours, but they don't develop the secondary flavours typical of burgundy." Today, Australian winemakers have learned the lesson. As Jeremy Oliver put it in his Online Report: "Nobody is making a good Pinot Noir in Australia without an appreciation of *terroir*." But anyone making Pinot Noir outside Burgundy faces a common problem. In the words of Steve Pannell of BRL Hardy: "Burgundy has left an indelible mark on the variety." Even today, when winemakers have realized that the variety requires very specific conditions, there is no real recognizably Australian type of Pinot. The winemakers still inevitably follow the Burgundian model and, not surprisingly, find it exceptionally difficult to emulate.

Pinot, says Peter Gago, "is an even more unforgiving variety; you have to have all the variables". To get the right quality of grapes, he will only buy those grown on cool hillsides. "I won't buy Pinot Noir from below 400 metres [1,312 feet]," he declares, and even then "You have to educate the growers to keep crops down and to pick at the right moment."

Pinot, unlike Shiraz, only acquires its serious tannins, texture, and flavours just before vintage – hence the limited quantity, a mere 1,100 cases, of "real" Pinot Jago makes from fruit from the Adelaide Hills. Nevertheless, his 1999 vintage had all the hallmarks of a serious burgundy.

Few of the Australian winemakers have accepted that the right conditions include the dense planting characteristic of Burgundy: 10,000 vines to the ha, four times the Australian norm. Today some of the best Australian winemakers, such as Brian Croser at Petaluma and Andrew Pirie at Piper's Brook, crowd their vines, which is the only way to produce the finest results with Pinot Noir. As many as 500 Australian estates are trying to grow the fickle variety, though the majority of the Pinot is used to make sparkling wines. Real successes are localized, and then only in truly cool-climate regions, most of them in the south of the continent and in Tasmania. This is not surprising. As Brian Croser explains, in most Australian vineyards you get "brighter sunlight for shorter periods" – because the vineyards are closer to the equator than those in Burgundy. The favourite regions for Pinot include southern, seaside Victoria, above all the Mornington Peninsula south of Melbourne, and Gippsland, where the wild variations in temperature from year to year can wreak havoc – as they did in 2002 when very little wine was made.

Australian winemakers have similar problems with Merlot. Most Australian Merlots are too simple and fruity, unable to develop secondary aromas. As Michael Hill-Smith says, they are "desperately trying to be Cabernets". Many of them, he adds, are "overoaked, lack the silky texture concentration and fruit density that truly great Merlot can achieve". As elsewhere in the world there are particular problems with phenolic maturity; the period of perfect maturity is so short, thus greatly reducing the period during which the grapes can be harvested.

The same trends of growing regional specialization can be seen with that increasingly fashionable variety, Sauvignon Blanc. As Philip Shaw says, it was planted in the wrong areas in the past, but "Now we've found we can make a crisp, herbal style of Sauvignon. It's not too New Zealand-like, but it's still very exciting." This is especially the case in the Adelaide Hills, home to fine wines from Nepenthe and Shaw & Smith, producers of long, fleshy, grassy wines without the overpowering aromas of some of their New Zealand competitors. Even more complex wines may emerge when more Australians copy the winemakers of Bordeaux and blend Sauvignon Blanc with Semillon. Typically, a blend from Cape Mentelle has a lovely Semillon oiliness together with a fragrant Sauvignon nose.

Semillon is one of the continent's oldest favourites. Indeed, most of the vines imported in the early nineteenth century by Captain Sturt and others from Cape Town were various types of Semillon. In its historic home, the Hunter Valley, Semillon was called variously Hunter Riesling, Hunter Chablis, and Hunter Burgundy. There, and in a few other regions, the variety leads a double life. When young it is simple, charming, and aromatic. It then goes into a sulk, but emerges between its fifth and seventh birthdays as a truly deep, complex, almost waxy wine. Clarke and Rand quote Bruce Tyrrell's explanation: "Semillon has a structure and acidity like Riesling; it's like Riesling in everything except flavour."

Hunter Semillon that is not going to spend any time in oak can be picked much less ripe to make use of the acidity, while grapes destined for oak should be picked riper to stand up to the wood. The smidgin of botrytis found in the grapes, what with the rain in the growing season, "doesn't necessarily hurt; it's useful for the complexity and aroma it brings. . . Given ten years or more in bottle [Hunter Semillon] underwent a miraculous transformation, acquiring tastes of nuts, honey, and lightly browned buttered toast." But people won't afford the extra expense. As a result, only a handful of producers, notably McWilliams with its Mount Pleasant Elizabeth, and Tyrrells with its Vat 1, are prepared to keep it that long. Yet Semillons *can* last. At the Yalumba museum tasting, a 1970 Semillon made by Lindemans in the Hunter (it was called Chablis) had acquired lovely toasty/vanilla overtones while the 1943, also from the Hunter, had rich, dry, almondy, sherry overtones.

Of the nearly thirty other varieties separately listed in *The Australian and New Zealand Wine Industry Directory,* there are a number which, like Semillon, are survivors from the early days. Outside Australia, Verdelho is largely confined to Madeira, where the few remaining vineyards produce some of the island's most subtly nutty wines. In Australia, it has a reputation for mediocrity, although a handful of producers, mostly in Western Australia, produce finely concentrated, fruit-and-nutty, Madeira-type wines.

By contrast, Grenache, apart from a handful of offerings made from truly aged vines (many, especially in the Barossa, were unfortunately ripped up in the mid-1980s), is as characterless in the southern as it is in the northern hemisphere. Nevertheless, its inadequacies are being taken as a challenge. "It was just rosé; we're getting over that now," says Steve Pannell. Other varieties from the Rhône Valley – for Shiraz goes with what Max Allen has rightly described as "earth wines" – are attracting more attention. They include Mourvèdre (known as Mataro in Australia), Marsanne – still best-known as the wine from Chateau Tahbilk served to the young Queen Elizabeth in the mid-1950s – and Roussanne, the variety with which Marsanne is automatically associated.

For a long time, the growers were inhibited from trying new varieties, even those obviously suited to the continent's generally warm climate. The situation was worst in South Australia, with its rigorous anti-phylloxera measures. The importation of new varieties into the state was forbidden from 1900 to 1966, and even then imports from outside the state – above all from outside Australia – were strictly controlled, resulting in lengthy delays. What with finding the right sites and waiting for the vines to grow and the wine to mature, the time frame for trying new varieties is still at least a decade, and generally closer to twenty years.

Historically, the search for new varieties has been led by Yalumba and

Brown Brothers, largely because of the enthusiasm of Peter Wall at Yalumba and John Charles Brown. Their tradition is now followed by Brian Walsh at Yalumba and Mark Walpole at Brown Brothers. Walpole is a real varietal fanatic who has no fewer than sixty varieties in his own half-ha (1.2-acre) plot as well as parcels of varieties such as Touriga and the Zinfandel that apparently does very well in the King Valley. Two types of Touriga are included in the finest ports, but Walpole doesn't know which one he has. Yalumba, the leader in producing the delicately floral Viognier, one of the most promising new varieties, took over fifteen years to bring it to market after it was first planted in 1980. Yalumba even held a seminar on the variety in August 2002. Again it's a "site-specific" variety. Yalumba's Oxford Landing Viognier, made from Riverland fruit, is a typically heavy, but its three other offerings – Growers Limited Release from the Barossa, the Heggies from the estate in the Eden Valley, and above all the Virgilius from the best of the Barossa grapes – are complex, seriously floral wines.

Other promising varieties include Pinot Gris (or Grigio), which is thoroughly at home in cool climates. Nepenthe, in the Adelaide Hills, and Brown Brothers both make particularly clean, refreshing, and popular wines, though the best probably comes from Henschke. So the list goes on. Zinfandel is promising, although it needs years to absorb the (American) oak. So does the Spanish Tempranillo, now being widely planted; Brown Brothers is one of the firms that has made a success of the variety. Australia is now the largest grower of Petit Verdot, a variety that is irregular in cool regions but ripens every year in the Riverland, and, crucially, retains its acid in a warm climate.

The search for such new varieties is not just a matter of scientific interest. The British market, unlike the Australian, is open not just to new wines but also to new varieties. Some of the more adventurous buyers are even looking for new blends, like that of Malbec and Ruby Cabernet being produced by Angove's at the express request of British supermarket chain Waitrose. "When we can get a good niche," says Ross Brown, the chairman of Brown Brothers, "when we can bring out new styles ahead of the rest of the industry, we generate a lot of interest, especially in export markets. In many ways our Orange Muscat and Flora is a much easier sell in the UK than just another Cabernet or Chardonnay."

The biggest opportunity lies in Italian varieties. As David Gleave, a highly respected British importer of Italian wines, pointed out at a recent seminar in London: "Of the Old World countries only Italy is holding its own. . . maybe the Australians are realizing that a resurgent Italy could be a bigger threat than a complacent France." The Australian pioneer of Italian varieties was the Italian-born Dr Thomas Henry Fiaschi, who imported some Italian varieties for his vineyard near Sackville Reach on the Hawkesbury River northwest of Sydney. But his vineyard, like so many others, disappeared in the 1920s. Today, winemakers and nursery staff are trying out a number of varieties, with very varying degrees of success.

One problem is the ignorance, not only of drinkers, but also of winemakers. Dr Roderick Bonfiglioli of Chalmers Nurseries says firmly, "If the client cannot pronounce it, or does not appear to know much about it, we try to discourage them." Garry Crittenden, who is based at Dromana, in the fashionable Mornington Peninsula south of Melbourne, became one of the leaders of the pack after a visit to Italy where he studied regions, varieties, and styles that might be as suitable for hot Australian conditions as they are for the Sicilian summer. He could not get proper clones of new varieties. "Much of the earlier material," he said, "had been smuggled in, and was clearly inferior. . . One load I bought was unsaleable as Dolcetto, which was what it really was, but perfectly saleable as Malbec, which the grower swore it was." Crittenden made life even more difficult for himself by trying to ferment his Italian grapes as if they were Cabernet Sauvignon, which did not help the quality of the wine.

The most bloody-minded grape is Nebbiolo, the variety used in Barolo, that rugged Italian red wine, a variety described by one winemaker as "Pinot Noir with attitude. If you try and improve the colour, you end up with tannins that are simply too aggressive." When it was planted in Mildura it didn't even go red but ended up an unappetizing orange colour. It also has a nasty habit of providing a lot and a little fruit in alternate vintages and, needless to say, it requires a very specific climate. Nevertheless, James Halliday believes that Nebbiolo could become "the 'other' Pinot Noir, difficult, very site-specific but well worth persevering with". The "buzziest" Italian variety today is Sangiovese, the basis of Chianti, which, says Vanya Cullen, a leading winemaker in Margaret River, "will be the red variety for Australia".

Max Allen is betting not on the Sangiovese, which is "leading the Italian charge", still less on Nebbiolo ("too far out of the Australian drinker's experience to achieve anything more than niche notoriety"), but Barbera, responsible for "very attractive, very approachable wines". He could be right, for Browns now sell 150 tonnes worth of Barbera to Britain. Chain of Ponds, owned by the Amadios, a family of Italian descent, is making a fascinating blend of Barbera and Grenache. Clearly the Amadios are expansion-minded, having hired Zar Brooks from d'Arenberg and a new chief winemaker, Neville Falkenberg, formerly senior maker of white wines at Southcorp. There is clearly more to come, for Mark Walpole can now offer a regular supply of excellent clones from Italian nurseries and can also reel off the many and various varieties that intrigue him, including Nosiolo, Sagrantino, and Aleatico.

To increase the choice, the CSIRO continues to produce new varieties. The first four – Tullila, Goyura, Taminga, and Tarrango – were introduced in the 1980s and were designed for warm, irrigated regions. Of the four, only Tarrango, an Australian-bred hybrid that mixed Touriga Nacional, one of the finest wines from the Douro, and the characterless Sultana (Thompson Seedless), has made much of an impact. Mark Walpole defines it as "a big cropper with high acidity". In the hands of the Browns it emerges as Australia's potential equivalent to Beaujolais: crisp, light, and fruity. Only a handful of growers have tried Gamay, the variety used in Beaujolais, and none to any great effect. It's too early to tell if other CSIRO varieties brought out in the mid-1990s – Tyrian, Cienna, Vermilion, and Rubienne – will catch on. They are all hybrids of Cabernet Sauvignon and Sumoll, a traditional Spanish variety that Jancis Robinson, the British authority on grape varieties, says is "fading". But, says one distinguished winemaker, "They're on the wrong track. Instead of trying to improve old varieties, they're producing new varieties without necessarily knowing where to grow them." More useful to the average winemaker is the work of the South Australian Vine Improvement Committee, set up in the 1970s to distribute selected clones through an establishment at Nuriootpa in the heart of the Barossa.

One of the biggest differences between wines in Australia and those made in Europe is not the varieties, but the use of water, which is forbidden in France, for instance, and rare elsewhere. By contrast, irrigation is normal in Australia, the driest continent on earth, and South Australia is the driest state in the continent. Not surprisingly – with the exception of the Hunter and Coonawarra – there is little rain during the growing season, and without water the grapes simply shrivel. There are two distinct types of irrigation: one as an insurance policy against dry seasons, the other as an inherent part of grape-growing, as practised above all on the banks of the Murray River. Today, less than forty per cent of Australian wine is grown without the help of water, although there has always been a premium for grapes from dry-grown areas. In 1967, Max Lake quoted premiums of about twenty-five per cent.

The use of water illustrates a point I made earlier: Australian producers treat grapes just as they would any other fruit. They are quite prepared to use a whole range of mechanical equipment, including not just mechanical harvester, and pruners but more exotic items such as pre-pruners, wire lifters, and vine trimmers. Much of this equipment is imported from European countries like France, Spain, and Italy, thus weakening Old World arguments against the use of such aids. Mechanical harvesting, which arrived in the 1970s, was especially suitable in the hotter regions where grapes could be picked in the cool dead of night, though the clumsy, early machines got badly stuck in the appallingly rainy 1983 vintage in Coonawarra. The widespread use of machinery that needs room to operate is one of the reasons why Australians plant vines far more widely apart than is usual in the best winemaking regions in Europe.

The "anything goes" or, if you prefer, "all's fair in love, war and Australian winemaking" attitude reached a climax with Peter Clingleffer of the CSIRO, an advocate of, at most, minimal pruning, what might be described as the "let it all hang out" school of cultivation. This helped productivity, particularly in the Murray River region, but it proved increasingly unsuitable for premium varieties and in marginal regions. In the King Valley, for instance, minimal pruning delayed ripening by a full week. Eddie Price at Amberley Estate in Margaret River claims to have "every trellising system known to man and a couple of our own". For him, minimum pruning means that "through viticultural Darwinism, the strongest will prevail with small bunches – and small grapes – on the outside". "It works," he says, "but the fruit is never so concentrated – in Margaret River anyway: Of course in Coonawarra, the natural concentration may be so great as to need diluting."

To outsiders, anything seems to go in Australia in the actual making and maturing of the wine. The attitude seems to be "if it ain't unhealthy it's okay". Even though the formation of the National Food Authority in 1991 triggered a strengthening of controls over winemaking, the wine industry is still largely controlled by individual states. As a result, there are only a few examples of winemakers being taken to court. While Tyrrell's was relatively unaffected in 1988 when Murray was found to be using sorbitol (a banned substance), Kingston Estate in the Riverland suffered badly after it was found guilty of unethical winemaking techniques. These were revealed when a group of American students working the vintage at Kingston found that the winemakers were using silver nitrate (a substance that reduces sulphur and sulphuric acid) which is banned, even though its two ingredients, sulphur dioxide and hydrogen peroxide, are both legal. Also added were ethanol liquid, red tannin, and fermenting Sultana juice on red skins taken from Cabernet Sauvignon. Kingston was banned from exporting for six months: a bad blow since it had been the country's ninth biggest exporter, and it seems unlikely to survive in the long term as an independent business.

Because of their attitude, Australian winemakers are perfectly happy to use the artificial yeasts scorned by most serious European winemakers. But then, Australians have always been looking for special yeasts. According to Ernest Whitington in *The South Australian Vintage*, published in 1903, Edmond Mazure, a well-known grower of French origin, "applies the French germ when he wants to produce a wine of a French character and the Spanish *levures* for sherry-making". Australian winemakers claim that they are aiming, above all, at naturalness: "simply trying to preserve the qualities in the original fruit" in the words of one winemaker. But today they're going further, with specialized enzymes to enhance Riesling aroma and flavour, although one yeast widely used for Rieslings gave an overly pronounced character of "tropical fruit salad", which, in chemists' language, translates as acetate esters.

Specialist chemical manufacturers are now developing hybrid yeasts, which, they claim, are totally different from the genetically modified variety is forbidden in Australia. They include, as well as the normal commercial yeast *Saccharomyces cerevisiae*, another strain, *Saccharomyces paradoxus*, which is resistant to low temperatures. Australians are not alone. It is thought that the gooseberry/cat's pee characteristics of many modern Sauvignon Blancs, especially those from New Zealand, are due more to the yeast than the grapes.

Another major difference between European and Australian wine-making lies in what is added during fermentation. The French have often accused the Australians of making "industrial" wine because of their use of acid to rectify the imbalance between the acid and the sugar level in the grapes inevitable in hot climates. The accusation is classic chutzpah given that in some of their greatest wine regions such as Bordeaux and Burgundy, the French can add enough sugar to strengthen the final wine by a couple of degrees, as well as, (though less legally) a spot of acid here and there. In fact, both substances are used to create the proper balance in the final wine, and most palates can detect when too much has been used. Any excess sugar is not "grapey," while excess acid leaves a dry film on the palate.

That said, Australian controls are pretty lax. Although no sugar can be added to wine in Australia, up to six grams of acid can be added for every litre of wine. Moreover, Chris Hatcher of Beringer Blass is not alone in believing that "If you add the acid before the fruit is pressed, then it is much more easily intergrated than if it is added later" – which does not give it the chance to dissolve naturally as the wine matures. Nevertheless, some of the country's best winemakers don't really like the practice. As Mark Lloyd of Coriole, maker of probably the country's finest Sangiovese, puts it: "It's really nice to make a red wine where you don't have to add acid." Most winemakers add the acid during fermentation if efforts to avoid using it at all have proved unsuccessful.

The problem, which derives from the warmth of the climate, was exacerbated by the switch from fortified to table wines. This created problems for growers in irrigated regions who had previously been paid according to the amount of sugar in their grapes, and thus the strength of the wine made from them. When the grapes were needed for table wines, their grapes often required the addition of too much artificial acid to correct the balance. Still, every practice is continually being questioned in the hope of improvement. Alan Hoey of Yalumba points out that the heat of 2001 did less damage than it would have five years earlier. "Many people are managing their vineyards and water better," he explains. "Vines are generally in better balance. If that heatwave had hit here five years ago, there would have been a lot more trouble."

People forget just how backward the Australian wine industry was as late as the 1980s. During the 1983 vintage, there was a lot of rain during the harvest and a great deal of rot. As Chris Hatcher remembers, "Many people didn't have a clue what to do." In addition, and rather belatedly, winemakers are trying to cater for people who wish to avoid added chemicals and preservatives in their wines. Following its success with Banrock Station, BRL Hardy now sells a no-preservative Shiraz. There are even moves toward sustainability. At Cape Mentelle, David Hohnen states that "Organic viticulture has no disadvantages in a climate where there is no rain in spring and summer. It's cheaper as well."

Even more belatedly they have turned their attentions to the problems created by the overuse of oak: one of the biggest – if not *the* biggest – fault in Australian winemaking. But Peter Lapsley, a well-known winemaker, puts it another way: "It's not that a wine is overoaked; it's just that the oak is under-wined." Too many wines, red and white, are sold too young after overexposure to new oak. This has greatly contributed to the notion that Australian wines are too harsh and unforgiving, and thus not as fruity and "consumer-friendly" as they should be. Worse, the use of artificial oak additives makes for "artificial" wines.

But habits are changing. Consider the case of one of the finest, Peter Lehmann's Stonewell Barossa Shiraz. As Andrew Wigan, the estate's winemaker, told Max Allen that in the late 1980s, "The more oak we could get into the wine, the better we thought it would be. We were driven by wine shows: we'd make big bruisers for the local boys – one hundred per cent American oak, all new, all barrel-fermented, two-and-a-half years in barrel. They'd win gold medals and we'd think 'Jesus, this is the way to go'."[3] He now realizes that these wines were not easily drinkable. They would fail the classic "Would you like another glass?" test. And above all, European buyers didn't want too much oak. So from 1996 on, Peter Lehmann started introducing the less violent French oak. Another reason for going easy on oak casks is financial: an estimated forty-five per cent of the A$100 million (£35.7 million) spent on oak by Australian winemakers every year is wasted because the wine is not actually improved by its time in wood.

There are some dubious, but unfortunately widespread, practices

[3] Max Allen, *Harper's*, August 24, 2001.

relating to the cost of oak. An extreme example occurred when, in the absence of anyone in authority at one highly respected winery, the journalist Philip White took delivery of several drums of liquid "essence of chips". The winemaker later insisted that the chips were "for experimental purposes only".There are three levels of substitution for the immensely expensive oak casks which add up to an Australian dollar (£0.36) a bottle to the cost of a wine. At the lower end are the essences, such as those received by White; then come oak pellets or chips. Windy Ridge Winery of Foster in South Gippsland, for example, soaks reds with lumps of wood, "finishing with strong oak flavours and grip on the cheeks". A five-centimetre (two-inch) lump goes into Pinot, and a six-centimetre (2.4-inch) lump into Cabernet Sauvignon and Malbec. Even if these pellets are treated, they still give a dusty feel to the wine and are disastrous for white wine. Recent research claims that chips are satisfactory if they are added pre-fermentation; they give that over-oaky, under-fruited feel if added after malolactic fermentation. But Chris Hatcher is blunt. "I hate chips," he says flatly. "I don't know the provenance of the wood or its age or type."

The oak staves often lowered into the vats of more expensive wines fulfil one of the two tasks carried out by casks: they allow a chemical relationship between the wood and the wine. Today, the oak's second role, the gentle oxidation of the wine provided by the interstices between the individual staves, can be provided by "micro-oxygenation", a technique now increasingly used in winemaking, albeit only in red wines, in which the wine is drip-fed with oxygen. The combination of micro-oxygenation with staves should produce a result akin to immersion in a cask, with the advantage of greater control, not only of the rate of injection of oxygen, but also through the ability to blend the age and origin and thus the nature of the wood being used by putting individual staves of different types of wood into a single vat.

Not only do practices change, so do winemakers' aims. In the 1960s, Ron Haselgrove, a distinguished winemaker at Mildara, was, says Len Evans, "a fanatic for trying to evolve a style of red wine which was like a Bordeaux". As Evans put it in the 1980s: "Today we go for a Twiggy kind of wine: delicate, delightful, with almost ethereal qualities. . . charming, vital with never a hint of blowsiness."

In the 1980s, Nick Bulleid wrote: "Perhaps through a residual cultural cringe, we saw the pendulum swing toward early-picked reds often around eleven per cent alcohol, in which winemakers were chasing an unnatural "European" elegance. Now, perhaps with an overconfidence driven by ten years of export success, it has swung to reds, where maximum impact of fruit, alcohol, and tannin is all-important, with scant regard for balance, subtlety, and companionship with food."

The unhappy, and often unfair, association of Australian wines with excess strength and richness is so strong, says Bulleid, that "There are many instances of elegantly styled Australian Shiraz being returned by disappointed customers to overseas wine merchants because they were expecting big, oaky, McLaren Vale Shiraz."[4] The swing away from "European" styles has led to criticism of the many young winemakers who go on a sort of grand tour of the better European vineyards, lest they adapt Old World habits. But as one of them puts it: "Most of us are using the experience to develop and polish our own styles of wine."

While wood is a vital factor in making many Australian wines, for the makers of Australia's famous dessert wines, or "stickies", the oak cask in which the wine matures is merely a neutral container. More important is the blending. Mick Morris takes a drop of wine from the most antique of the casks to add to a glass of a youngster, a five-year-old, say, to prove that the wine he inherited from his father fifty years ago transforms the younger, deepens it, renders it infinitely more complex. "A tablespoon [15 millilitres] does wonders for fifty gallons [227 litres]," says Morris laconically. Fortunately for them, the old wines sold by Morris and his fellow winemakers in Rutherglen are increasingly appreciated. Robert Parker recently awarded an average of ninety-eight points to three of Bill Chambers' Muscats and three of his Tokays.

Unfortunately, the same cannot be said for the handful of Australian "ports," and "fino" and "amontillado sherries" – terms that have to be put in quotation marks because they cannot be sold as such outside Australia. Delicious though some of them may be, they are now virtually unsaleable, the "sherries" because of competition from Spain, the "ports" because there is no appropriate name for them. Nevertheless, the best of them can have a deeply satisfying raisinness derived from the Grenache and Shiraz from which they are made.

[4] Nick Bulleid, reported in the *Wine Industry Journal*, September–October 2001.

All the many and various threads in Australian winemaking over the past thirty years come together in the sparkling wines. The finest examples of these difficult-to-make wines depend acutely on a balance between high levels of acid and fruit, achievable, in theory anyway, only in cool-climate vineyards. Unfortunately, many of the wines resemble the best-selling but flabby Golden Gate produced by Miranda from the usual suspects, like Doradillo and Gordo. Still, Australian winemakers have always shown great ingenuity in making the best of what they had. They used the *charmat* process in which, although the wine is matured in bottle as in Champagne, the lees are removed after the bottles have been emptied into a vat. This not only saves a lot of money, it proves to be an advantage for British drinkers. As Chili Hargreaves of Beringer Blass points out, such wines benefit from the longer period they enjoy following disgorgement as they are transported halfway across the world. The best, though nowhere near Champagne, often have delicious overtones of crisp Granny Smith apples. The quality greatly improved as Pinot Noir and Chardonnay grapes became more readily available and the whole sector, led by Seppelt and newcomers like Yellowglen, moved upmarket in the 1980s.

The first major attempt to echo Champagne practices came from Moët & Chandon's vineyard in the Yarra Valley. After a number of name changes dictated by the changing policies of the parent group, the wine is now called "Green Point by Chandon". After parallel stylistic developments, it is now yeasty and elegant, and as good as a decent non-vintage Champagne. The rosé is even better: crisp and fruitier than the often too-jammy wines produced in Champagne itself.

The future of upmarket Australian fizz lies in the use of "Tassie fruit," a rarity because there are relatively few vineyards in Tasmania that have any Chardonnay or Pinot Noir to spare for the production of sparkling wine. The two stars are the Piper's Brook fizz introduced in 2000 by Andrew Pirie after a major effort ("five years and A$5 million [£1.78 million] and nothing to show for it yet" was his lament) and the Arras being produced by Ed Carr of BRL Hardy, probably the finest maker of sparkling wine in Australia. It is of a previously unachieved depth and complexity. There's likely to be more soon, as a number of firms – especially Hardy – are planting extensively in Tasmania.

There's better to come. As Ed Carr points out: "We haven't even begun putting Tasmanian reserve stocks away for later blending. We haven't begun to find the best little Tasmanian spots for vineyards. This is a business in its infancy. There's so much left to do." Even now the confidence shows in the way that the excellent Jansz is advertised as "méthode Tasmanoise", nose-thumbing the French refusal to allow the term *méthode champenoise* to be used outside Champagne itself.

For me, the supreme example of the Australian recovery of its vinous heritage and the end of any form of cultural cringe comes from the increasing popularity of the ridiculous-sounding "sparkling Shiraz", a nineteenth-century specialty reintroduced in a fit of retro-chic in the late 1980s. Its rich but not cloying blackberry sparkle was recognized when one from Seppelt, most traditional of Australian sparkling-wine producers, won a trophy at the 1999 International Wine Challenge. The last word on this wine must be left to a necessarily anonymous winemaker: "Nick, there's a baby in every bottle. We had a few cases in the office; after a few weeks half the girls were pregnant and the rest were unlucky." There speaks the authentic voice of unreconstructed Australia.

12

Surprisingly Healthy

*Our approach is perhaps closer to, say, an agricultural approach to
managing people in modern times than it is to a corporate view.*

ROBERT HILL-SMITH

The new millennium started with an event that transformed the whole
structure of the Australian wine industry and threw into doubt the future
independence of even its biggest players. The earthquake was caused by
the "merger", announced on February 27, 2001, of Southcorp and
Rosemount Estates. Officially it took the form of a bid by Southcorp,
which bought Rosemount for A$1.4 billion (£500 million). The payment
was in the form of 94.3 million shares and a cash payment of A$881
million (£315 million), making the Oatley family one of the richest
in Australia. The Oatleys also promised to retain at least a tenth of the
new Southcorp's capital for a decade, but would not bring their total
shareholding above 19.9 per cent for the following two years.

One of the alleged motives for the deal was to keep Southcorp in
Australian hands, for by the end of the twentieth century, foreign vultures
were hovering over the remaining independent companies. The "new"
Southcorp has considerable defences, not just in the shares directly
owned by the former Rosemount shareholders, but through a further
considerable slice in the hands of loyal – that is, nationalist – shareholders unlikely to sell to a foreign bidder.

The official announcement at the time had stated that Oatley would be
deputy chairman, and in theory, the Rosemounters could be outvoted by
the former Southcorp directors. But within a few weeks, it became clear
that Rosemount, which represented the majority shareholders, would be
taking charge of a group immediately nicknamed "Rosecorp", with all

four of the top jobs going to former Rosemount directors. Bob Oatley became chairman, his son-in-law Keith Lambert CEO, Chris Hancock marketing director, and Philip Shaw was to be in charge of winemaking. Lambert's claim that "neither company took over the other" rang rather hollow, for it was clearly what the stock market would call a "reverse takeover" in which the smaller partner takes control.

Nevertheless Lambert was undoubtedly sincere when he said that the new team was "trying to extract the best from the people and resources of both sides". Rosemount knew that it needed most of the Southcorp people. "Rosemount had a problem," admitted Philip Shaw, "in that we did not have a depth of [managerial] resource." There was no doubt in anyone's mind that Southcorp had lost its way. As one old hand said of Lambert after the merger, "At least he has a vision of what he wants to do with the business. You couldn't really say that of the people who were running Southcorp immediately before him."

Lambert, a Canadian executive who had worked in senior positions at Fosters, had stepped in at Rosemount in the years when Hancock was (miraculously) recovering from serious health problems. When the Rosemount people arrived, they found that "Southcorp was a management-free zone," as one insider put it. "Under the old Southcorp, there was bureaucracy without a sense of direction," said another survivor, grateful to be working for a single boss rather than a network of committees. Even the managers of the successful cellar door-cum high-grade restaurant at Magill Estate felt the sense of liberation.

By the standards of a normal industrial takeover, the initial reorganization, which included the sacking of up to 200 executives and winemakers, was not excessive. But Lambert was an outsider without any real charisma whose career had included a number of such upheavals. He did not appreciate that aspects of the reorganization would be perceived as terribly brutal so it came as no real surprise when he was sacked in early February 2003 after a shock reduction in profits.

Contributing to the problem was the shiftiness of the previous management. For example, they had never told Mario Micheli of the merger talks when they hired him as European director just before the deal was announced. In the Barossa Valley, Philip Shaw saw that there were more winemakers at Nuriootpa than those listed by Southcorp. He refused to visit the wineries until those whose names the "old" Southcorp had omitted – because they were destined for the chop – had been told of their fate, which the former executives had obviously been hoping to blame on the Rosemount management. Moreover, shock at the brutality seems odd given that in the 1990s Penfolds had behaved in a far more heavy-handed fashion, which led such distinguished winemakers as Phil Laffer to go off to its great rival, Orlando Wyndham.

The first victims of the Southcorp-Rosemount merger were the so-called "marketing experts" hired by the previous regime whose major qualification appeared to be their lack of experience in the wine business. Yet Bruce Kemp, former CEO of Southcorp, had understood that wine was a special product. As he once said, "You don't get subjected to vintages in other industries." Next, the top team of makers of white wine was peremptorily sacked in the middle of the vintage, which created a major stir. The new managers claimed that their immediate subordinates, left in charge, were a first-rate group. At the same time the winemakers were reorganized into "regions" enjoying greater independence.

Some of the makers of red wine were obviously unhappy at a new policy that involved a vast increase in production of the more commercial wines from the Penfolds range. As a result, John Duval, formerly the group's chief winemaker, found himself confined to the finer wines, up to and including Grange, and subordinated to Philip Shaw. He had been introduced to wine ("cherry and lemonade or port and lemonade") by his grandfather, who had worked at Chateau Reynella for fifty-four years. Duval had joined Penfolds in 1974 and was immediately involved in the production of Grange. Twelve years later he took over as only the third guardian of the Grange shrine, but in July 2002, Duval left after months of clearly agonizing indecision. Yet movement was not only one way. At much the same time, Shaw hired Glen Jones, previously chief white winemaker for BRL Hardy.

Within three months of the merger, Philip Shaw – who refuses to call himself "chief winemaker" – had shown that he had a clear idea of where he was going. He appreciated the fact that Southcorp "had very good viticultural expertise, probably the best in Australia", way ahead of his own company (although in early 2002, David Murdoch, the chief viticulturalist he had inherited with the merger, departed). By contrast, he felt that "The winemakers were probably underrepresented at the top end at the corporate level." More important from a quality point of view, the winemakers were overly involved with blending, and he wanted to "put the emphasis back onto the making of wine, right from the vineyards". Fortunately, like its major competitors, the "old" Southcorp had invested heavily in vineyards capable of producing premium varieties; the new enlarged Southcorp now owns 6,900ha (17,050 acres), probably the largest vineyard holding in the world.

The new management immediately got rid of Southcorp's only non-wine remnant, the water-heater business, which provided enough money to recoup the cash element in the takeover bid for Rosemount. The clear ambition was a single-minded determination for the new group to be a major, if not the biggest, player in the global wine market – "architects of the new world order" is an expression I have heard used.

The next element in the strategy, to abandon the bulk wine business, at least outside Australia, and to concentrate on a relative handful of major premium brands, was sensible. The old Southcorp had been a production-driven business; switching the spotlight to marketing involved stopping lots of half-finished, half-abandoned projects. The house cleaning also involved writing off A$25 million (£8.9 million) from an inventory of lower-grade wine and the labels and bottles which were no longer required. The concentration was a necessity. While Rosemount had seventy products, Southcorp had 1,200, of which over 200 were in the still-declining fortified wine business. While Rosemount received an average of A$88 (£31) per case of wine across all markets, Southcorp received a mere A$55 (£20). Over half of the new Southcorp's sales came from three brands – Penfolds, Lindemans and Rosemount – with dozens of others making up the balance.

At the time of writing, the new management has already sold, or is try-ing to sell, a number of brands. One of the first was Hungerford Hill, which was sold to Cassegrain for development as a New South Wales regional wine to be made by Philip John, a much-respected winemaker who left Southcorp as a result of the shake-up. The new Southcorp is clearly not going to continue the policy of its predecessor: clinging to all the brands it does not intend to develop. Others sold or for sale include Blues Point, Edwards & Chaffey, Thirsty Fish, and Tulloch: "the forgotten brand of several owners". A number of brands, some better-known than others, remain in limbo. They include Killawarra, Leo Buring, Fifth Leg, Great Western, Kaiser Stuhl, Matthew Lang, Tollana, Salinger, Fleur de

Lys, Drumborg, Sunday Creek, Chalambar, Corella Ridge, Sheoak Springs, Harper's Range, Terrain, Moyston, and Rouge Homme in Coonawarra; the winery has been sold as surplus to requirements, the brand retained.

Of the other brands owned by the "old" Southcorp, Queen Adelaide is a major player in providing "fighting varietals", including the best-selling Chardonnay, within Australia. Seaview is a major brand in sparkling wine. The boutique winery group brings together such jewels as Coldstream Hills and Devil's Lair, white Wynns will be the key to boosting sales of wine from Coonawarra, a region where the group owns nearly 600ha (1,483 acres) of vines. Seppelt, most neglected of companies, is being revived as a brand specializing in wines from Victoria, made largely made from Shiraz.

Of the big three, it is Penfolds that brings a gleam to the eye of the new management, who see opportunities, above all, in the United States, where the impetus had been lost during the 1990s and where Lindemans Bin 65 had benefited from being an official sponsor for the 2000 Sydney Olympics. The push makes perfect sense, since Penfold's average selling price is nearly double that of Lindemans – and thirty per cent higher even than Rosemount. Even though Penfold's sales were boosted by the presence of Grange and Bin 707 on the wine lists of many of the country's best restaurants, sales had grown from 1.2 million to only 1.9 million cases in the four years up to 2000, and had been completely outpaced by Rosemount. The campaign for a brand labelled, not inaccurately, "Australia's most famous wine" involves not only the relatively low-end wines such as Rawson's Retreat (production of the Bin range is likely to be limited by lack of fruit of the appropriate quality), but also new brands, of which the first, called Thomas Hyland, was launched with a Shiraz and a Chardonnay. The aim is to provide a complete range for the United States down to Koonunga Hill (which is now on allocation, with every buyer receiving only a proportion of its requirements) at $10 (£6.25) and Rawson's Retreat at around $8 (£5).

A major problem for the group in Europe was the abrasive behaviour of the senior Rosemount sales director. Before he left, a number of excellent sales staff had gone and he had alienated some key customers. Mario Micheli, a late hiring by the "old" administration, followed a policy of abandoning the "own-brand" market – where wines are sold under the name of a major customer like a supermarket chain – and, before he left in late 2002 brought in some of his former colleagues from Anheuser-Busch in the USA. The aim is to transform Penfolds into a brand as big as Lindemans (or Rosemount, for that matter) with sales way above the 200,000 cases the current sales staff inherited. Global ambitions can also be seen in France, where the new management is developing the James Herrick winery in Provence, although the founder left shortly after the merger. By concentration on a single variety, inevitably Chardonnay, he had developed sales of over 150,000 cases. The new regime is also backing the highly promising experiment in transplanting clones of Shiraz from the Kalimna vineyard – heart of Grange – to the Central Coast region of California, where Southcorp could soon be producing up to 400,000 cases of wine.

A mere three months after the merger, Southcorp confirmed a long-projected joint venture with Mondavi to make super-premium brands in both California and Australia. Both wines aimed at the top end of the market, an echo of Mondavi's successful and long-established joint venture to produce the Opus One prestige wine in partnership with the Rothschild family of Mouton-Rothschild.

But for all its apparent dominance in Australian terms, Southcorp remains vulnerable because of the upheavals, a fragility shown by a May 2002 profits warning unwisely issued by the executive in charge of relations with investors, which severely set back the group's share price. Unfortunately, the analysts seemed unable to understand either the vagaries of the wine business – shown by the three difficult vintages in the first years of the third millennium – or the efforts being made by the "new" Southcorp to lift the group's profitability to something approaching that of the "old" Rosemount. But in early 2003 a profits warning showed the effect of the group's internal upheavals.

The situation gives rise to the fear that wine will follow the beer business, in which there are only six significant players, and in which the big players have a substantial stake in the only family-controlled brewer, Coopers, a favourite of Australian beer-lovers. Australia's wine industry now appears hopelessly top-heavy, with the big four accounting for around eighty-five per cent of the sales, the top twenty another ten per cent, and the other 1,400 or so wineries scrabbling over the remaining six per cent. Hence there is a double fear: that the medium-sized companies will inevitably be taken over, and that hundreds of smaller wineries will prove unviable. This fear is reinforced by an ever-increasing concentration of the retail side to the business. In early 2002, the troubled Coles Myer group, one of the big two that dominate retail wine sales, announced that it would be expanding its outlets. Both Coles Myer and Woolworths have been finding ways of wriggling out of the restrictions in Victoria, which, in theory, limited them to ten per cent of the outlets.

The most dramatic proof that such fears were justified was the takeover in early 2002 of Brian Croser's Petaluma group, which had been quoted on the stock exchange in 1993 to provide capital for acquisitions. During the 1990s, Croser used the funds to take over a number of other vineyards, mostly in cool-climate regions such as Pemberton and the Mornington Peninsula, but also including Mitchelton, a sizeable and troubled venture in the Goulburn Valley near Tahbilk. Croser, like other disciples of Evans and Evans, did not take to business naturally; he had never really succeeded in melding these holdings into a dynamic group. Petaluma was therefore easy (though overpriced) prey for New Zealand brewer Lion Nathan, which had just lost Montana, the dominant force in New Zealand's wine industry, to the British Allied-Domecq group. The battle showed that all wine companies were vulnerable, with both breweries and spirits groups realizing that they were operating in flat markets, but that premium wine was both a growing and a profitable business. Croser was clearly shaken to the core. "At the time," he says, "I felt sort of numb and anaesthetized."

The rush for shelter led to several friendly takeovers. In 2001, the Wingara Wine Group, which owns the Katnook Estate in Coonawarra and the Riddoch and Deakin Estate labels, sold a controlling interest to Freixenet, a major producer of cava sparkling wines. Then Moët & Chandon bought Mountadam, the venture launched by the Wynn family after they had sold their first business. And soon after Andrew Pirie had launched his long-awaited sparkling wine to general acclaim, he sold Piper's Brook to a private company headed by a Melbourne-based member of the Thienpont family, Belgian wine merchants famous for their vineyards in Pomerol, which include Vieux-Certan and Le Pin. Pirie's reasoning was simple: he felt that a bid was inevitable and he preferred it to be friendly.

When Allied-Domecq bought five per cent in Peter Lehmann's firm, a stake increased to ten per cent in May 2002, the end seemed to be nigh. There was also the fear that deals like those of McWilliams with Gallo and Jim Beam, and Andrew McPherson and Alister Purbrick with Brown-Forman, could lead to takeovers, as did the partnership of BRL Hardy and Constillation. Nevertheless, some Australian investors are counter-attacking. The International Wine Investment Fund has already invested in Michel Laroche, one of the best growers in Chablis, in the firm of Gabriel Meffre, a leading merchant in the Rhône Valley and in two British merchants Vinoceros and Bibendum.

There have been doubts about the survival even of family-controlled firms, dozens of which had already disappeared into the maw of the bigger firms – for example, those in the Southcorp portfolio. Mike Paul dismissed medium-sized companies as merely "less successful large ones", to which Robert Hill-Smith replied with the words of Anita Roddick of Body Shop fame: "Anyone who thinks you have to be big to be a nuisance has obviously never slept with a mosquito."

To survive in the middle ground, firms need a core brand or concept. But, whatever the marketing experts might say, there appear to be no real rules as to the "survivability" of different sizes of companies. Some of the privately owned companies look reasonably secure if – a big if given the history of such businesses, and not only in Australia – family share-holders don't get too greedy. McWilliams has its increasingly successful connections with Jim Beam and Gallo. Yalumba has a staple fighting brand with Oxford Landing, as well as a well-balanced portfolio of different varieties to respond to the ever-increasing demand for niche wines – an advantage enjoyed on a larger scale by Browns with its wide range of varietal wines. For his part, Robert Hill-Smith reckons that, by 2004, Yalumba will be processing 35,000 tonnes of grapes, enough for about two million cases. As for the future, he says, "We love to control our own destiny. We are not very good partners."

By contrast, Bruce Tyrrell has found that his sales of 350,000 cases of Long Flat Red (named after a local place), made largely from bought-in fruit and wines, do not make the brand big enough to provide adequate margins. He has put the brand up for sale. He still has a well-respected range of upmarket wines, and a healthy mail-order business, to guarantee his independence. For its part, De Bortoli has moved successfully upmarket, first with its icon Noble One botrytized Semillon, and more importantly, with its venture into the Yarra Valley.

Graham Cranswick-Smith provides probably the best illustration of the problems of medium-sized companies without any special advantages. By profession he's a marketing man whose entry into wine was through a management buyout of the winery in Griffith, where he worked. This had been owned by Cinzano – and thus controlled by International Distillers and Vintners, a major wine and spirit group. In his first years Cranswick-Smith was largely dependent on bulk contracts, which, he says, "provide a basic cash flow and if the wine is good enough it can be diverted into one of the brands".

Nevertheless, he had to change banks twice to raise enough finance, and in 1997, the third, Westpac, told him to float his young company, which raised A$12 million (£4.29 million). But then he overreached himself by buying Australian Premium Wines, which included the prestigious Haselgrove brand and the bulk Mildura wines, as well as the winemaking capacity he sorely needed by then. His own brand, Barramundi, was doing well, especially in Britain, based on his basic philosophy of relying on exports, "low-cost grapes, and winery and marketing skills". But in April 2001 he had to sell Haselgrove. Sales overall were slightly down in a booming but increasingly competitive market, and his Australian distributor, Hill Group, went into liquidation. Hill owned three wineries. Another winery owner, Barrington International, which had bought Haselgrove from Cranswick-Smith, also went under in early 2002 with debts of over A$25 million (£8.9 million). By the time of the 2002 harvest, Cranswick-Smith was having to pay growers A$100 (£36) a tonne if they did not harvest their grapes and a mere A$180 (£64) if they did because he had contracted to buy too many grapes. His problems naturally dragged down the price of shares and in June 2002 he "merged" with Evans & Tate in what was effectively a takeover by the ambitious West Australian firm. The dangers of investing too much were dramatically demonstrated in August 2002, when Gartner Wines went under after investing A$30 million (£10.7 million) in its winery.

At least two major ventures are designed to meet the increasing demand, above all from major US importers, for reliable, good-value, own-brand wines. Andrew McPherson and Alister Purbrick seem well-established in the Goulburn Valley with a wide range of customers in Britain, the US, and even France. More problematic is the "merger" in early 2002 of Simeon and Brian McGuigan. In the 1990s, Simeon had grown into one of the biggest crushers, with two modern, low-cost wineries, both on the Murray River, one putting through over 100,000 tonnes of fruit and the other 75,000 tonnes – around the same quantity as Orlando Wyndham and nearly double the tonnage crushed by Beringer Blass. Simeon had had a long-term contract with its former owner, Orlando Wyndham, which had spun it off some years earlier while retaining a fifteen per cent interest. But Simeon got into trouble promoting a "blackberry nip" and was forced into a merger with Brian McGuigan. Chairman of the combined group is David Clarke, chairman of Macquarie Bank and a long-term wine-lover – not surprisingly, since his father had been Maurice O'Shea's auditor.

Typical of Sydney's business elite, Clarke had bought a property in the Hunter Valley in 1982 and had founded a winery, Poole's Rock, which remains his pride and joy. In 2002, he bought the former headquarters of Tulloch because it provided a perfect cellar-door outlet for his wines. He divides the healthier parts of the industry as a whole into two: the biggies and the small ("up to 100,000 cases the economics are good"), and he clearly intends to be involved at both ends. Clarke and McGuigan do not aim to own many vineyards. "They're simply not economic at the levels of profitability demanded by public companies," says Clarke, "so we only own a few key sites."

The merged company, named McGuigan and backed by all the financial resources that Clarke can provide, represents a new force in Australian wine and is reckoned to be much bigger than the size of any other company outside the big four. The new company will have an unprecedented capacity to provide retailers with wine for their own brands (although, in fact, the big four may not be too unhappy about easing themselves out of the bulk wine business). McGuigan sells to a number of major British supermarket chains such as Tesco and Sainsbury, and has established a joint venture with major British distributor Waverley Vintners to produce a range of wines under the Moondarra label at prices below those of most Australian wines. Outsiders are concerned about the quality of the wines, or rather their suitability for modern tastes. McGuigan is renowned for wines, both white and red, with a certain amount of residual sugar and designed to appeal to unsophisticated tastes. He believes that "people talk dry but drink sweet", which may be becoming less and less true. To ensure that it continues to receive its own style of wines, Orlando Wyndham has now installed a permanent supervisor in the Simeon winery.

Despite takeovers, the number of quoted wine companies keeps growing. In 1990, there were only three valued at $640 million (£400 million), while ten years later there were seventeen. By that stage, five more had been taken over, and therefore de-listed, while the survivors were valued at $2.7 billion (£1.7 billion). Needless to say, listing involves wheeling and dealing. Soon after Margaret River winery Xanadu was floated, it bought the virtually bankrupt Riverland firm of Norman Wines. But inevitably, any firm that goes public is vulnerable, and not only to external pressure.

Simon Gilbert, a well-respected winemaker, is a clear example of the clashes inevitable because of different time-frame expectations of private investors almost inevitably looking for a quick return, and a winemaker who knows how long it takes vines, the grapes they produce, and the wines made from them to become profitable. Gilbert had assembled a group of investors to build a major winery, costing A$17 million (£6.1 million), in Mudgee. He planned to rely on contract winemaking to make a profit while he established his own wines – even his cheap Card Series includes an excellent, nutty-floral Verdelho and a well-made Cabernet/Merlot. But the investors are restless and he is having to refinance the venture. Nevertheless, his previously excess facilities are now profiting from the lack of crushing and winemaking capacity, which had lagged behind the growth in the area of vineyards because investment in the equipment did not attract such favourable tax treatment.

There is still an ever-increasing demand for high-quality grapes of premium varieties even though the big four have extensive estates in key regions. As Hugh Cuthbertson, formerly of Beringer Blass, explains, "Plantings don't make balance sheets look good," because they are such a long-term investment. So it is cannier for major groups to rely for the majority of their requirements on growers and vineyards financed by outside investors. A typical supplier is Cabonne, at Cudal, north of Orange, crushing 20,000 tonnes in what is by far the largest winery in the region. Cabonne is now a listed company, but developed the winery in conjunction with a number of "farmers", in fact investors, who provided the capital while Cabonne managed the vineyard and the winemaking.

There are lots of other cases soundly based on long-term contracts with major groups, such as Belvidere near Langhorne Creek, crushing 10,000 tonnes. Boar's Rock in McLaren Vale was established in 1997 on Californian lines, crushing over 8,000 tonnes of grapes for major clients. There a consultant "keeps an eye on things". Most of the big syndicated groups, such as Kirribilly and FABAL in South Australia, and Blaxland in Victoria, have specialized in single-vineyard projects on a large scale and have concentrated on specific market segments. Exceptionally, Rutherglen Estates is planting up to 400ha (988 acres), largely with Shiraz, on the back of an eight-year contract with Southcorp. Unusually for such invest-ment, the vineyard also includes some experiment al plantings of a real, typical Sangiovese, some rather primitive if spicy Durif, and it is selling a nice, soft blend of Chardonnay and Marsanne.

While there are a number of sharp operators looking only to attract naïve investors, the more reputable financial advisers insist that clients think in terms of returns without taking the tax advantages too much into account. Such advisers are also wary of investors who are in it for the prestige, so they can boast about the wines with which they are involved. Nevertheless, the tax relief available on vineyards – as on other agricul-tural holdings – is still not to be sneezed at. The government provides a number of special allowances, including accelerated depreciation on equipment and special deductions for irrigation systems. Most impor-tantly, the vines themselves are tax deductible through relief from the highest rate of tax, provided only that the investment lasts five years. This means that after that time, the taxpayer can claim an allowance to set off against his income, thus reducing the actual investment by forty per cent or more. There's even more profit if investors borrow, raising the theoret-ical return from, say, a nominal fourteen per cent to forty-five per cent over ten years by increasing the amount put into the project.

The wine industry has proved so attractive that up to A$3 billion (£1.07 billion) has been invested in new vineyards, of which about half has been through private syndicate groups. The balance has been invested by firms like BRL Hardy and Simeon, big private groups like Orlando and Brown Brothers, and specialized groups like Nepenthe, Geoff Hardy, and Brian McGuigan. Investors include a wide range of wealthy individuals, with the usual representation of doctors. As one financial adviser put it, "Consultants are well off because they charge too much, have too much spare time, and are rotten golfers on the whole." With growth has come some spivvy advisers and an increasing number of ignorant investors. Too many of them are not even aware that they can only expect any profit at all from "their" vines three years after they are planted, and then only a small one, and that it will take up to ten years for the full income stream to come through. Many of them are putting their money into wineries without any definite contract to back the investment – and indeed, into some "virtual wineries" without any assets at all. Historically, the vast majority of these schemes had a guaranteed cash flow from pre-arranged contracts with big wine companies. By contrast, only four of eighteen recent projects had a contract of any sort with the majors, and half had contracts only with themselves – that is, associated "paper" winemaking companies – leaving it up to the managers to market and sell the wine.

The investment stream is having to face increasing competition from other horticultural and agricultural business opportunities such as plantations of blue gums, radiata pines, olives, and tea trees. Some of these alternative investments, especially those that involve planting trees, have received special treatment from a government that is fully aware of the surplus of grapes in part due to the lavish tax treatment of investors. As one leading adviser says, "Our farmers are asking for the government to clamp down on the special tax reliefs because they don't want any more grapes in the ground that are not contracted. At present, the government has done nothing but the tax office is putting tighter interpretations on the existing law to reduce the effectiveness of the timing of the deductions." In fact, investors have learned their lesson, though probably too late and plantings have plummeted dramatically.

The relief provided to small wineries and, above all, to the now-hard-pressed growers by the reduction in investor-led new plantings is a long way off, since the schemes so energetically promoted at the end of the 1990s and around the turn of the millennium are not yet producing. In theory there should be room for both the traditional growers on their family farms and the new investors. Demand is growing, and the proportion of bought-in grapes is invariably high; at Brown Brothers it's seventy-five per cent.

The whole of Australia is now coming to resemble Champagne, another region of blended wines produced by firms that are renowned for the value of their brands, but (with a few exceptions) can supply only a small proportion of the grapes they require. In the 1980s, in Champagne, and a decade later in Australia, the growers held the whip hand, hence the famous question: "How can you tell a rich from a poor grower in Champagne? Why, the poor ones have to wash their own Mercedes."

The slump of the early 1990s changed the terms of trade in Champagne, though not as drastically as they did in the first two years of the twenty-first century in Australia. The average price of grapes in Australia fell by around five per cent in both 2000 and 2001. Because the price had risen so regularly in the previous decade, at double the rate of the cost of living, it was still over two-thirds higher in 2001 than in 1990. As one major buyer put it, "In the last ten years these guys have made fools of us." They were helped by the slackness of the old regime at Southcorp. One employee arranged a long-term contract for himself at a healthy A$1,000 (£357) a tonne – up to four times the market value of the grapes before he was sacked.

Orlando Wyndham pioneered a grading system for growers in the mid-1990s, one of the ways through which the firm maintained the quality of Jacob's Creek. Its pool of vineyards consists of 10,000 "plots," none of more than four ha (ten acres). Phil Laffer was so short of viticulturalists to supervise the growers that he was prepared to recruit any promising graduate with a degree in agriculture. The growers' offerings are now divided into five grades. Their ranking is decided by the simplest of methods: how the grapes taste when harvested. Prices are decided by the use to which their grapes will be put. At Southcorp, the grading system is now systematized, with over twice as much being paid for fruit for the upmarket "Bin" wines as for those used in making Koonunga Hill. There is an astonishingly wide price range overall – from A$300 (£107) a tonne to the A$2,000 (£714) a tonne paid for the very best fruit from Coonawarra, and the stellar A$10,000 (£3,571) a tonne paid for fruit destined to go into Grange.

The range of prices is matched by the extraordinary variations in the relationships between growers and their customers. On one hand there is genuinely friendly mutual respect: the growers chewing Peter Lehmann's *Metwurst* and exchanging incomprehensible Barossa jokes; the plaque in the entrance hall at Yalumba celebrating growers who have been supplying the family for generations; the several hundred growers who are shareholders of BRL Hardy as well as suppliers; the jolly Italians lunching with Geoff Merrill in McLaren Vale – which they insist should be renamed "Ferrari Vale" after their team's successes; and those who supply the Browns, many of whom had followed market trends by switching from tobacco to grapes in the 1970s, a change encouraged by Browns. These growers, says Peter Brown "had green thumbs". "In many cases they were the same people who came to us with demijohns to buy wine." At the other extreme there are the victims – some of whom deserve their fate through carelessness or arrogance – who are suffering and whose problems are likely to get worse. There are the growers who were left with no one to sell to after Normans, a major winery near Renmark, went under in 2000, leaving stranded many growers who, through greed, had left the security of a contract with Berri-Renmano.

The change in the balance of supply and demand is recent. In 2000, a small vintage meant that the large processors could not refuse any fruit, however inadequate. Today, the reverse is the case. "My worst job," says one major buyer, "is having to tell growers that their grapes aren't up to standard, perhaps [this was 2002, a notoriously difficult year] because they had been too mean to spray against downy mildew. I've had growers' wives collapsing in tears in my office."

"The penny has still not dropped at the bottom end," says another. "There's still the assumption that our requirements will continue to increase." "We dropped twenty per cent of our growers," says Phillip Shaw bluntly, "because they weren't quality/yield-based." Those able to agree on five-, eight- or ten-year contracts with major buyers such as Karadoc find that their precious piece of paper contains a strong quality statement. Indeed, when Keith Lambert came to Karadoc to address 300 growers, the first such talk by a chief executive of Southcorp, his message was simple: "We will buy only good grapes."

The changes are not merely financial; they are also psychological and social. As Philip White put it in his newsletter, with typically exaggerated panache: "Rural Australia is only just learning to cope with the newly industrialized wine business. Gone are the old cute cellars where councillors and parliamentarians went for a smoke and a free red while they discussed the wine biz with their local grape cocky." By contrast, the new industrial wineries "run twenty-four hours a day, make heaps of noise from traffic and machinery, give off the occasional noxious aroma, use toxic chemicals, and really piss off local residents".

If growers are having to knuckle under, at first glance small wineries are even worse off. Brian Croser is typically blunt: "They are water-skiing behind the *Queen Mary*." By 2002, there were over 1,400 wineries in Australia. The figure is nearly four times the number in 1983 when the *Australian Wine Directory* first published exact figures. At one point it was reckoned that a new winery was being opened every three days, although the pace has slowed noticeably.

Yet there is no reason why the vast majority of the smaller wineries should not survive. The danger area is reckoned to start at above 100,000 cases, with all the extra staff and equipment required. The result is that a fully commercial operation requires total sales of a million cases, unless the company enjoys a good enough reputation to ask premium prices for its wines. It has to be remembered that Bordeaux, which is still two-thirds the size of Australia in terms of wine production, accommodates over 8,000 estates offering 12,000 brands. In Australia, say insiders, 600 of the 1,400 wineries are hobby farms owned by outsiders for whom profitability is a low priority – not as important as the pleasure and social status derived from owning a vineyard.

Victoria, with an enormous and still not totally exploited "home market" provided by the inhabitants of Melbourne, has the highest proportion – three-quarters of the total in the state – of small wineries, that is those crushing less than a hundred tonnes. Many of them look well-placed to survive on a combination of cellar-door sales, reinforced by the substantial mail-order business often generated by visitors whose details are obviously recorded at the time of their visit. But this is only if their wines are above the average and their cellar doors are within reach of a major city, or – like Brown Brothers – on a tourist route to a major holiday destination. Under these conditions, cellar-door outlets catering for the increasing number of drinkers not content with the relatively limited range of wines available in the major retailers are a superb means of avoiding the pressure from the increasing power of the major groups and the limited number of specialist wine merchants. Indeed 1,164 producers, over eight in ten of the total, have a cellar-door outlet by which they can cater for the growing desire – seen also in the French habit of buying direct from the producer – of personal purchasing.

Nevertheless, the cellar door will not help vineyards in relatively isolated regions such as the extreme southwest of Australia (though not, obviously, Margaret River, that long-established holiday region) as well as Mudgee and Orange. Moreover, Adelaide may prove to be too small a centre to justify the growing number of cellar-door operations in the many wine-growing regions within easy reach of the city.

The problems were clearly demonstrated by the story of the National Wine Centre in Adelaide, a lovely building at the edge of the Botanic Gardens, a park that attracted 1.3 million visitors a year: more than any other government-owned property. The gardens were also a haunt for tourists, and food- and wine-lovers, and an attractive situation to house the national wine organizations already headquartered in Adelaide. After the mini-scandals over consultancy fees, overpayment for websites, and the like, usual with any such project, the centre opened in 2001. Because of over-optimistic forecasts, it immediately started to lose money, and in early 2002, the newly elected Labour government of South Australia asked the wine industry to join it in an attempt to raise revenues by a fifth and cut costs by a tenth. By the autumn the centre had been closed.

The model for other regions is, of course, the Hunter Valley. Visitor numbers reached the million mark in 1997 and were up by a half three years later, over two-thirds from Sydney. Not surprisingly, the direct sales and mail-order customers garnered as a result of such visits can amount to eighty-five per cent or more of a winery's total sales. "If it's a bad day at Bondi, it's a good day at the vineyards," they say – though it is difficult for visitors from the Old World to understand that, for Sydneysiders, the beach is the everyday norm while the Hunter is an attractive alternative. As a result, the valley is now the second most important tourist destination in New South Wales and the fifth or sixth in the whole of Australia, with 3,000 hotel bedrooms and 400,000 overnight or corporate visitors bringing in income reckoned to be A$560 million (£200 million) and creating 4,900 jobs. The most elegant accommodation is provided by Len Evans's new Towers development. The Hunter's success, especially now that the cellar doors are offering wines from all over Australia, is not surprising. As Bruce Tyrrell points out: "It's because we're closer to the real action in the marketplace."

A classic Hunter development is Tamburlaine, a winery established in the 1960s but expanded since 1985 by its psychologist-owner Mark

Davidson, who claims that it has the biggest cellar-door sales in the Hunter. Tamburlaine sells up to 60,000 cases, virtually all of them at the cellar door or through a wine club that has 10,000 members, 5,500 of them from Sydney, with a claimed ninety-three-per-cent renewal rate. One great advantage of the cellar door is that it is "easier to sell unusual varieties to buyers who say they don't know anything about them", including Verdelho and Chambourcin from Tamburlaine's ninety-two-ha (227-acre) estate in Orange.

The possibilities around Melbourne are even greater because the cellar-door industry is less developed, and one region, the cool-climate Mornington Peninsula, is one of the city's favourite resort areas. In the past, a number of entrepreneurs have tried, with mixed success it has to be said, to develop vineyards and wineries with an in-built restaurant and cellar door that should have provided the project's basic profits. In Sunbury, near Melbourne, one revived winery, Goona Warra, funded by tax-minimizing investors, relies on wine for only a third of its revenue. The rest comes from a hospitality centre based in a rebuilt Victorian winery. The centre accounts for half the sales of Goona Warra's wines, which are actually made miles away.

A similar concentration on the cellar door was part of the business plan of the Palandri development founded by Darrel Jarvis in Margaret River. In 1999, Jarvis was removed from the Heytesbury Group, owned by Janet Holmes à Court, who now owns the Vasse Felix winery herself. Jarvis aimed to rely on the continuing demand for wines from the region, on his open contempt for many of its other winemakers, and on the elaborate hospitality centre he built. Spending nearly a third of the Palandri revenues on marketing, the formula has yet to prove itself. Jarvis' former employer has taken a different strategy, showing some of her outstanding collection of Australian paintings at her winery as an attraction.

There are many festivals and events organized by well-established wineries. At the Barossa Vintage Festival, held in April every other year, visitors can taste the newly made wine – an idea now copied in the Clare Valley. Each winery teams up with a prominent restaurant to provide a dish to match a glass of wine. In Margaret River, Amberley arranges food festivals with a dozen different fish dishes. Leeuwin Estate, the entertainment pioneer in the region, has gone even further. Its famous Art Series of wines has labels inspired by those devised by the late Baron Philippe de Rothschild for Mouton-Rothschild. Today, the estate, a mere three hours south of Perth, has become a major tourist centre with good food and a serious art collection, complete with works by Sidney Nolan, topped by now – world-famous concerts. The concerts started in 1985 when the London Philharmonic Orchestra schlepped to what must have seemed like the back of beyond, a precedent followed in subsequent years by artists ranging from Dame Kiri Te Kanawa to James Galway – and Tom Jones.

Wine tourism is not confined to serious winemaking regions. Indeed, tourism is considered so attractive that the potential of sales to tourists can be more important than a region's potential for making decent wines. This applies above all north and south of Sydney, in unpromising regions such as the south coast around Nowra, and on the Hastings River to the north. There the French-descended family, the Cassegrains, decided to diversify into viticulture in 1980 as part of a real-estate development. It was easier to attract tourists than to grow grapes, and the weather was too wet for anything except the hybrid Chambourcin. The same applies to most of the wineries in Queensland. The ultimate in wine tourism is the not overly distinguished wine made at Chateau Hornsby, a property established by Denis Hornsby, an enterprising pharmacist, in Alice Springs in the scrubby, baking-hot Northern Territory.

Wine tourism is also spreading to foreign visitors to Australia. In 1999, before the boost provided by the Sydney Olympics, 450,000 international visitors, over one in ten of the total, included a visit to a winery in their trip. The percentage was obviously greater in well-known regions like the Barossa Valley, where the figure was over two in five, and this despite the relative paucity of direct international air links between Adelaide and Europe. Promoters (and state tourist agencies) are naturally talking up the idea of attracting visitors from countries where Australian wine is gaining ground: Germany, Switzerland, Belgium, the Netherlands, and even France. *That* would be the day.

13

Tomorrow Is Another Day

The day when age and quality in an Australian wine will be acknowledged as noblesse – *worth a price, and justifying a host in offering it to his guests – on that day the wine industry will be established in the colonies.*

HUBERT DE CASTELLA

James Halliday is among those who have made the positive case for the future of Australian wine.

"Australia enjoys many natural advantages over the majority of its European competitors," he wrote: *"a warm and generally dry growing season; abundant land suited to viticulture; an unpolluted environment; a strong technical base provided by world-class research and teaching facilities; and the absence of excessively restrictive legislation. It produces wines which are distinctively Australian and at prices which the markets of the world have judged to be most attractive. There is every reason to suppose that it will retain and indeed build on those advantages in the decades ahead."*

Halliday was writing in 1998, and, if anything, the outlook has improved since then, with continuing proof that the taste for Australian wine is not confined to Britain. Against most predictions, exports continued to rise in the first years of the third millennium, up in value by seventeen per cent, reaching the A$2 billion (£714 million) mark during 2002, although the average price paid by foreigners slipped slightly. Increases in value are unlikely to keep pace with the actual amount of wine being shipped, as the surplus of generally not top-level grapes grows and becomes available for export, since the domestic market is simply not going to be able to absorb the increased quantity of wine.

Given the reduced price of grapes, the early years of the twenty-first century could witness a second wave of exports, of lower-value wines, competing in the lower half of the world market, where Australia has so far been virtually absent. Australia could also repeat its success farther upmarket by offering wines that are far more professionally made and marketed than their equivalents from the Old World – or much of the New, for that matter.

Not surprisingly, there is a pervasive fear that the image of "Brand Australia" will be diluted by sales of bulk wines unworthy of the country. Nevertheless, after a delay caused largely by the unwillingness of at least one major group to accept controls on bulk exports, the regulations have been tightened. Today, bulk wine can be sold only to approved bottlers. This is easy in Britain, where there are many responsible bottlers such as Stowells, or in countries like Canada and Scandinavia where the business is in the hands of government monopolies. But in France, Germany, and Holland in particular, there's a danger that, as one winemaker puts it, "The wine will be blended with crap and then passed off as Australian."

The surplus arises from late 1990s increases in planting from between 2,500 and 3,000ha (6,178 and 7,413 acres) annually in the early 1990s to over 16,000ha (39,536 acres) in 1998. After forty-per-cent rates of growth in the last two years of the millennium, the total rose only by six per cent in 2000-1 and is now virtually static. Yet by 2001, the total area under vines was well over 150,000ha (370,650 acres), nearly treble the level at the depth of the slump of the 1980s. Because the increase consisted largely of red-wine grapes, it is here that the surplus is being felt first, and it is likely to grow as the plantings of the late 1990s reach full production. The surplus will obviously be concentrated in warm-climate regions, above all along the Murray River, as the supply of grapes, (virtually all of them from premium varieties) from cool-climate regions grows. By 2010, the cool-climate regions could be out-producing warmer regions.

Since grapes account for around a quarter of the wholesale cost of wine, any reduction in their price is welcome to everyone involved – except, obviously, the growers themselves. In 2002, a vintage notable for lower-than-average yields, there was a surplus of over 20,000 tonnes, and growers were starting to riot – so far, without much effect. This practice could become a habit if experience in the south of France, where growers have been restive on and off for nearly a century, is anything to go by. Their discontent may well be exacerbated by an associated phenomenon, whereby all the major players are persuading or forcing their growers, above all in Riverland, to reduce their yields, sometimes dramatically. This policy will also reduce any possible surplus as the rate of increase in grape production will inevitably be less fast than the rate of planting new vineyards.

The major groups will be increasingly able to make better wines because of their new-found ability to choose their grapes, and thus answer the basic problem confronting Australian winemakers: the blandness of many of their biggest brands. The reason for the lack of quality was simple. In the later years of the 1990s, the makers were having to work miracles to produce even acceptable wines from, frankly, below-par grapes.

At the time of writing domestic sales are growing only slowly, although they are moving up-market. Indeed, although sales of casks are increasing, this is because the premium casks are taking sales from cheaper wines sold in the bottle. The move upmarket does increase the pressure on the warm regions; the surplus will have to find outlets abroad since the quantities available for export could more than double, with an additional forty-three million cases. In that case, exports would have to rise to over three-fifths of production. This should not be impossible since they already account for well over two-fifths of the total. Nor should the forecasts be taken too seriously, for they assume reductions in productivity of up to a mere fifteen per cent for the red wines from warm-climate regions – far lower than the reductions might be in reality, given the colossal pressure being exerted by the big buyers to reduce yields.

The industry's attitude toward the rate of growth in the domestic market could well be overly pessimistic. The figures from the *Wine Industry Journal*, March–April 2002, show that the proportion of the adult population who were wine-drinkers increased from under forty-four per cent in 1995 to over fifty-two per cent three years later. Moreover, the increase is greater in the older sections of the population, aged from forty-five upward. This is inevitable and will increase, as the oldest inhabitants who habitually drank beer or fortified wine for most of their lives die out and are replaced by increasingly well-off baby-boomers for whom table wine has become a natural drink. Even the growth of imports, at a rate far exceeding that of consumption, could be a favourable factor, since it demonstrates drinkers' steady move upmarket, a further challenge to the local industry.

But Australia has a small population, and the wine market will never be able to absorb more than a small proportion of the ever-increasing supplies of wine. As a result, in the words of Hugh Cuthbertson, producers have to "export or be damned". Yet they don't need to dominate the world trade in wine, or even aspire to the same commanding position elsewhere as they have in Britain. Indeed, an eventual loss of market share sooner rather than later in their principal market is inevitable, even though it will probably be masked by an increased demand for wine. The outlook in Britain is particularly difficult for the thousands of winemakers outside the big four, since the supermarkets that dominate the business in Britain are offering a steadily more restricted range of wines and are exerting ever-increasing pressure on their suppliers.

That said, even within Britain, the market is by no means saturated. Both Southcorp and Beringer Blass are now exploiting the fact that Australian wines are far less well-established in the on-trade sector – pubs, restaurants, and the like – than they are in retail outlets (the off-trade) by teaming up with leading specialist distributors. At the moment the on-trade market is dominated by the French and the Italians. Even German wines, whose reputation has slumped over the past decade, have a bigger share of the market than the Australians. As John Hoskins, a well-respected pub owner, put it at a recent conference, the range of Australian wines in the average English pub or restaurant is decidedly limited. "Pubs have 'one of everything'," he said, "and these generally involve an Australian Chardonnay or Semillon/Sauvignon; they're big sellers but that's it. Australia, unlike France, is limited by the lack of well-known Australian regions." Moreover, he added, "Australian wines are what [people] normally drink at home, so when they go out they want something different."

The Australian obsession with the British market, which will surely top out (in terms of market share, anyway) sooner rather than later, ignores the fact that both Germany and the United States are bigger markets – though not bigger importers – and ones where the Australians have not yet reached their full potential. Massive growth is proving easier in the United States than in Germany, where so great a percentage of the market is held by the "hard discounters" who buy purely on price. But Australian wines still have less than one per cent of the total market in Germany, so there is obviously room for growth.

In the United States, the percentage of imported wines has increased in recent years, although even now they account for only an eighth of the market, of which the Australians have less than a quarter. Even before the new Southcorp started its offensive with Penfolds, total sales were already above A$500 million (£179 million): two-and-a-half times their level a mere three years ago, a growth rate reminiscent of the golden days in Britain. By 2002, sales were rising faster even than they ever had in Britain, and for the same reason: the lack of decent, mid-priced, properly marketed wines from other sources. As one exporter put it, "We haven't scratched the surface yet. It's like Britain in the 1980s." But exports are increasingly, and dangerously, dependent on those to Britain and the United States, which together account for nearly three-quarters of the total. Elsewhere in Europe, while the Scandinavian countries are increasingly interesting markets and the Swiss are ideal clients, some countries, like Spain and Italy, are virtually closed to all wine imports.

But there could be a joker in the pack: France. The forecasters – though notably not among the major firms – assume that the French market is virtually closed to the Australians. Yet France is a country where imports are leaping ahead, albeit from a very low base, and where shoppers are used to buying even the best wines from the all-powerful supermarkets. Like their British equivalent fifteen years ago, the French supermarkets lack wines, like those from Australia, that combine guaranteed quality with value for money and are promoted by modern marketing methods. Inevitably, the Australians face obstacles, there as elsewhere, cultural as well as economic. The Americans, for instance, are bound to offer a particular welcome to the wines of Chile (though not for premium offerings) if only because of the increasing proportion of Americans of Hispanic origin. The Dutch and, to a lesser extent, the Germans are equally open to wines from South Africa. Then there is the widespread assumption in Asia, above all in Japan, that the finest luxury products (wine included) necessarily come from France – and the best fresh fruit and vegetables from Chile.

Australia has some advantages in Asia. It is likely that Asian Generation Xers, born between 1961 and 1980, will turn to wine, and that so many of the younger generation now being educated in Australia will return home as ambassadors for the country's wines. The same factor has already proved of considerable use to the Americans. The industry is now pitching deliberately to the young worldwide, with wines like Hardy's Wicked range but has found that the young prefer better wines.

Australian winemakers can probably rely on making fewer mistakes than many of their competitors. Some French regions, notably the Côtes du Rhône, are echoing Australian success in Britain with a simple campaign based on offering sturdy, fruity, reliable red wines. But the bulk of the French winemaking community is still hampered not so much by the rules – ridiculous though they sometimes are – that govern the production of wine in France as by the still-widespread assumption that if a grower or a cooperative produces a wine, it will sell itself and the state should play its part in disposing of even, indeed especially, the grottiest wines. Many of the Australian "flying winemakers" are making good-value, technically correct wines in regions such as the south of France, which can also naturally produce "bottled sunshine." They are, however, often hampered by the idleness and lackadaisical attitude of the French cooperatives with which they are working.

The Italians certainly pose a threat, though whether they – or the Spanish for that matter – have the same internal discipline, and financial and commercial clout as their Australian competitors is another matter. The same applies to the threat posed by the rest of the New World, notably South Africa, Chile, and Argentina. Some of the most powerful US producers, potentially also the most powerful rivals, are allied with the Australians one way or another, and most of the rest – with the obvious exception of the extremely aggressive Gallo – seem to treat exports as ways of ridding themselves of surplus wines rather than the object of a sustained campaign. This is precisely how they behaved in the late 1980s, at a time when they played a far more important role in the British market than did the Australians.

A bigger worry for Australian winemakers has nothing to do with the competition; it is the industry's historic overreliance on the ever-shrinking, ever-more saline supply of water, above all from the Murray River and its tributaries. Although the biggest user of Murray water is the city of Adelaide (with attendant problems in disposing of waste), growers in the Adelaide Hills still have to battle for their share of water for their vineyards. The fundamental problem is the long-term limit imposed by the supply of water of an appropriate quality. According to Chris Hatcher, "The key to the future is the availability of water," which, to him, is a necessary ingredient in making wine throughout Australia. In fact regions are already being selected only if they have a reliable, clean, water supply. Coonawarra, for example, always had plenty of water.

The whole question of water is bedevilled by states' rights, for the thirsty growers of South Australia are downstream from New South Wales, Victoria, and Queensland, and hence receiving what they perceive, rightly, as less than their fair share of the precious liquid. Today, the federal government is trying, with limited success, to introduce a proper conservation policy. This would have to include a steep increase in the price of water – today a mere quarter of what it ought to be. By introducing a system of rationing by price they could ensure that the present, already greatly reduced, flow of the Murray–Darling system is maintained and the growing and dangerous proportion of salt in the water reduced. But local political pressure in all four states prevents governments from charging the proper price for water, which is used in much greater quantities by farmers growing cotton and rice, not to mention irrigated pastures for cattle. Fortunately, farmers can grow more grapes than cotton or rice with a given allocation of water, so an increasing quantity of land is likely to be diverted to grapes, thus reducing the overall demand for water.

The problem is not confined to the Murray River. There is an ever-increasing use of artesian water, but this is liable to be very salty, and its use results in a steady fall in the level of the water table. The pressure for increased production is having dreadful effects. A company called Barossa Infrastructure is building a pipeline from the Murray to a local reservoir to provide what is called "drought-proofing" for the valley. As Max Allen puts it: "Sucking water from an already overstressed river system would be a PR nightmare for the Barossa" – as well as a major environmental problem.

Unfortunately, there's not enough suitable water for the present area, let alone future plantings. Philip White reports the words of a local grower: "The new water [from the pipeline is] not so salty as what we've been pumping out of the aquifer," the underground water previously used. To make matters worse, just before the state election in the spring of 2002, the South Australian government approved another pipeline, this time to the Clare Valley, which was never going to allow its bigger neighbour, the Barossa, to put one over it.

The same process can be seen in Langhorne Creek, whose size was always limited by the reach of the flooding of the Bremer River. There was a good fresh aquifer there, but greed and ignorance saw it overexploited until it turned too saline to use. So the local politicians, led by Dean Brown, then premier of South Australia, arranged new irrigation permits with the Murray–Darling Commission, which allowed new pipelines to irrigate the higher ground with water from Lake Alexandrina. That saw the creek explode in a rush of prospective growers. In 1991, there were 471ha (1,164 acres) of immaculately tended vineyard at Langhorne Creek. But by mid-1997, with what one observer describes as "the premier's extra squirt", there were about 2,500ha (6,178 acres), and the locals thought that might double by 2002 to about 5,000ha (12,355 acres), a clearly unsustainable level which had already been reached by the end of the millennium.

To the grape-growers' credit, the amount of water used to produce a tonne of grapes is diminishing sharply. The formerly dominant system of flood irrigation is now largely a thing of the past, and the use of overhead sprinklers is declining rapidly. With this method, over a quarter of the water is lost by evaporation in hot weather, with the further danger of sunburn on the wet leaves. In the past, drip irrigation, which was introduced from Israel in the late 1960s and uses a mere fifteenth the amount of water compared with flood irrigation, was relatively expensive, but it is now within the financial reach of most growers. The control it provides and its relatively low cost have also enabled growers in previously unirrigated regions to regulate their yields in dry years and compete on a more equal basis.

The latest weapon in the fight to economize with water is partial root-zone drying (PRD), a development important enough to be included on the list of the hundred most important Australian technical innovations in the twentieth century. As the name implies, it involves simply watering each side of the vine (or any other fruiting tree or shrub) alternately, thus, obviously, halving the quantity of water required compared even with classic drip irrigation. The results, according to Dr Peter Dry, include reduced vegetative growth, better vine balance, and the same quantity –

and better quality – fruit for a given quantity of water. The results are the same in every type of irrigated vineyard.[1]

The development of PRD is just one example among many of the new-found confidence among Australian winemakers. As Steve Pannell puts it: "We're not trying to copy anybody any more." This confidence is perhaps best shown in the attitude to cork – and its alternatives. "Australians were always the most demanding customers of the cork producers," says James Halliday, "so much so that Amorim [one of the biggest firms in the business] had to establish a factory in Australia." And when the Australians decided that the level of cork taint was too high, they were prepared to make what Halliday calls a "declaration of cultural independence", by experimenting with plastic closures and, above all, with Stelvin screw-caps. They were also greatly influenced by their customers among the British supermarkets who were simply not prepared to accept the per-centage – between one and five, depending on who you listen to – of wine that was more or less corked, less fresh and fruity than it ought to have been.

Screwcaps had been introduced several decades ago by enterprising companies like Brown Brothers and Yalumba but had the reputation of being used only for cheapos ("from the bottom up" as one winemaker put it). Nevertheless, they had at least proved that the closures did not affect the wines, however long they were aged. But screwcaps did not receive general recognition until 2001, when many of the producers of the best Rieslings in the Clare Valley banded together to use Stelvin, proving that they kept the wine fresher and more aromatic – a vital point with the vari-ety – than cork. The idea was first suggested to them by two British wine writers, Oz Clarke and Charles Metcalfe, who were shocked at the effect of cork on their wines.

Despite fears to the contrary, the public loved them; one producer who had some bottles with cork stoppers couldn't sell them. Since then, the declaration of independence has spread. The Clare producers were fol-lowed by the New Zealanders of Marlborough with their prestigious Sauvignon Blanc, but an even greater boost came in the spring of 2002, when Southcorp, which had previously been hesitant about screwcaps, announced that, as from the 2002 vintage, it would bottle all its Rieslings

---

[1] Peter Dry, *Wine Industry Journal*, January–February 2002.

using them. Their acceptability has been greatly increased recently by the development of improved screwcaps – and by the widespread adoption of screwcaps by Tesco.

Screwcaps are a sign of the restlessness of the Australian character, a sort of divine discontent, an attribute perhaps best expressed in the well-known remark by Peter Lehmann: "Why do we make so many types of wine? Because we know how boring it would be to wake up every morning and just be able to make Château Lafite." "If," says Lehmann's winemaker Andrew Wigan, "we don't make a better wine than last year we're pissed off." "I won't hire anyone," says Robert Hill-Smith, "who isn't excited every day during vintage."

This restlessness also shows in the willingness of increasing numbers of Australians to have a go, even in previously untried regions. New entrants are emerging at each end of the spectrum. Max Allen contrasts two of them: the large Reschke estate in Coonawarra and Stoney Rise in Langhorne Creek. After working in financial markets, Burke Reschke returned home and launched Empyrean, a Cabernet far fleshier than the region's benchmark wines, at the astounding price of A$690 (£246) a case wholesale or A$115 (£41) a bottle retail. The whole idea, as Allen says, "is back to front from the traditional method of establishing a brand". "In this case," he says, "the 'flagship' has come out first, to be followed by lesser wines. By contrast, the youngsters behind Stoney Rise are aiming squarely at their own Generation X. Stoney Rise, they say is the name of a 'sweet little surf break just down the road from Robe' and their wine, as befits a decidedly Rhônian offering, is called 'Cote de Robe'."[2]

Both initiatives have in common that essential factor for success: a clear idea of the eventual buyers of their wines. The newcomers are reinforced by experienced winemakers whose companies have been taken over – the most prominent examples include Tim Knappstein, the Wynns, and Kym Tolley, a descendant of the Penfold-Hylands and the Tolleys, two of the most famous names in the history of wine in Australia, whose Penley Estate wines are some of the best out of the Coonawarra.

Nevertheless, there are risks. In a speech made to a French audience in early 2001, Mike Paul pointed to a number of dangers likely to be encountered by producers in the New World, in particular in Australia.

[2] Max Allen, *Wine Industry Journal*, January–February 2002.

These included a destructive similarity between the wines they are offering and the problem posed by the fact that the major producers are publicly quoted companies looking for returns that are usually simply not available in the wine business. Fortunately there are at least three institutionalized checks on the quality of wines being sold abroad, and thus, in effect, at home, because winemakers in general will not make separate qualities for exports. The first is the control on the quality of exports, even of bulk wine. The second is the show system. Many of the shows have become monsters; there are over 2,000 wines at the most prestigious national and state events, involving individual classes of over 300 and 250 wines to taste a day, with foreigners, especially the British, walking out because they are unable to take the pace and top judges having to devote five days, which they can ill afford, to each show. The shows are far less important than in the days, not so long ago, when they were essential to weed out the large number of wines that were so ghastly they could be rejected immediately. Moreover, the medals they award are becoming less important because other criteria – the opinions of consumers and retailers outside the country and medals at international competitions, above all the International Wine Challenge in London – are seen as more important.

It is difficult to see how the show system can be modernized. There are rivalries between individual states and separate regions, and, as Jeremy Oliver points out, the shows are so profitable. "Most [of the 62] wine shows," he wrote, "are owned and conducted by the wine committees of their state's agricultural societies" and the rules vary wildly, with some – including the Melbourne Show, responsible for administering the prestigious Jimmy Watson Trophy – allowing unfinished wines in cask. In 2002, the trophy was dealt a further blow when it was awarded to a wine entered as from the Hill of Gold vineyard in Mudgee. It soon emerged that it was Rosemount's Traditional blend of Merlot and Cabernet Sauvignon which, as Jeremy Oliver says it, "has as much to do with Mudgee as the Jimmy Watson itself has to do with credibility".

Other problems include the sheer number of wines to be tasted, the eligibility of judges whose wines are entered, the ability of major groups to flood shows with wines entered under different names. Shows do retain a crucial role, if only in keeping a check on the less prestigious wines. Chris Hatcher expects all his winemakers to get at least a bronze for their A$8 to A$9 (£2.86 to £3.21) wines. At BRL Hardy, Steve Pannell says that while shows cost the firm A$250,000 (£89,285) a year, they do provide a "guideline for customers" and greatly help to improve quality, especially of white wines.

As many producers of the country's top wines started to neglect the shows, the industry managed to acquire a rough-and-ready control system for its better wines. It took the form of that essential status symbol for winegrowers, a class system, one that grew in importance during the 1990s. It was largely the work of a half-English immigrant, Andrew Caillard. He is a descendant of John Reynell of Reynella and grandson of the old lady who had sold Reynella to Hardy's in the 1970s. He associated Langton's, the auction house he runs, with Christie's. "They'd been slow in Australia compared with Sotheby's," he says, "so they were looking for a competitive edge." Since then, not only has Langton's run regular wine auctions but it has established a generally recognized classification system for Australian wines. As Caillard surveys the ever-upward trend of prices, especially for the icon wines (a spur for the winemakers), he finds that his buyers reflect the democratic nature of the country and are not confined to the narrow stratum of wine snobs who dominate the market elsewhere.

Langton's encourages Australians to think in terms of buying wines for laying down, a necessary lesson, for the best Australian red wines, which need the longest time to mature, are almost invariably released for sale well before they are ready to drink. The new management of Southcorp has started releasing some of Penfolds' best wines a year earlier than had been the case. This is damaging to their reputation, if only because ninety-eight per cent of wine is still drunk within two days of being bought. Few houses have proper – let alone cool – cellars to keep wine. Bruce Tyrrell claims that when an old customer was shown a robust 1988 Cabernet and told that "this needs to go into a cellar for at least six years", he replied: "Son, at my age I don't even buy green bananas."

But help may be on the way – from Colchester, an unremarkable town east of London. In early 2002, John Thorogood, of the respected Colchester-based wine merchant Lay & Wheeler (agent for Henschke among other icon wines), was strongly recommending that "customers who buy wines at opening prices" – that is, when they're first put on the market while still being matured in wood casks – should consider many Australian wines for laying down "as they would fine wines from

Bordeaux, Burgundy, the Rhône, or Tuscany". Yes, fine Australian reds really are keepers and they can be purchased at price levels which make proprietors in some European regions blush with embarrassment.

But Lay & Wheeler are dealing with a tiny percentage of Australian wines. For the majority, it is clear that the "bottled sunshine" image and reality of the past decades will have to be put on a diet. The sun will have to shine through a muslin veil of elegance rather than through an oak cask darkly. "Brand Australia Lite", as it were, would be the answer. Even worse, if – as, to be fair, is already happening – the wines do slim down, and become more consumer-friendly, the perception of strength may remain entrenched enough to reduce their appeal. Fortunately there's already a trend toward lighter white wines: Riesling, unoaked Chardonnay, Sauvignon Blanc either alone or blended, Bordeaux-style with Semillon, wines that have the advantage of accompanying admirably the Asian and fusion cuisine that has become increasingly popular, not only in Australia, but throughout the Western world.

Unfortunately, the slimming process is likely to be impeded by the spotlight shone on some of the country's biggest wines by Robert Parker, the all-powerful American guru who loves his wine rich 'n' sexy and, almost invariably, made in such small quantities that they are called "*vins de garage*" in France and "tin-shed wines" in Australia. Through a process of overextraction, these wines (in Bordeaux as well as Australia) break Philip White's sensible rule that "an acre of ground can't produce more than an acre of flavour – there's a finite amount of flavour in an acre".

Chris Ringland, one of the best winemakers in the Barossa Valley, was able to release his 1996 Three Rivers at A$535 (£191) a bottle, "a not insubstantial rise" in Jeremy Oliver's words, on the A$65 (£23.20) he had charged for the previous vintage. The reason: a perfect one-hundred point score from Mr P. The American allocation was sold out within three weeks. These, wrote Oliver, are "blockbuster wines that are in many ways the quintessential oversized, flamboyant, in-your-face style that makes Australia's top reds so distinctive". More seriously, however, too many winemakers in regions, notably Coonawarra, whose wines ought to be fine and elegant, are trying too hard to produce unnaturally rich, Parker-ized wines, as are many of their colleagues in that other cool-climate region, Bordeaux .

But all this is dodging the issue. "It's a bit like being a forecaster at the

Bureau of Meteorology," says Robert Hill-Smith. "You do a forecast today and it evolves into another one tomorrow." For him "the most important brand is Australia" is not Barossa or even his own Yalumba, "because if that brand fails – for whatever reason – then we all fail". And to achieve that, he adds, "Australia must lift its game with more styles, more structure and elegance and more generosity to the whole wine world." This raises a crucial skill: the ability to guess or forecast future demand for individual varieties, if only because of the long lead time, at least ten years, required to change. This is a quality for which such wily veterans as John Charles Brown and Deen De Bortoli have been noted in the past. In the late 1990s, when the cry was for more red wines, De Bortoli and his son Darren were telling his growers to plant white varieties.

The attacks on the blandness, the "fruit-driven" style of so many Australian wines, was already under way before British wine-writers waded in at the turn of the millennium. One of those, Andrew Jefford, wrote in the London *Evening Standard* that Australian winemakers must "learn to step back from the spotlight and allow nature to fashion and shape their wines. . . Many Australian winemakers, constrained by fear, technology and company accountants, don't yet dare to make real, natural Australian wine." Such winemaking involves behaving like great winemakers throughout the ages, allowing the grapes themselves, the qualities of the sites where they were grown, and their natural qualities to come through in the final product, uninfluenced by acid and not unbalanced by too much oak. Nevertheless, the wines should also show what has been described as the "ultimate Australian [qualities], which include value and consistency."

It all adds up to that old Shakespearean truism: "To thine own self be true." The message has got through. When he was awarded the Jimmy Watson Trophy in 1998, Steve Pannell said simply: "We must continue to make wines we want to drink."

Bibliography

In his book *Wine and Scalpel*, Dr Max Lake lamented that "There has been little, if any, tradition of wine scholarship in Australia." That was written in 1967, when his books were being published by a small publisher in Brisbane. Fortunately, since then, an extensive literature on the subject has grown up. The books I found most useful are marked with a star.

Aeuckens, Annely et al., *Vineyard of the Empire: Early Barossa Vignerons 1842–1939*, Australian Industrial Publishers, Adelaide, 1988

Allen, Max, *Crush: the New Australian Wine Book*, Hardie Grant, Melbourne, 2000

Australian and New Zealand Wine Industry Directory, Winetitles, Adelaide, 2002

*Beeston, John, *Concise History of Australian Wine*, 3rd edition, Allen & Unwin, St Leonards NSW, 2001

*Beeston, John, *The Wine Regions of Australia*, 2nd edition, Allen & Unwin, St Leonards NSW, 2002

Bell, George and Bishop, Geoff, in Aeuckens, Annely et al., *Vineyard of the Empire: Early Barossa Vignerons 1842–1939*, Australian Industrial Publishers, Adelaide, 1988

Benwell, WS, *Journey to Wine in Victoria*, Pitman, Melbourne, 1960

Bishop, Geoffrey C, *Mining, Medicine and Winemaking*, Angove's, Renmark, 1986

Bleasdale, Rev John I, *On Colonial Wines*, Mason, Firth & McCutcheon, Melbourne, 1873

Burden, Rosemary, *A Family Tradition in Fine Winemaking*, Hardy's, Adelaide, 1978

Busby, James, *Treatise on the Culture of the Vine*, [1825], reprinted David Ell Press, Hunters Hill, 1979

Busby, James, *Journal of a Tour Through Some of the Vineyards of Spain and France*, [1833], reprinted David Ell Press, Hunters Hill, 1979

Castella, Hubert de, *John Bull's Vineyard*, Sands & McDougall, Melbourne, 1886

Clarke, Oz, *New Classic Wines*, Mitchell Beazley, London, 1991

Clarke, Oz and Rand, Margaret, *Grapes and Vines: a Comprehensive Guide to Varieties and Flavours*, Websters-Little Brown, London, 2001

Cox, Harry, *The Wines of Australia*, Hodder & Stoughton, London, 1967

Davison, Graeme, Hirst, John and Macintyre, Stuart (eds), *Oxford Companion to Australian History*, Oxford University Press, Melbourne, 1998

Dunstan, David, *Morris of Rutherglen*, privately published, Rutherglen, 1989

Dunstan, Keith, *Not a Bad Drop: Brown Brothers*, Australian Scholarly Publishing, Kew VIC, 1999

Evans, Len, *The Australian Complete Book of Wine*, Books for Pleasure, Sydney, 1976

Grasby, W Catton, *The Coonawarra Fruit Colony*, Vardon & Pritchard, Adelaide, 1899

*Halliday, James, *Wine Atlas of Australia and New Zealand*, revised edition, HarperCollins, Sydney, 1998

*Halliday, James, *A History of the Australian Wine Industry 1949–1994*, Australian Wine and Brandy Corporation with Winetitles, Adelaide, 1994

Heddle, Enid Moodie, *Story of a Vineyard: Chateau Tahbilk*, [1960], reprinted by Lothian, Melbourne, 1985

The House of Seppelt 1851–1951, The Advertiser Printing Office, Adelaide, 1951

James, Walter, *Barrel and Book: a Winemaker's Diary*, Georgian House, Melbourne, 1949

Kelly, Alexander, *The Vine in Australia*, Sands, Kenny, Melbourne, 1861

Knightley, Philip, *Australia: the Biography of a Nation*, Jonathan Cape, London, 2000

Laffer, HE, *The Wine Industry of Australia*, Australian Wine Board, Adelaide, 1949

Lake, Dr Max, *Classic Wines of Australia*, Jacaranda Press, Brisbane, 1966

Lake, Dr Max, *Vine and Scalpel*, Jacaranda Press, Brisbane, 1967

Linn, Rob, *Yalumba and Its People*, Samuel Smith & Sons, Angaston SA, 1999

Macarthur, William, *Letters on the Culture of the Vine, Fermentation, and the Management of Wine in the Cellar*, Statham & Forster, Sydney, 1844

Mayo, Oliver, *The Wines of Australia*, new edition, Faber & Faber, London, 1991

Norrie, Philip, *Past South Australian Wine Doctors*, Organon, Lane Cove NSW, 1994

Norrie, Philip, *Past Victorian Wine Doctors*, Organon, Lane Cove NSW, 1994

Norrie, Philip, *Wine Doctors of Sydney*, Organon, Lane Cove NSW, 1994

Norrie, Philip, *Past New South Wales Wine Doctors*, Organon, Lane Cove NSW, 1997

Oliver, Jeremy, *Evans on Earth*, Lothian Publishing, Melbourne, 1992

Osmond, Robert and Anderson, Kym, *Trends and Cycles in the Australian Wine Industry 1850–2000*, University of Adelaide, Adelaide, 1998

Parkes, WS, Cowerford, Jim and Lake, Max, *Mines, Wines and People: a History of Greater Cessnock*, Council of the City of Greater Cessnock, Cessnock NSW, 1979

Pike, Douglas (ed), *Australian Dictionary of Biography*, Melbourne University Press/Cambridge University Press, Melbourne/London, 2000

Ramsden, E, "James Busby: the Prophet of Australian Viticulture," *Journal of the Proceedings of the Royal Australian Historical Society*, vol 26, 1940

Rankine, Bryce, *Evolution of the Modern Australian Wine Industry*, Ryan Publications, Adelaide, 1996

Robinson, Jancis, *Vines, Grapes and Wines*, Mitchell Beazley, London, 1986

Robinson, Jancis (ed), *The Oxford Companion to Wine*, 2nd edition, Oxford University Press, Oxford, 1999

Simon, André. *Wines, Vineyards and Vignerons of Australia*, Lansdowne Press, London, 1966

Tetaz, John, *From Boudry to the Barrabool Hills: the Swiss Vignerons of Geelong*, Australian Scholarly Publishing, Kew VIC, 1995

Thudichum, JLW and Dupre, Auguste, *A Treatise on the Origins, Nature and Varieties of Wine*, Macmillan & Co, London, 1872

Trollope, Anthony, *Australia and New Zealand*, George Robertson, Melbourne, 1873

Ward, Ebenezer, *The Vineyards and Orchards of South Australia*, [1862], Sullivan's Cove, Adelaide, 1979

Whitington, Ernest, *The South Australian Vintage 1903*, Friends of the State Library of South Australia, Adelaide, 1997

Useful periodicals:

Decanter, *Harper's* and *Australian and New Zealand Wine Industry Journal*

On-line resources:

*Oliver, **Jeremy**, *OnWine Report*, www.onwine.com.au

Index